BLOND'S ADMINISTRATIVE LAW

SULZBURGER & GRAHAM PUBLISHING LTD.
165 West 91st Street
New York NY 10024

(212) 769-9738
(800) 366-7086

BLOND'S ADMINISTRATIVE LAW

By
Neil C. Blond
Brett I. Harris
Michele F. Kyrouz
Mark Monack

Edited By
John Marafino

Also Available in this Series:

Blond's Torts
Blond's Evidence
Blond's Property
Blond's Contracts
Blond's Income Tax
Blond's Family Law
Blond's Corporations
Blond's Criminal Law
Blond's Corporate Tax
Blond's Civil Procedure
Blond's International Law
Blond's Criminal Procedure
Blond's Administrative Law
Blond's Constitutional Law
Blond's Multistate Questions

ISBN 0-945-819-15-3

printed in the USA

Abbreviations used in this book

BA — Bonfield & Asimow, State and Federal Administrative Law

BS — Breyer & Stewart, Administrative Law and Regulatory Policy: Problems, Text and Cases

GB — Gellhorn, Byse, Strauss, Rakoff & Schotland, Administrative Law: Cases and Comments

CD — Cass & Diver, Administrative Law: Cases and Materials

S — Schwartz, Administrative Law: A Casebook

MM — Mashaw & Merrill, Administrative Law: The American Public Law System, including the 1989 Supplement.

TEXT CORRELATION

Blond's Administrative Law	BA	BS	GB
Chapter 1 Due Process	22-104	545-560 699-852	209-225 545-656
Chapter 2 Problems in Administrative Adjudication	105-190	425-465 853-938	862-918 946-984
Chapter 3 Adjudicatory Procedure	191-243	513-544 625-632 939-1006	657-728 795-834
Chapter 4 Rulemaking v. Adjudication	244-281	466-512	269-314
Chapter 5 Rulemaking Procedure	282-419	561-624 633-698	226-268 315-347 834-861 919-945
Chapter 6 Government Control	420-535	41-184 375-424	47-208
Chapter 7 Open Government	536-560	1185-1260	729-794
Chapter 8 Scope of Review	561-627	185-374	348-544
Chapter 9 Availability of Review	628-741	1007-1184	985-1208

Blond's Administrative Law	CD	S	MM
Chapter 1 Due Process	415-502	331-444	83-109 174-249
Chapter 2 Problems in Administrative Adjudication	631-784	445-533 594-650	273-316
Chapter 3 Adjudicatory Procedure	503-535	163-211 534-566 576-593	508-560
Chapter 4 Rulemaking v. Adjudication	265-322	303-321	385-412
Chapter 5 Rulemaking Procedure	323-414	229-302 567-575	413-507
Chapter 6 Government Control	3-102	1-162 322-331	1-82 110-173
Chapter 7 Open Government	869-946	212-228	561-622
Chapter 8 Scope of Review	103-180	791-870	250-272 317-384
Chapter 9 Availability of Review	181-264 536-630 785-868	651-790	623-934

How To Use This Book

"You teach yourself the law, we teach you how to think"
- Professor Kingsfield, The Paper Chase

Law school is very different from your previous educational experiences. In the past, course material was presented in a straight-forward manner both in lectures and texts. You did well by memoriz-ing and regurgitating. In law school, your fat casebooks are stuffed with material, most of which will be useless when finals arrive. Your professors ask a lot of questions but don't seem to be teaching you either the law or how to think. Sifting through voluminous material seeking out the important concepts is a hard, time-consuming chore. We've done that job for you. This book will help you study effective-ly. We hope to teach you the law and how to think.

Preparing for class

Most students start their first year by reading and briefing all their cases. They spend too much time copying unimportant details. After finals they realize they wasted time on facts that were useless on the exam.

Case Clips

Case Clips help you focus on what your professor wants you to get out of your cases. Facts, Issues, and Rules are carefully and succinctly stated. Left out are details irrelevant to what you need to learn from the case. In general we skip procedural matters in lower courts, we don't care which party is the appellant, petitioner etc. because the trivia is not relevant to the law. Case Clips should be read before you read the actual case. You will have a good idea what to look for in the case, and appreciate the significance of what you are reading. Inevitably you will not have time to read all your cases before class. Case Clips allow you to prepare for class in about five minutes. You will be able to follow the discussion and listen without fear of being called upon.

This book contains a case clip of every major case covered in your case book. Each case clip is followed by a code identifying the case book(s) in which it appears as a principal case. Since we tried to accommodate all the major casebooks, the case clips may not follow the same sequence as they do in your text. The easiest way to study is to leaf through your text and find the corresponding case in this book by checking the table of cases.

"Should I read all the cases even if they aren't from my casebook?"

Yes, if you feel you have the time. Most major cases from other texts will be covered at least as a note case in your book. The principles of these cases are universal and the fact patterns should help your understanding. The Case Clips are written in a way that should provide a tremendous amount of understanding in a relatively short period of time.

Hanau Charts

When asked how he managed to graduate in the top 10 percent of his class at one of the 10 most prestigious law schools in the land, Paul Hanau introduced his system which included charts now called Hanau Charts.

A very common complaint among first year students is that they "can't put it all together." It is difficult to read 100 pages of material and then understand how it fits in with material read weeks or months earlier. It's hard to spend an entire day reading cases about a defense and then to understand the relationship between the defense and other defenses when you have read cases for three or four other classes in between. Hanau Charts will help you put the whole course together. They are designed to help you memorize fundamentals. They reinforce your learning by showing you the material from another perspective.

Outlines

More than one-hundred lawyers and law students were inter-viewed as part of the development of this series. Most complained that their casebooks did not teach them the law and were far too voluminous to be useful before an exam. They also told us that the commercial outlines they purchased were excellent when used as hornbooks to explain the law, but were too wordy and redundant to be effective during the weeks before finals. Few students can read four 500-page outlines during the last month of classes. It is virtually impossible to memorize that much material and even harder to decide what is and is not important. Almost every student interviewed said he or she studied from homemade outlines. We've written the outline you should use to study.

"But writing my own outline will be a learning experience."

True, but unfortunately many students spend so much time outlining they don't leave time to learn and memorize. Many students told us they spent six weeks outlining, and only one day studying before each final!

Mnemonics

Most law students spend too much time reading, and not enough time memorizing. Mnemonics are included to help you organize your essays and spot issues. They tell what is important and which areas deserve your time.

Table of Contents

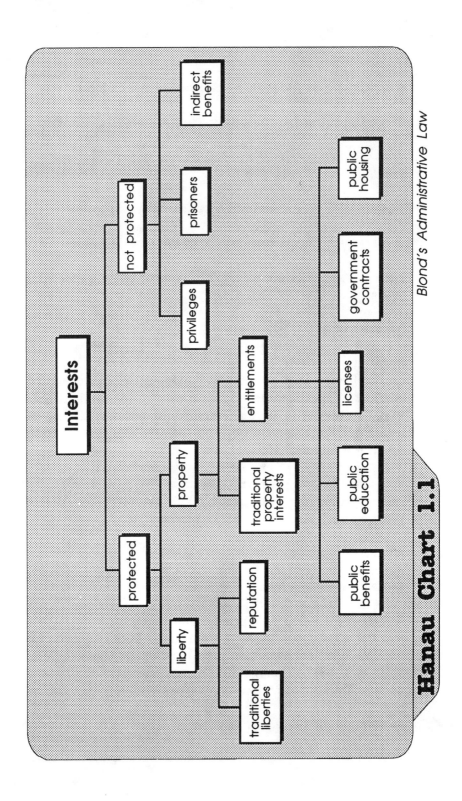

Blond's Administrative Law

Hanau Chart 1.1

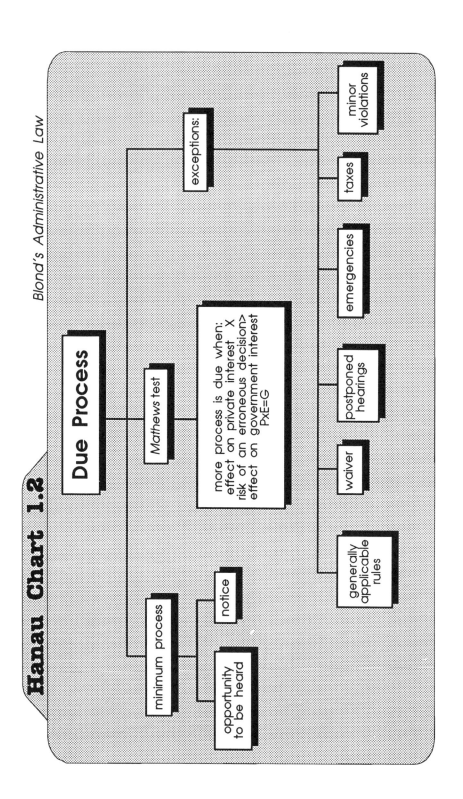

Hanau Chart 1.2

Blond's Administrative Law

Due Process

Mathews test

more process is due when:
effect on private interest X
risk of an erroneous decision>
effect on government interest
PxE=G

exceptions:

minor violations

taxes

emergencies

postponed hearings

waiver

generally applicable rules

minimum process

notice

opportunity to be heard

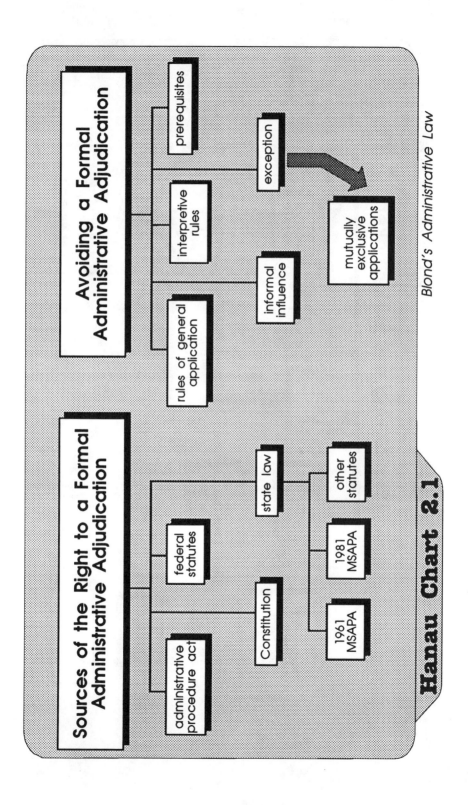

Sources of the Right to a Formal Administrative Adjudication

- administrative procedure act
- federal statutes
  - Constitution
    - 1961 MSAPA
  - state law
    - 1981 MSAPA
    - other statutes

Avoiding a Formal Administrative Adjudication

- rules of general application
- interpretive rules
  - informal influence
- prerequisites
  - exception → mutually exclusive applications

Blond's Administrative Law

Hanau Chart 2.1

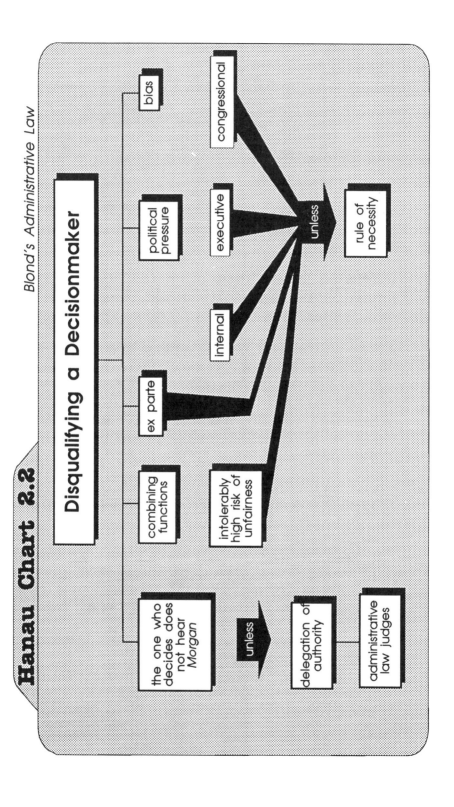

Hanau Chart 2.2

Blond's Administrative Law

Disqualifying a Decisionmaker

- bias
- political pressure
- ex parte
  - congressional
  - executive
  - internal
  - intolerably high risk of unfairness
  - *unless* → rule of necessity
- combining functions
- the one who decides does not hear *Morgan*
  - *unless* → delegation of authority → administrative law judges

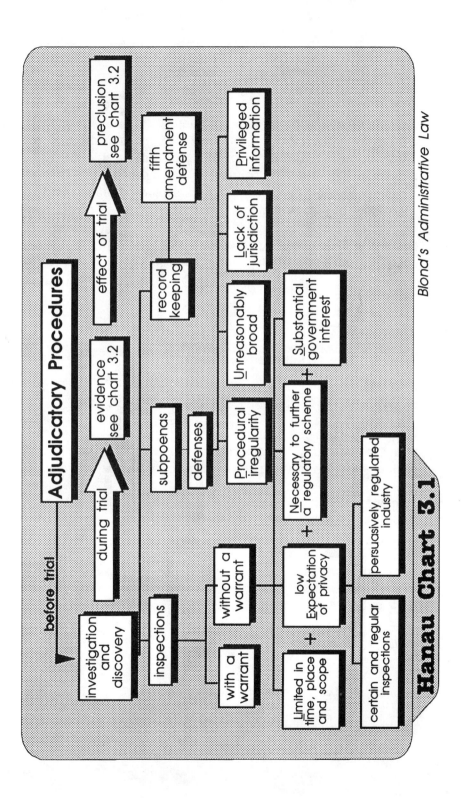

Adjudicatory Procedures

before trial

during trial

effect of trial

preclusion
see chart 3.2

evidence
see chart 3.2

investigation and discovery

record keeping

fifth amendment defense

subpoenas

defenses

Privileged information

Lack of jurisdiction

Procedural irregularity

Unreasonably broad

Substantial government interest

Necessary to further a regulatory scheme

inspections

without a warrant

with a warrant

low Expectation of privacy

+

Limited in time, place and scope

+

certain and regular inspections

persuasively regulated industry

Blond's Administrative Law

Hanau Chart 3.1

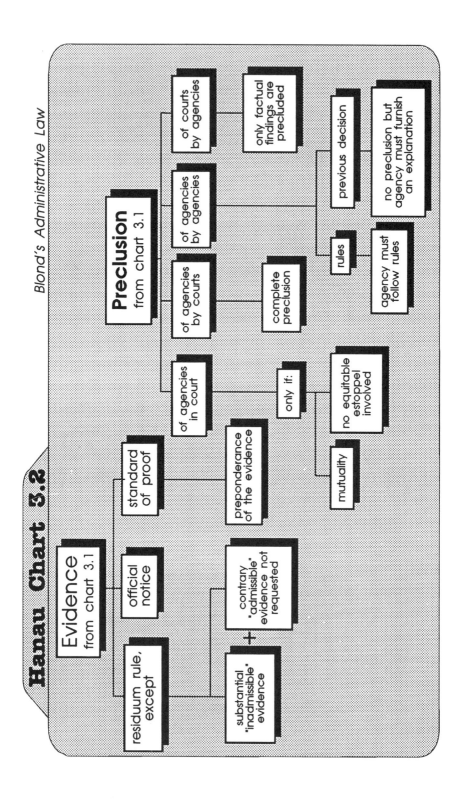

Hanau Chart 3.2

Blond's Administrative Law

Evidence
from chart 3.1

- official notice
- residuum rule, except
  - substantial "inadmissible" evidence + contrary "admissible" evidence not requested
- standard of proof
  - preponderance of the evidence

Preclusion
from chart 3.1

- of agencies in court
  - only if:
    - mutuality
    - no equitable estoppel involved
- of agencies by courts
  - complete preclusion
    - agency must follow rules
- of agencies by agencies
  - rules
  - previous decision
    - no preclusion but agency must furnish an explanation
- of courts by agencies
  - only factual findings are precluded

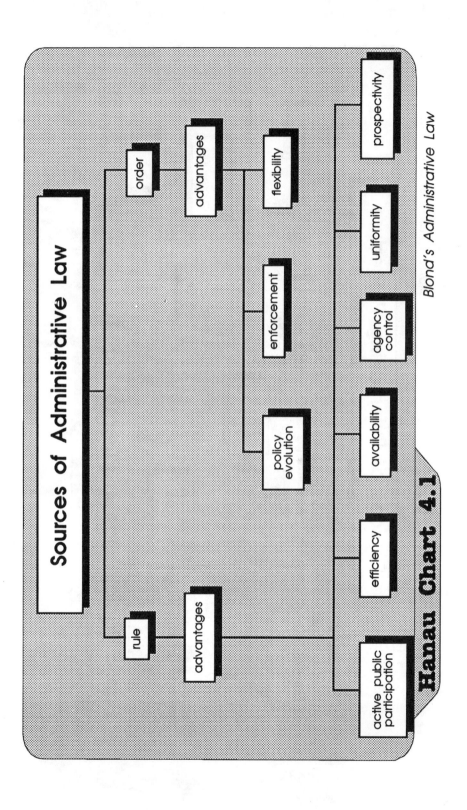

Sources of Administrative Law

order
advantages
flexibility
enforcement
policy evolution
prospectivity
uniformity
agency control
availability
efficiency
active public participation
rule
advantages

Hanau Chart 4.1

Blond's Administrative Law

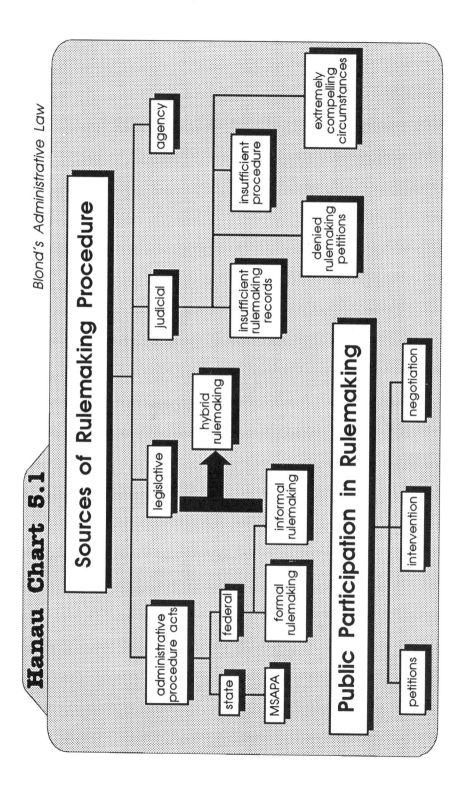

Hanau Chart 5.1

Sources of Rulemaking Procedure

- legislative
  - administrative procedure acts
    - state
      - MSAPA
    - federal
      - formal rulemaking
      - informal rulemaking → hybrid rulemaking
- judicial
  - insufficient rulemaking records
  - denied rulemaking petitions
  - insufficient procedure
    - extremely compelling circumstances
- agency

Public Participation in Rulemaking

- petitions
- intervention
- negotiation

Procedural Differences in Rulemaking

	formal	hybrid	informal	MSAPA
notice and comment	notice only	yes	yes	yes
standard of bias	completely impartial	unalterably closed mind	unalterably closed mind	not mentioned
publication	federal register	federal register	federal register	public record
regulatory analysis	no	no	no	yes
ex parte ban	total	limited	no	no
oral proceedings	yes	rarely required	no	upon request

Hanau Chart 5.2

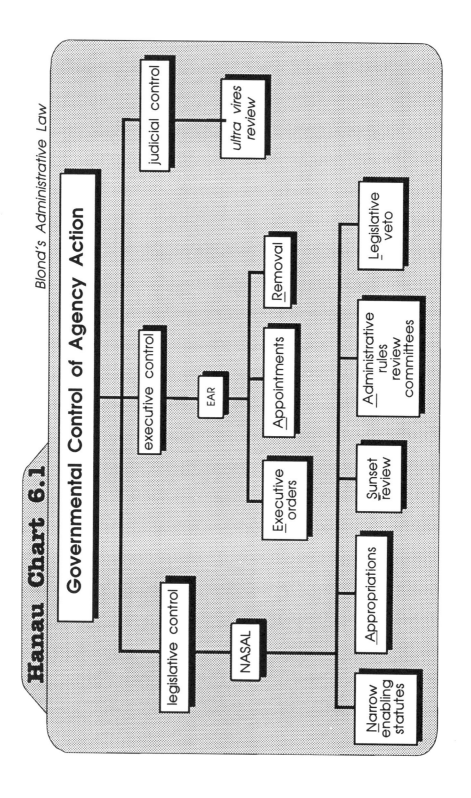

Hanau Chart 6.1

Governmental Control of Agency Action

- judicial control
  - ultra vires review
- executive control
  - EAR
    - Executive orders
    - Appointments
    - Removal
- legislative control
  - NASAL
    - Narrow enabling statutes
    - Appropriations
    - Sunset review
    - Administrative rules review committees
    - Legislative veto

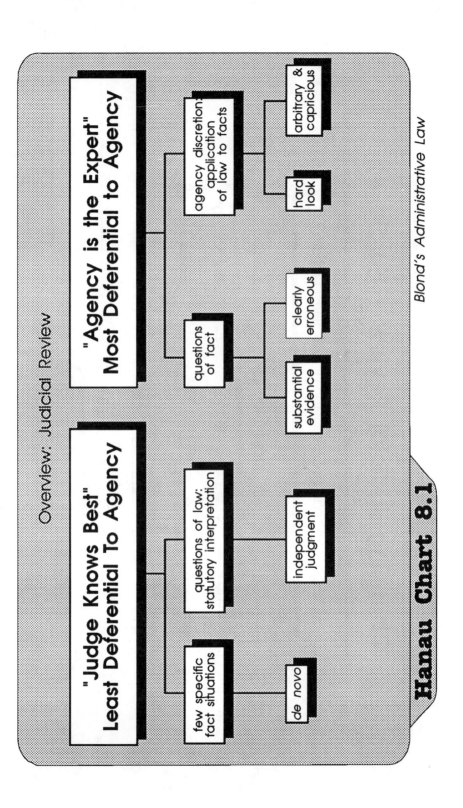

Overview: Judicial Review

"Judge Knows Best"
Least Deferential To Agency

"Agency is the Expert"
Most Deferential to Agency

few specific fact situations

questions of law: statutory interpretation

questions of fact

agency discretion: application of law to facts

de novo

independent judgment

substantial evidence

clearly erroneous

hard look

arbitrary & capricious

Blond's Administrative Law

Hanau Chart 8.1

Hanau Chart 9.1

Obtaining Judicial Review - Hurdle #1

Does the federal court have jurisdiction?

jurisdiction

agency enabling statute

general jurisdiction statutes

Federal Question 28 U.S.C. sec. 1331

Mandamus 28 U.S.C. sec 1361

Obtaining Judicial Review-Hurdle #2

Does sovereign immunity bar the action?

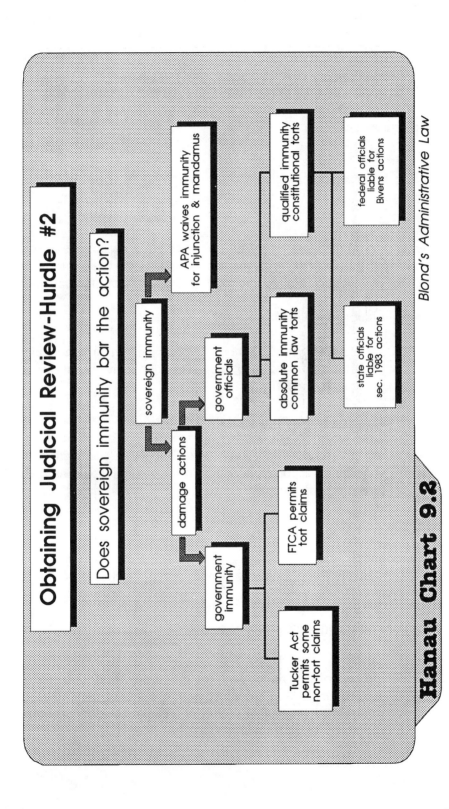

- sovereign immunity
  - APA waives immunity for injunction & mandamus
  - government officials
    - qualified immunity constitutional torts
      - federal officials liable for Bivens actions
    - absolute immunity common law torts
      - state officials liable for sec. 1983 actions
  - damage actions
    - government immunity
      - FTCA permits tort claims
      - Tucker Act permits some non-tort claims

Blond's Administrative Law

Hanau Chart 9.2

Hanau Chart 9.3

Obtaining Judicial Review - Hurdle #3

Is judicial review precluded?

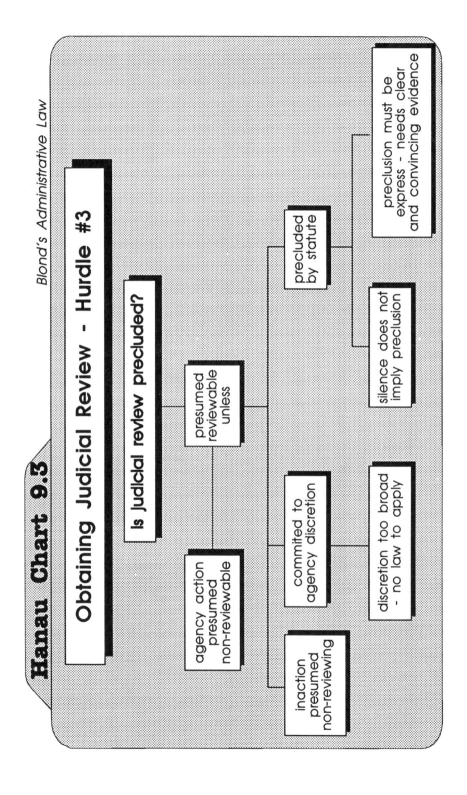

presumed reviewable unless

- precluded by statute
  - preclusion must be express - needs clear and convincing evidence
  - silence does not imply preclusion

agency action presumed non-reviewable

- committed to agency discretion
  - discretion too broad - no law to apply
- inaction presumed non-reviewing

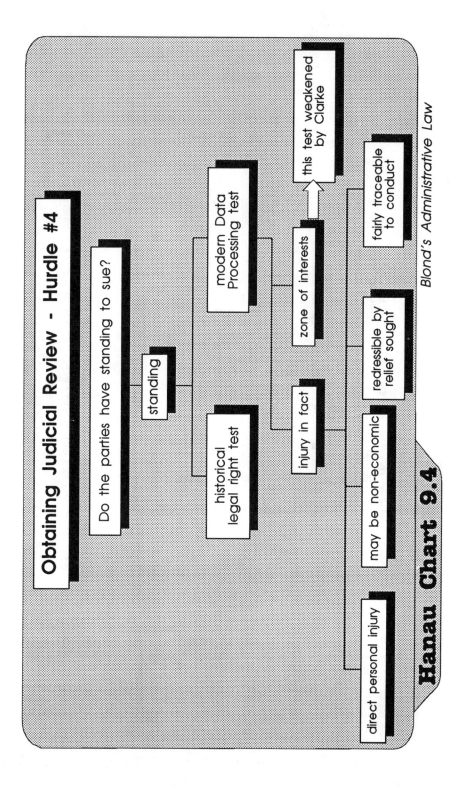

Obtaining Judicial Review - Hurdle #4

Do the parties have standing to sue?

standing

historical legal right test

modern Data Processing test

injury in fact

zone of interests

this test weakened by Clarke

direct personal injury

may be non-economic

redressible by relief sought

fairly traceable to conduct

Blond's Administrative Law

Hanau Chart 9.4

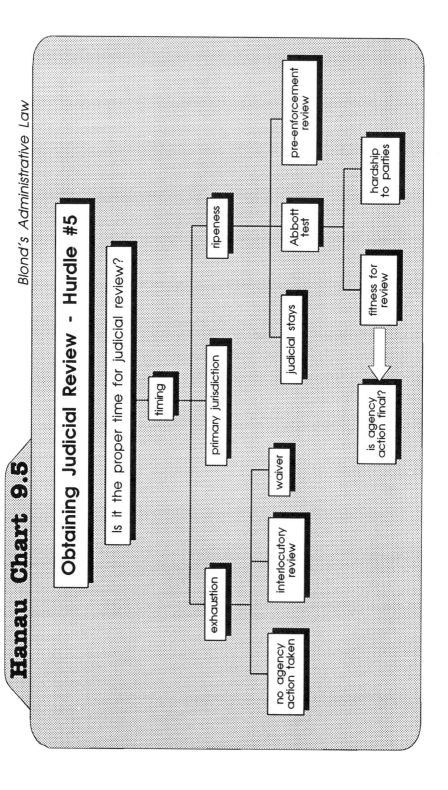

Obtaining Judicial Review - Hurdle #5

Is it the proper time for judicial review?

timing

ripeness

primary jurisdiction

judicial stays

Abbott test

pre-enforcement review

hardship to parties

fitness for review

is agency action final?

exhaustion

no agency action taken

interlocutory review

waiver

Chapter 1

DUE PROCESS HEARING RIGHTS

I. INTRODUCTION

The Fifth Amendment and § 1 of the Fourteenth Amendment, which restrict the federal and state governments respectively, prohibit administrative agencies from depriving any individual or corporation of "life, liberty, or property, without due process of law." But defining the interests protected by these Due Process Clauses and the process due those protected interests presents a complicated issue for the courts. Also, states may create interests by statute, which are also protected by due process. This chapter will explore the limits of property and liberty interests and due process requirements as they apply to administrative agencies that may infringe on those interests.

II. TRADITIONAL INTERESTS

Where an individual has no rights regarding what was lost, that person has a privilege, which can be taken without due process. A protected right is commonly known as an interest, or protected interest.

Traditionally, rights were restricted to property that could be actually owned, such as real estate and chattel. Abstract interests, such as a driver's license, or government entitlements, such as welfare and disability payments, were privileges, not rights.

A. Property

  1. Physical property owned by an individual or corporation is protected by due process.

2. Property interests are created and defined by statute or state law. Once created, they may not be withdrawn without due process of law.

B. Liberty

1. The freedom to act and to use one's property as one wishes is protected by due process.

2. Liberty interests are defined by the Constitution.

III.   POST-*GOLDBERG* INTERESTS

Beginning with *Goldberg v. Kelly* in 1970, and as definitively stated in *Board of Regents v. Roth* in 1972, many interests that had previously been considered a privilege, like government entitlements and licenses, have been reinterpreted as protected rights requiring due process before the government may eliminate them.   Of course, traditional interests are still protected; they are merely supplemented by these additional interests.

A. New Property Interests (Government Entitlements)

Mnemonic: BELCH

1. Public Benefits

a. Public benefits such as welfare, Medicaid, and retirement pensions.

b. There is a property interest in the continued receipt of these benefits once they are granted.

c. There is no property interest in qualifying for benefits. No property right is conferred until receipt of the benefits begins.

    d. There is no property interest in maintaining a constant level of benefits; legislatures may alter benefits without affording recipients due process.

    e. There is a property interest in receiving the proper amount of benefits as determined by law.

2. Education

    a. States have created a property right to receive a public education.

    b. Students also have a liberty interest in freedom from excessive corporal punishment.

3. Licenses
There is a property interest in the continued possession of a government issued license, such as medical, driver's, and architectural.

4. Government Contracts

    a. The government may refuse to grant or renew a contract for any reason, without affording the recipient due process.

    b. Guaranteed government employment contracts (i.e., classification as a "permanent" employee) may not be terminated without due process.

5. Government Funded Housing
Like other government benefits, a right to continued receipt of government subsidized housing may not be terminated without due process. But additionally, a tenant may not be evicted from a particular housing unit without being afforded due process, even if other public housing is available.

B. New Liberty Interest (Reputation)

There is a liberty interest in preserving one's reputation, as long as the violation of this right contains both the following elements:

1. The statement must be published, untrue, and alleging a moral defect.

2. The damage to reputation must be accompanied by a change in status (such as the loss of a job).

C. Exceptions

1. Privileges
   The old privilege/right distinction still remains in some isolated areas of the law.

   a. Scope
      A privilege is subject to all conditions set forth in the relevant statute without regard for due process.

   b. Examples:

      i. Immigration
         The ability to enter the country is a privilege. In contrast, once an immigrant has entered the country, deportation may not occur without due process.

      ii. Qualifying for Entitlements
          Qualification for any public benefit is a privilege. Legislatures set the standards, and they are not limited by due process. Public benefits include all the post-*Goldberg* property interests, such as Medicare, a license of any sort (medical, driving, etc.), public housing, a government contract, etc.

2. Prisoners
   Normally, courts will not investigate alleged violations of a prisoner's due process rights unless:

   a. Prison conditions violate other constitutional norms; or

   b. State law grants the prisoner a protected interest.

3. Indirect Benefits
    Beneficiaries may only sue for what is directly due them. A regulation that indirectly affects the quality of benefits, but does not reduce or terminate them may not be challenged. For example, closing an unemployment office denies no benefits, but makes receipt more difficult.

IV.   WHAT PROCESS IS DUE?

A. Minimum Due Process

Before any protected right is infringed, at least minimum due process must be afforded the holder of that right.

1. Elements
    Minimum due process must include an opportunity to be heard and notice of such an opportunity.

2. Limitations

    a. A minimum due process hearing need not be judicial in nature.

    b. An opportunity to be heard will usually be oral in nature.

        Exception: Where the safety of others might be endangered, such as a prison hearing.

    c. An opportunity to be heard need not be "face-to-face."

    d. Decision makers need not be independent or have legal training, as long as they are competent.

B. The *Mathews v. Eldridge* three-pronged test

1. When To Apply It

   a. To determine whether a given agency's procedure affords sufficient due process;

   b. To determine what process is due an individual whose rights are threatened; and

   c. To determine whether due process must be given before rights are taken away (i.e., a pre-termination hearing).

2. How To Apply It
   Mathews Calculus: $\underline{P} \times \underline{E} > \underline{G}$

   Weigh the effect on the $\underline{P}$rivate interest, multiplied by the risk of an $\underline{E}$rroneous decision, against the effect on the $\underline{G}$overnment interest to determine whether more process is due.

   a. Effect on the Private Interest
   Look at the severity and the duration of the loss, as well as historical limitations on that interest.

   b. Risk of an Erroneous Decision
   Look at the necessity of an oral presentation, the rate of reversal after judicial review, and possible alternatives to the present procedure.

   c. Effect on the Government Interest
   Look at the cost of a due process hearing and the burden of an increased number of cases upon the agency.

3. Problems with *Mathews*

   a. The calculus does not take into account the importance of a hearing to a complainant's sense of self-worth.

b. Disregards importance of a pre-termination hearing when complex factual issues are involved.

c. Narrowly defines the costs and benefits of a hearing.

d. Utilitarian approach ignores the constitutional values encompassed by due process.

e. Unscrupulous claimants may request a pre-termination hearing only to keep undeserved benefits coming. This increases agency costs in unnecessary lawsuits, and benefits paid to unqualified recipients.

f. Courts are forced to write administrative procedures.

g. Agencies may resent judicial intervention and ignore new procedures.

h. Complicated hearings may be unfair to uneducated claimants.

i. Adversarial hearings may hamper cooperation between agencies and recipients.

C. Irrebuttable Presumptions

1. Defined
   Irrebuttable presumptions are factual assumptions, made by a statute or agency, which a party is never allowed to attack in court.

2. Constitutionality
   Irrebuttable presumptions violate due process when that presumption is not necessarily or universally true in fact, and when the state has reasonable alternative means of making the crucial determination. *Stanley v. Illinois.*

D. Methods of Dispute Resolution

1. Judicial Review
Where an agency and a recipient disagree whether benefits should be disbursed, the dispute is often resolved through judicial review of the agency decision.

2. Administrative Law Judges
Instead of judicial review, many agencies use administrative law judges as impartial decision makers.

3. Non-Judicial Dispute Resolution
Agencies may also use many non-judicial methods of dispute resolution, such as school disciplinary actions, prison parole boards, and tenure review.

4. Every method of dispute resolution must preserve due process.

E. Exceptions

1. Generally Applicable Rules
Where everyone affected by a statute or an agency rule is affected equally, no process is due, even where substantive rights are infringed.

2. Waiver

a. Due process rights may be waived.

b. A statute or regulation may deem due process rights waived by a lapse of time.

3. Postponed Hearings

a. A pre-determination due process hearing may be held at any time before a final decision has been made.

b. Where only property rights are affected, postponement of an opportunity to be heard will not violate due process.

c. Judicial review will satisfy due process only where *Mathews* does not require a pre-determination hearing and where judicial review allows a party to adequately present his case *de novo.*

4. Emergencies

   a. Where immediate destruction of property is necessary to prevent a nuisance, no due process is required.

   b. In times of war, liberty and property rights may be infringed without due process.

5. Taxes
   Property may be summarily taken for the purpose of collecting unpaid taxes, as long as post-seizure adjudication is available.

6. Minor Violations
   De minimis deprivations of property and liberty do not require due process.

V.   MASHAW'S MODELS OF ADMINISTRATIVE JUSTICE

Professor Jerry Mashaw has identified three administrative philosophies behind dispute resolution. These philosophies are independent of each other and often contradictory. When analyzing a specific agency's procedures, it is sometimes helpful to determine which philosophy most closely applies.

A. Bureaucratic Rationality

1. Defined
   Decisions should be accurate and efficient, using standardized procedures and cost-benefit analyses. Individual attention and subjective analysis are low priorities.

2. Policies Emphasized

    a. Ensure accurate agency decisions.
    b. Ensure consistent agency decisions.
    c. Police the government's use of discretion.
    d. Create a record to aid subsequent judicial review.

B. Professional Treatment

1. Defined
Decisions should provide appropriate support to a recipient, utilizing personal examination and counseling to create a rapport between the caseworker and client. But this must occur within the framework of an objective standard of rules. However, decision makers would be neither independent nor, in many cases, impartial.

2. Policies Emphasized

    a. Give claimants a sense of self-worth.
    b. Give claimants a forum for their grievances.
    c. Allow claimants to understand and accept agency decisions.
    d. Maintain a cooperative spirit between caseworker and recipient.

C. Moral Judgment

1. Defined
Decisions should be fair and equitable. Standardized procedures are discarded in favor of ad hoc decisions on the merits. Consistency in decisions is not a goal; moreover, case-by-case analysis is often inefficient and costly.

2. Policies Emphasized

    a. Ensure that program goals are realized.
    b. Provide claimants with individualized responses.
    c. Make the agency accountable for its policies.

CASE CLIPS

Goldberg v. Kelly (S.Ct. 1970) BA, BS, GB, CD, S, MM
Facts: New York State welfare payments were discontinued without an evidentiary hearing.
Issue 1: Must the government provide for an evidentiary hearing before the termination of welfare-type benefits, which is normally considered only a privilege?
Rule 1: (Brennan, J.) The recipient of welfare entitlements has a protected property interest in the continued receipt of those benefits and, thus, is entitled to an evidentiary hearing before benefits are terminated. The distinction between privilege and right is abolished.
Issue 2: Must the pre-termination hearing be judicial in nature?
Rule 2: A hearing must occur before termination of benefits and need only provide the recipient an opportunity to present oral arguments and evidence on questions of fact, confront or cross-examine witnesses, counter opposing evidence, and retain an attorney before an impartial decisionmaker who must produce a record of his reasons behind his determination.
Dissent: (Black, J.) This decision hinders the government from denying funds to those not legally entitled to receive them. Welfare is mere charity from the government and not a protected interest. The government will withhold deserving people from its lists until an exhaustive determination of validity has been made. Since welfare programs are new to the nation, its regulation should be left to the legislature.
Dissent: (Burger, C.J.) The cost of an evidentiary hearing may be a heavy burden on an administrative agency.

Board of Regents of State Colleges v. Roth (S.Ct. 1972)
BA, BS, GB, CD
Facts: D discharged an untenured professor without a statement of reasons or an opportunity for a hearing.
Issue: Is continued state employment a protected interest requiring a satisfaction of due process requirements prior to termination?
Rule: (Stewart, J.) A state employment contract does not constitute a constitutionally protected interest; thus, due process need not be afforded prior to its termination.

Dissent: (Marshall, J.) Every citizen who applies for a government job is entitled to it unless the government can establish some reason for denying employment.

Hewitt v. Helms (S.Ct. 1983) BA

Facts: Helms, a prisoner, was effectively restricted to solitary confinement for forty-five days without a hearing.

Issue 1: Under the Fourteenth Amendment, does a prisoner have a liberty interest in remaining in a general population cell?

Rule 1: (Rehnquist, J.) There is no liberty interest in remaining in a general population cell. As long as conditions imposed do not otherwise violate constitutional norms (such as free speech or the freedom to practice religion), the Court will not review whether an inmate's treatment violates the Due Process Clause.

Issue 2: When will a state law grant to a prisoner a liberty interest in remaining in a general population cell?

Rule 2: Although the enactment of procedural guidelines does not generally indicate the creation of a liberty interest, where the law uses mandatory language and requires specific pre-conditions before imposing solitary confinement, a liberty interest is created.

Dissent: (Stevens, J.) The liberty interest derives from natural law, not from the Constitution, and not from Pennsylvania state law.

Note: Other portions of the case, printed later in the casebook, are discussed below.

Cleveland Board of Education v. Loudermill
(S.Ct. 1985) BA, GB, S, MM

Facts: Generally, civil servants are "at will" employees who may be fired without an opportunity to be heard. However, under Ohio law a civil servant may only be terminated for "cause."

Issue 1: Does a law that restricts termination of government employment create a property interest?

Rule 1: (White, J.) When a government employee may not be terminated without "cause," state law has created a property interest in freedom from unlawful termination.

Issue 2: When a state creates a property right, is termination of that right subject to due process limitations?

Rule 2: All protected rights, even those created by the state, require notice and an opportunity to be heard, as well as a *Mathews* analysis (see below). Procedural aspects of a state law will be analyzed separately from the substantive right created.

Concurrence: (Marshall, J.) The employee deserves more due process than notice and an opportunity to be heard. Whenever evidence is disputed, a government employee should be entitled to present witnesses and confront and cross-examine opposing witnesses.

Dissent: (Rehnquist, J.) No property interest was created by Ohio law. Even if one had been, the procedural aspects of this property interest is indistinguishable from its substantive aspects. Furthermore, the balancing test creates unpredictable and inconsistent decisions.

Mathews v. Eldridge (S.Ct. 1976) BA, BS, GB, CD, S, MM

Facts: Disability payments were discontinued without an evidentiary hearing.

Issue: When is an evidentiary hearing required before the loss of a property interest?

Rule: (Powell, J.) Anybody in risk of the loss of a liberty or property interest must be given notice and some sort of opportunity to be heard. But, in determining whether an evidentiary hearing is required before the final determination of benefits, three factors must be weighed. First, look at how the private interest will be affected, including degree of loss and length of loss. Second, look at the risk of an erroneous decision, including the necessity of oral presentations, the rate of reversal after judicial review, and possible alternatives to the present procedure. Finally, look at how the governmental interest will be affected, including the incremental costs of pre-determination hearings, and the burden on scarce fiscal and administrative resources.

Dissent: (Brennan, J.) The Court understates Eldridge's need for disability benefits. The Court also improperly considers the availability of other forms of public assistance in terminating benefits.

Hewitt v. Helms [Part II] (S.Ct. 1983) BA

Facts: Helms, a prisoner, was effectively restricted to solitary confinement for forty-five days without a judicial-style hearing.

Issue: What due process must be afforded a prisoner with a liberty interest in remaining in a general population cell?

Rule: (Rehnquist, J.) An informal, nonadversarial proceeding is sufficient due process protection of an inmate's liberty interest in remaining in a general population cell. An inmate must receive some notice of the charges against him, and an opportunity to present his own views, whether in writing or orally, which the decisionmaker must review. Periodic review of an isolated inmate's circumstances is also required.

Dissent: (Stevens, J.) Due process requires an opportunity to make an oral presentation, initially and at each review.

Walters v. National Association of Radiation Survivors (S.Ct. 1985) BA, GB

Facts: Final authority to determine veterans' benefits rested in the Board of Veterans' Appeals (BVA). According to a statute passed in 1864, a veteran's legal counsel could not charge more than ten dollars per case.

Issue: May Congress restrict the amount an attorney may charge when representing a petitioner of non-financially need-based government benefits at an administrative hearing?

Rule: (Rehnquist, J.) Although restricting access to expert representation, attorney fee limitations, absent a strong showing of probability of error, do not deny due process to claimants in "informal and non-adversarial" proceedings.

Concurrence: (O'Connor, J.) Fee limitation has not been proven to pose a risk of erroneous deprivation of rights in this general case, but may be invalid "as applied" in future individual proceedings.

Dissent: (Stevens, J.) The right to consult an attorney falls firmly within due process, which cannot be assigned a value for the utilitarian *Mathews* test. Furthermore, this law is outmoded and paternalistic.

Londoner v. Denver (S.Ct. 1908) BA, BS, GB

Facts: Denver City Council assessed a tax against Londoner, a property owner and taxpayer, without affording him the opportunity for an oral hearing.

Issue: What process is due a taxpayer whose tax is assessed by an administrative agency?

Rule: Before an agency levies a tax, the taxpayer must be given notice and an opportunity for an oral hearing.

Bi-Metallic Inv. Co. v. State Board of Equalization
(S.Ct. 1915) BA, BS, GB, S

Facts: All property taxes in the county were increased 40 percent without providing for an opportunity to be heard.

Issue: Must a property owner be given an opportunity to be heard whenever taxes are increased?

Rule: (Holmes, J.) Where all concerned are treated equally by the statute (i.e., a law that is applied generally to all taxpayers or citizens), due process does not require an opportunity to be heard.

Atkins v. Parker (S.Ct. 1985) BA

Facts: Congress changed the food stamp program, reducing or eliminating benefits for many households. Massachusetts sent notice informing families of the change and giving them an opportunity to request a "fair hearing," during which time their present level of benefits would be frozen.

Issue 1: What notice is required for recipients of a change in government benefits?

Rule 1: (Stevens, J.) Notice must plainly inform each family of the availability of a hearing and that benefit levels would be frozen, but not as to the particulars of the new law.

Issue 2: Do recipients have a property interest in a constant level of benefits?

Rule 2: The Due Process Clause of the Fourteenth Amendment creates no property interest in a constant level of benefits and does not require Congress to maintain current levels of entitlements.

Dissent: (Brennan, J.) Because of mistakes by Massachusetts, many households were deprived of their proper level of entitlements, even under the new law. Reductions in a recipient's proper level of entitlements is an infringement upon a property interest requiring due process considerations.

Bailey v. Richardson (1951) BS, GB

Facts: P had been employed by the Civil Service Commission until the Commission's "Loyalty Board," acting upon information from undisclosed sources, investigated her alleged disloyalty to the government. P answered all interrogatories and received an administrative hearing, but was still discharged by the Board.

Issue: May the government discharge an employee on grounds of disloyalty without a judicial hearing?

Rule: Since non-appointed government employment is a privilege and not a right, no due process is violated by discharge without a hearing.

Dissent: Dismissal for loyalty is a punishment requiring a judicial hearing. The dismissal also violated the First Amendment right to free speech.

Greene v. McElroy (S.Ct. 1959) BS

Facts: Greene's security clearance was revoked because of anonymous allegations that the Defense Department refused to disclose.

Issue: May administrators withhold the identities of anonymous informers by claiming that the information is a "military secret"?

Rule: (Warren, C.J.) Without express authority by the President or Congress, an agency that withholds an informers' identity violates an individual's due process.

Dissent: (Clark, J.) There is no right to military secrets, so no hearing was necessary at all. Furthermore, the security clearance program was properly authorized.

Cafeteria & Restaurant Workers Union v. McElroy (S.Ct. 1961) BS, GB

Facts: Brawner (P) had worked at M&M Restaurant on a naval base for more than six years before being denied access to the base (and thus her job) as a security risk. She received no hearing on the merits of the discharge, nor specifics about the cause of the firing.

Issue: Does denial of access to a government job without a hearing constitute a violation of due process?

Rule: (Stewart, J.) Access to a government job is not a protected interest, thus, denial of access does not violate due process. A government employee may be discharged at will for any valid reason that is neither arbitrary nor discriminatory.

Dissent: (Brennan, J.) This decision allows an employer to discharge an employee for an arbitrary or discriminatory reason by saying the discharge occurred for a rational reason, since the employer's decision will not be reviewed. Furthermore, being labelled a "security risk" will impair P's future ability to garner employment.

Southern Ry. v. Virginia (S. Ct. 1933) BS

Facts: By state law, the state highway commissioner could, without affording notice or a hearing, require a railroad to build an overhead road crossing, or even to eliminate one.

Issue: What due process must an agency afford a company before commanding it to perform an action affecting property interests?

Rule: (McReynolds, J.) Before any property interest may be taken by administrative action, notice and an opportunity to be heard must be afforded.

North American Cold Storage Co. v. Chicago
(S.Ct. 1908) BS, GB

Facts: Officials refused to allow deliveries to or from a warehouse, effectively shutting down the business, after the company refused to turn over forty-seven barrels of poultry that the City claimed had become putrid.

Issue: When may the government destroy private property without due process?

Rule: (Peckham, J.) If not destroying the property may in itself constitute a nuisance, that property may be summarily destroyed without violating due process.

Bowles v. Willingham (S.Ct. 1944) BS, GB

Facts: Congress authorized the Office of Price Administration (OPA) to fix rents according to its discretion. Rents were declared frozen at April, 1, 1941, levels. Those ordered to change their rents in accordance with an OPA order could only contest the order through judicial review after the fact.

Issue: Must a landlord be able to contest a rent regulation order before it goes into effect?

Rule: (Douglas, J.) Post-determination judicial review is sufficient due process for a taking of goods, as long as the judicial review is adequate.

Perry v. Sindermann (S.Ct. 1972) BS, GB

Facts: Sindermann had been employed for ten years under a series of one-year contracts at Odessa Junior College, which had an informal tenure program. Sindermann had "understood" that he had tenure.

Sindermann claimed his contract had not been renewed due to statements he had made.

Issue 1: Does lack of a formal guarantee of government employment preclude an employee from claiming a violation of First Amendment rights?

Rule 1: (Stewart, J.) The government may not terminate or refuse to renew employment on the basis of an employee's constitutionally protected behavior, even if the employee has not been guaranteed continued employment.

Issue 2: Does an implied guarantee of continued government employment constitute a protected property interest that requires satisfaction of due process before termination?

Rule 2: An implied guarantee of continued employment requires satisfaction of due process before the government can refuse to renew an employment contract.

Concurrence: (Burger, C.J.) State law determines whether an implied guarantee exists.

Arnett v. Kennedy (S.Ct. 1974) BS

Facts: Kennedy, a Civil Service employee, was fired. Federal law provided that Civil Service employees may not be fired without cause and procedures to protect that right.

Issue 1: Where a statute that confers a property right to government employment also creates procedural methods to terminate that employment, may the procedures be separated from the substantial right in a due process analysis?

Rule 1: (Rehnquist, J.) Where legislation creating a protected interest concentrates on procedural measures, the substantive right may not be considered separately.

Issue 2: Where a discharge occurred due to allegations of dishonesty, must there be a pretermination hearing?

Rule 2: Post-termination proceedings are sufficient to give a discharged employee "an opportunity to clear his name."

Concurrence: (Powell, J.) Procedural measures must be considered separately from the substantive right, and must comport with due process requirements. Here, it does.

Dissent: (Marshall, J.) Procedures must satisfy due process. The stigma associated with termination "for cause" is sufficient to require pretermination hearings before an independent and impartial decision-maker.

Goss v. Lopez (S.Ct. 1975) BS, S

Facts: Students were suspended from high school without an opportunity to be heard.

Issue: Does a student's suspension without a hearing satisfy due process requirements?

Rule: (White, J.) Given the high risk of error and the rights of the students, minimal process is due. The students must be given oral or written notice, an explanation of evidence against them, and an opportunity to present their own version of the facts.

Dissent: (Powell, J.) This constitutes an unnecessary intrusion into the management of public schools. Furthermore, the statute that confers this right not to be suspended contains procedural safeguards that cannot be separated from the right conferred. Finally, a due process hearing is not justified given the low chance of erroneous suspensions.

Bishop v. Wood (S.Ct. 1976) BS

Facts: The City Manager of Marion terminated the employment of a policeman without affording him a hearing. A policeman is classified as a "permanent employee" by a city ordinance.

Issue 1: Does a permanent public employee have a property interest in continued employment that is protected by due process?

Rule 1: (Stevens, J.) Since only state law can create a property interest, where state law determines that a policeman is an "at will" employee, there is no property interest in continued employment.

Issue 2: Does a discharge for "false and defamatory" reasons constitute an infringement on a liberty interest in reputation?

Rule 2: Where the reasons for termination of employment, even if "false and defamatory," are made public only after termination, no defamation has occurred.

Dissent 1: (Brennan, J.) Before a state law is construed as not granting a property interest, the Court should look at whether there was an objectively reasonable belief that an interest was created.

Dissent 2: (White, J.) A property interest in continued employment was created by state law. This interest requires due process protection.

Paul v. Davis (S.Ct. 1976) BS

Facts: Davis, a reporter, was identified in a police flyer as an "active shoplifter" but had never been convicted of shoplifting.
Issue: Does a government induced injury to one's reputation qualify as a loss of a liberty interest requiring a due process hearing before such an occurrence?
Rule: (Rehnquist, J.) Defamation alone is insufficient to constitute a loss of any liberty interest.
Dissent: (Brennan, J.) Interest in one's reputation is a protected liberty interest.

Meachum v. Fano (S.Ct. 1976) BS, GB

Facts: After several fires, several state prisoners were transferred to a less favorable prison after a hearing before an internal review board, but without an opportunity to confront or cross-examine opposing witnesses.
Issue: May a state transfer prisoners without satisfying the due process elements required in other judicial proceedings?
Rule: (White, J.) Unless the state itself provides a right, a state may restrict a convict's liberty as long as doing so does not otherwise violate constitutional norms (such as free speech or the freedom to practice religion).
Dissent: (Stevens, J.) Liberty is an inalienable interest, and any "grievous loss" of it may be limited only in accord with due process.

Ingraham v. Wright (S.Ct. 1977) BS, GB, CD

Facts: Two students claimed their public high school's corporal punishment was "cruel and unusual."
Issue 1: Is corporal punishment of students cruel and unusual?
Rule 1: (Powell, J.) The Eighth Amendment does not apply; teachers may use any force that is not "excessive" and which the teacher believes is "reasonably necessary."
Issue 2: Is there a constitutional basis for relief from excessive use of corporal punishment?

Rule 2: Freedom from excessive corporal punishment is a protected liberty interest.

Issue 3: What due process is required?

Rule 3: A *Mathews* analysis is required in every case involving protected rights. The first factor (the private interest) should include an analysis of historical limitations of the interest.

Dissent: (White, J.) Corporal punishment should be limited by the Eighth Amendment if sufficiently severe. Tort action is inadequate to protect against such punishment.

Gray Panthers v. Schweiker (I) (1980) BS, S

Facts: Medicare procedures did not allow for opportunities to make oral presentations before affecting benefits, hearings in cases involving less than $100, or judicial review in cases involving less than $1000.

Issue: What minimal process is due a claimant with a property interest in continued receipt of government benefits?

Rule: A claimant with a property interest in continued receipt of government benefits must at least receive information regarding the original decision, a reasonable time and opportunity to present evidence supporting that claimant's position and, after the hearing, a "meaningful explanation" of the final decision.

Hahn v. Gottlieb (1970) BS, CD

Facts: Tenants of a federally subsidized private housing project objected to a twenty-eight dollar per month rent increase.

Issue: Do tenants of federally subsidized housing have a property interest in low rent requiring a due process hearing before a rent increase?

Rule: Under a *Mathews* test, the interest of a tenant of federally subsidized housing projects in affordable housing does not outweigh the government interest in efficient rent regulation. Thus, a hearing is not required prior to a rent increase.

O'Bannon v. Town Court Nursing Center
(S.Ct. 1980) BS, CD, MM

Facts: Medicare and Medicaid patients had to seek new facilities when the Department of Housing, Education and Welfare (HEW) decertified Town Court without a hearing.

Issue: Do Medicaid patients have an interest in remaining at a particular facility?
Rule: (Stevens, J.) The Medicaid statute confers upon patients a right to choose from a range of qualified facilities, but not a right to continuous treatment from any one particular facility.
Concurrence: (Blackmun, J.) Residents did have a property interest, but the decertification procedures afforded them due process.
Dissent: (Brennan, J.) Residents have a property interest in an expectancy of continued residency that was not afforded due process.

Swann v. Gastonia Housing Authority (1980) BS

Facts: Tenants of federally subsidized housing were notified within the thirty days required by the lease that their lease would not be renewed. The refusal to renew occurred without good cause.
Issue 1: Does the Low Income Housing Act (LIHA) creates a property interest in continued housing?
Rule 1: Tenants' reasonable expectations that they may remain in their rented homes beyond termination of the lease creates a protected interest under the LIHA.
Issue 2: Must an agency make a finding of good cause before terminating a property interest in the continued receipt of government housing by refusing to renew a lease?
Rule: Tenants' property interest in the continued receipt of government housing requires a finding of good cause before termination of a lease.
Note: On appeal, the Court of Appeals agreed that the tenants have a protected interest, but stipulated that good cause need not be proven before notice; eviction hearings provide adequate due process protection.

Board of Curators of University of Missouri v. Horowitz (S.Ct. 1978) BS, CD

Facts: Horowitz, a medical student, was dismissed for academic reasons without a trial-type hearing.
Issue: Does a student's expulsion require a quasi-judicial proceeding in order to satisfy due process?
Rule: (Rehnquist, J.) Academic evaluations, as opposed to disciplinary evaluations, bear such little resemblance to traditional fact-finding proceedings that judicial style proceedings are inappropriate.

Dissent in Part: (Marshall, J.) The distinction between academic and disciplinary evaluations is irrelevant; both pertain to the question of conduct.

Schweiker v. McClure (S.Ct. 1982) GB

Facts: The plaintiffs, who were denied Medicare benefits, received a hearing before a decisionmaker chosen by private insurance carriers, but paid for by the federal government.

Issue: Must a decisionmaker be appointed by the government and have formal legal training?

Rule: (Powell, J.) Legal training for a decisionmaker is unnecessary where knowledge of the law is not crucial to the decision making process. Furthermore, a decisionmaker must be unbiased, but not necessarily government appointed.

Heckler v. Campbell (S.Ct. 1983) CD, MM

Facts: Campbell was denied Social Security disability benefits because of the Administrative Law Judge's reliance on medical-vocational guidelines.

Issue: May an administrative decision regarding eligibility for benefits be based upon general guidelines?

Rule: (Powell, J.) General guidelines may be used to determine benefit eligibility.

Bell v. Burson (S.Ct. 1971) CD

Facts: Under Georgia law, an insured motorist involved in an auto accident must post a bond to cover all damage to other motorists, or else suffer suspension of his license and registration, without an opportunity for a hearing on the issue of liability.

Issue 1: Does a licensed motorist have a property interest in the continued possession of a driver's license?

Rule 1: (Brennan, J.) As continued possession of a driver's license may be essential to the driver's pursuit of a livelihood, a driver does have a property interest in its continued possession.

Issue 2: What process is due a motorist before a license may be suspended?

Rule 2: A driver must have notice and an opportunity for a hearing about issues appropriate to the nature of the case before his license is suspended.

Association of Administrative Law Judges v. Heckler
(1984) CD

Facts: The Department of Health and Human Services (HHS) evaluated Administrative Law Judges (ALJs) on two criteria. First, "allowance rates" determined statistically whether an ALJ overturned a disproportionate amount of cases. Second, "motion rates" analyzed whether the reasons set forth in decisions that the ALJ affirmed were consistent with the basis of the agency decisions.

Issue 1: Do ALJs have a liberty interest in a freedom to make impartial decisions?

Rule 1: An ALJ does have a protected interest in retaining its independence from HHS when adjudicating issues. However, this right is not absolute.

Issue 2: Did HHS's concentration on allowance rates infringe upon the ALJs' interest in the ability to make independent decisions?

Rule 2: HHS's concentration on allowance rates created an "atmosphere of tension and unfairness," which prevented the ALJs from exercising their right to decide cases impartially, thus infringing their interest in making independent decisions.

National Independent Coal Operator's Association v. Kleppe
(S.Ct. 1976) S

Facts: Coal mine operators accused of committing health or safety violations were given fifteen days to request a hearing before they were deemed to have waived that right.

Issue: May the right to a hearing be waived by implication?

Rule: (Burger, C.J.) Due process only requires an opportunity to be heard; the actual hearing may be waived expressly, or impliedly by an elapse of time.

Anaconda Co. v. Ruckelshaus (1972) S

Facts: Based on a contested factual study, the Environmental Protection Agency regulated the operation of an Anaconda copper smelter without an adjudicative hearing and without allowing Anaconda to present its own evidence.

Issue: When may an administrative agency create a rule affecting privately held rights without requiring satisfaction of due process?

Rule: To promulgate a rule affecting private rights without affording due process, a rulemaker must satisfy a two-part test. First, the action must not be directed at a single individual or corporation. Second, the proposed rule must not be dependent upon a determination of contested facts.

Hodel v. Virginia Surface Mining Assn. (S.Ct. 1981) S

Facts: The Surface Mining Act authorized the Secretary of the Interior to summarily and immediately shut down a mining operation whenever he determined that an operation had violated the law.

Issue: May a government administrator shut down an enterprise before affording a judicial-style hearing?

Rule: (Marshall, J.) Summary administrative actions that effect a deprivation of property rights are justified in emergency situations as long as the owner of the enterprise has an opportunity to be heard soon after the action.

Smith v. Liquor Control Commission (1970) S

Facts: The Liquor Control Commission revoked Smith's liquor license without notice or a hearing prior to revocation.

Issue: Can a state issued license be revoked without due process?

Rule: A license is a privilege, not a property right that may be revoked by the state at will and without due process.

Note: Future cases dispute this assertion. See *Celebrity Club, Inc. v. Liquor Control Commission*, below.

Gonzalez v. Freeman (1964) S

Facts: A federal corporation discontinued business with Gonzalez without affording prior notice or an opportunity for a hearing.

Issue 1: Does a private entity have a property interest in continued business relations with the government?

Rule 1: There is no right to do business with the government, but private entities doing business with the government have a protected property interest in being treated fairly by the government.

Issue 2: What process is due a private entity doing business with the government?

Rule 2: To protect the due process of a private entity with which it does business, an agency must provide standards regulating the termination of relations, notice of specific charges, an opportunity to refute evidence and cross-examine witnesses, and a recorded administrative decision.

Celebrity Club Inc. v. Liquor Control Commission (1982) S

Facts: Celebrity Club's liquor license was revoked without notice or an opportunity to be heard prior to termination.

Issue: Does the holder of a state-issued license have a protected property interest?

Rule: A holder of a state-issued license has a property interest in continued possession of the license, which may not be revoked without satisfaction of minimum due process requirements.

Salling v. Bowen (1986) S

Facts: In an experimental procedure designed to increase efficiency, the Social Security Administration Office retained full control over all pre-hearing processes, such as discovery, until immediately before the case was turned over to an Administrative Law Judge. All available evidence indicated that the new procedure was actually less efficient than allowing the ALJ to retain control.

Issue: May an agency handle disputes regarding its own agency until the very day that the dispute is reviewed by an independent decision-maker?

Rule: Applying a *Mathews* analysis, the recipients' interest in continued benefits and the increased likelihood of administrative error outweigh the unproven government interest in increased efficiency. Therefore, agency procedures violate due process when they put case files in the hands of the government advocate until the very day of the hearing.

Casey v. O'Bannon (1982) S

Facts: The Welfare Department closed several regional offices, forcing indigent applicants who could not travel to the central office to pursue appeals by telephone.

Issue: Does due process require a face-to-face hearing?

Rule: The use of speaker phones sufficiently reduces the chance of an erroneous decision (the second prong of the *Mathews* test) such that a face-to-face hearing is not required to satisfy due process.

United States Department of Agriculture v. Murry
(S.Ct. 1973) MM

Facts: Following statutory guidelines, the Department of Agriculture denied Murry's family of two-years worth of food stamps after her ex-husband claimed their nineteen-year old son as a dependent on his tax return.

Issue: Does a statute with an irrebuttable presumption (e.g., that a family with a child claimed as a dependent does not deserve public entitlements) necessarily violate due process?

Rule: (Douglas, J.) A statute with an irrebuttable presumption that is often contrary to fact is irrational an violative of due process.

Concurrence: (Marshall, J.) A hearing must be provided to anyone who claims that a statute aimed at certain abuses will not remedy those abuses, but instead will needlessly harm the claimant.

Dissent: (Rehnquist, J.) There is a rational relationship between a taxpayer's claiming of a dependent and his ability and desire to care for related recipients. This statute makes no irrational irrebuttable presumptions.

Note: Subsequently, in *Stanley v. Illinois*, the Supreme Court clearly articulated when an irrebuttable presumption violates due process: [I]t is forbidden by the Due Process Clause to [use an] irrebuttable presumption ... when that presumption is not necessarily or universally true in fact, and when the State has reasonable alternative means of making the crucial determination.

Califano v. Yamasaki (S.Ct. 1979) MM

Facts: Under the Social Security Act, the Secretary of Health and Human Services could recoup overpayments of disability payments by deducting the amount from future payments, except where the Secretary found that the recipient was without fault, or where recovery did either defeat the purposes of the law, or was against equity and good conscience. The Secretary did not provide an oral hearing before recoupment of overpaid benefits, either in cases of mistake or equity.

Issue: When a statute merely requires a "hearing," when is an oral hearing required?

Rule: When the language of a statute merely requires a hearing, oral hearings are necessary when decisionmakers must make subjective determinations. In cases of factual mistakes, which involve only an objective determination, a written hearing is sufficient, both statutorily and constitutionally.

Nash v. Califano (1980) MM

Facts: The Director of the Bureau of Hearings and Appeals instituted several reforms designed to cope with the backlog of cases for Administrative Law Judges (ALJs). Nash, an ALJ sued, but his case was summarily dismissed.

Issue 1: Do ALJs have a statutory right to decisional independence?

Rule 1: The Administrative Procedure Act vests ALJs with a limited right to be free from interference with their ability to make decisions.

Issue 2: Do ALJs have standing to sue based on infringement of this limited right?

Rule 2: ALJs do have a personal interest in their statutory right to make independent decisions, which gives them standing to sue from infringement of that right.

Chapter 2

PROBLEMS IN ADMINISTRATIVE ADJUDICATION

I. INTRODUCTION

Administrative agencies generally fulfill their statutory duties in two ways: adjudications and rulemaking. This chapter deals with some of the constitutional and institutional issues that agencies, courts, and the public face when dealing with administrative adjudications.

A. Models of Adjudicative Decisionmaking

1. Judicial Decisionmaking
   Administrative adjudications should be similar to judicial adjudications. The goals of such a system should be fairness and the litigants' acceptance of the decision and the administrative adjudicative process.

2. Institutional Decisionmaking
   The agency is a single unit, and the adjudicative branch just one method of enforcing agency goals. Agency personnel should work together in coming to a result as accurately and as efficiently as possible.

B. Purposes of Administrative Adjudications

1. Factual Determinations
   Where facts necessary to a determination are disputed, an administrative adjudication may perform factfinding roles similar to that of a common law jury.

2. Public Interest Determinations
   Congress often requires agencies to make policy determinations on the basis of a vague concept known as "the public interest."

Where an agency is unable to determine how best to serve that interest in a given case, a formal hearing on the matter must be held, even if no factual issues are disputed.

Legislatures generally require public interest determinations in two areas:

a. Mutually Exclusive Applications
Where there are more applicants than goods (e.g., broadcasting licenses, airline routes, or natural gas rights), agencies are generally required to award the application to the applicant who will best serve the public interest.

In limited cases (e.g., low power television and cellular radio system licenses), licenses have been awarded on the basis of random lotteries, as long as such a lottery comports with the public interest.

b. Minimum Standards of Quality
In some fields (such as medicine, mechanics, and drivers), an agency may be able to award an unlimited number of licenses. As long as applicants show they will operate in the public interest, as defined by minimum standards of quality, such applicants may not be rejected on the basis of either a market or random standard.

Some critics claim that this type of licensing (especially where the judges are members of the same profession who have already been licensed) serves to protect only privileged oligopolies, rather than the public benefit.

II. RIGHT TO AN ADMINISTRATIVE ADJUDICATION

A. When Must a Formal Adjudication Be Held?

1. Administrative Procedure Act (APA)
The federal APA does not mandate formal adjudicatory hearings. Any right to a hearing must come from another statute.

2. Federal Statutes
   A formal adjudication is required where Congress clearly intends that one be held. Courts often presume that Congress intended a formal adjudication when it uses the word "hearing."

3. Constitution
   Although *Wong Yang Sung v. McGrath* held that the formal procedures of the APA should apply whenever due process requires that an agency hold a hearing (See Chapter 1), many courts have declined to extend that ruling to areas where the court thought that formal proceedings would be inappropriate (such as prison discipline).

4. State Law

   a. Model State Administrative Procedure Act of 1961
      This act is nearly identical to the federal APA.

   b. Model State Administrative Procedure Act of 1981
      This act not only requires adjudication in every instance where a hearing is required but also sets up varying degrees of formality for adjudications in different situations.

   c. Additional Requirements
      The state legislature may place additional burdens to be met before an adjudication is warranted. But in the absence of those requirements, there are no common law restrictions on administrative adjudications.

B. Who May Attend a Formal Adjudication?

   1. Entitled Parties
      Section 554 of the APA requires an agency to notify all parties entitled by law to a formal adjudication of the impending proceedings. This notice requirement is similar to that required in rulemaking (See Chapter 5). A party may also petition an agency to conduct a formal proceeding.

2. Consolidation
Where two or more licensing applications are mutually exclusive, the granting of one necessarily deprives the others of that claim. In those cases, all claims must be decided in one proceeding. *Ashbacker Radio Corp. v. FCC.*

3. Intervention
According to § 554(c), any interested party may intervene in an evidentiary hearing. The term *interested party* has been steadily expanded in recent years to encompass almost anybody who can claim an interest. For further discussion, see the outline section on the Interest Representation Model in Chapter 7.

III. AVOIDING A FORMAL HEARING

Formal adjudications are often inefficient and time-consuming. Agencies that wish to resolve a dispute, promulgate a new code or regulation, or issue a license have used several methods to avoid the requirements of a formal adjudication.

A. Rulemaking

1. Rules of General Application
In those cases where a rule is promulgated to avoid litigation, the promulgated rule must be of general application. Where an agency rule affects a specific interest, as opposed to the interests of an entire class, a formal adjudicatory hearing is required.

2. Interpretive Rules
Rulemaking may be used to clarify and define the law that an agency must enforce, even where the agency is not explicitly authorized to conduct rulemaking. Such clarifications may avoid future litigation on those issues.

3. Prerequisites
An agency may issue general rules that set standards that must be met before a hearing is granted. The agency may also summarily reject applicants who fail to meet those standards.

Where it is unclear whether an applicant has met those standards, a hearing must be held.

4. Exception: Mutually Exclusive Applications
   An agency may not promulgate rules limiting the issues to be decided in a comparative hearing. All applicants' claims must be considered equally.

B. Informal Influence

An agency member may use his personal influence, including threatened rulemaking and adjudication, to cause private parties to adopt their own regulations or to resolve their own disputes without the use of formal agency action. Such "jawboning" or "raised eyebrow" techniques must cease, however, once agency action has begun. (See *ex parte* restrictions, below.)

IV.   DISQUALIFYING A DECISIONMAKER

A. *Morgan*: The One Who Decides Must Hear

In the late 1930's, the Supreme Court handed down several cases, collectively known as the *Morgan* cases, that defined the role of administrative decisionmakers in agency hearings. The courts and Congress have since further limited the definition of who may serve as decisionmaker.

The administrator who will make the ultimate determination of the disputed issues must also preside over the case. *Morgan I.*

1. Non-Reviewability of Decisionmakers
   Yet, a decisionmaker's mental processes may not be probed to determine whether an adequate review of the evidence was made. *Morgan II.* The agency need only establish that the relevant information was considered. *Morgan IV.*

2. Delegation of Decisionmaking Authority
   The head of the relevant department need not personally preside over every agency adjudication. The decisionmaker need not personally read every page of testimony put before the court. Decisionmaking authority may be delegated to subordinates or to administrative law judges. But, where a statute requires an individual to make a decision, any delegate must be instructed by that individual on how to vote.

3. The Administrative Law Judge (ALJ)

   Striving for unbiased and more efficient agency adjudications, Congress has established a system of agency judges to adjudicate many agency issues. The system is designed to provide adjudications with an agency's expertise, while freeing decisionmakers, to a limited extent, from undue agency influence. Now, there are more administrative law judges than federal court judges.

   a. Decisional Independence
      ALJs have a limited right to preserve their freedom from agency influence. ALJs have standing to sue for relief from infringement of this right. Several statutes, including the federal APA, establish this limited right.

   b. Expertise
      The decisionmaker need not have any formal legal training, given the desire for ALJs with significant experience in such specialized areas such as environmental health and safety and food and drug testing,

   c. Agency Review
      An agency may, at its discretion, review all decisions of ALJs. Any action on review, whether it be an affirmation, reversal, or even a refusal to review the decision at all, occurs wholly within the discretion of the agency. The agency need only furnish a decision explaining the grounds for the action.

d. Powers of an Administrative Law Judge

    i.   Administer oaths.

    ii.   Issue subpoenas.

    iii.   Receive relevant evidence.

    iv.   Hold depositions.

    v.   Hold conferences.

    vi.   Make procedural rulings.

    vii.   Question witnesses.

    viii.   Consider the adjudicatory record.

    ix.   Determine witness credibility and make factual findings.

    x.   Make decisions on the basis of a hearing record.

B. Combination of Functions

Agencies may perform many roles: legislator, investigator, policeman, manager, prosecutor, judge, and jury. Although combined functions are often tolerated within one agency, problems do arise when two or more of these functions are vested within one administrator and when a decisionmaker is supervised by an administrator who is responsible for the investigation and prosecution of cases.

1. Disqualification
To disqualify an agency adjudicator because of a combination of administrative functions (investigator, prosecutor, etc.), evidence must be presented that the risk of an unfair proceeding is "intolerably high." See *Withrow v. Larkin*.

2. Administrative Procedure Act
Section 554(d) of the APA forbids an administrative decision-maker who presides over a formal adjudication from conducting investigative or prosecuting functions for that case or a factually related one.

Exceptions:

MNEMONIC: **GEARS**

a. <u>G</u>overning body or administrator of an agency.

b. <u>E</u>stablishing codes of conduct for public utilities.

c. <u>A</u>pplications for initial licenses.

d. <u>R</u>atemaking.

e. <u>S</u>tatute expressly requires the same person to perform multiple functions.

3. Separation of Functions within an Agency
Often, agencies will take it upon themselves to produce separate divisions for investigating, legislating and adjudicating.

C. *Ex Parte* Communications

Ex parte communications will void a formal hearing where the communication "blemishes" the proceedings.

In determining whether agency proceedings have been "blemished," a court will consider:

1. The gravity of the communication.

2. The influence that resulted from the prohibited communication.

3. Whether the interested party benefitted from the communication.

4. Whether the communication was disclosed.

5. Whether requiring a new hearing would be useful.

D. Political Pressure

1. Internal Pressures
   Agencies may retain in-house or outside consultants to advise agency decisionmakers.

2. Executive Pressure
   Unless one of the agencies is "independent" of the executive branch (i.e., the Federal Reserve Board), communications among executive agencies are not prohibited and must be disclosed only where required by statute.

3. Congressional Pressure
   Congressional influence on an administrative adjudication is improper where:

   a. Congressional investigation focuses upon the mental decisional processes of a pending case; or

   b. The legislative agent applies pressure to consider factors not made relevant by the applicable statute; and

   c. That pressure affects the decisionmaking process.

E. Biased Decisionmakers

The existence of such a bias must be concretely established by the party upon whom disciplinary proceedings have been instituted. The party must overcome a presumption of agency integrity.

Decisionmaking bodies may not have a pecuniary interest in any proceedings before them. *Gibson v. Berryhill.*

Decisionmakers must also recuse themselves from a pending case where a disinterested observer may conclude that the agency has in some measure adjudged the facts as well as the law of a particular case in advance of hearing it. See *Cinderella v. FTC.*

F. Rule of Necessity

A decisionmaker who would normally have been disqualified may hear a case where no other substitute decisionmaker is available.

CASE CLIPS

City of West Chicago v. United States Nuclear Regulatory Commission (1983) BA

Facts: The Nuclear Regulatory Commission (NRC) granted the Kerr-McGee Corp. a license to operate a thorium milling plant without holding a formal adjudicatory hearing. The Administrative Procedure Act (APA) required a formal hearing whenever a statute calls for an adjudication made "on the record" after opportunity for a hearing. The applicable statute merely called for a "hearing."

Issue: Where a statute does not explicitly require adjudication made "on the record," when must a formal adjudicatory hearing, pursuant to the APA, be granted?

Rule: A formal adjudicatory hearing, pursuant to the APA, must be granted when required by due process or when Congress has clearly intended that a formal adjudication be held.

Milwaukee Metropolitan Sewerage District v. Wisconsin Department of Natural Resources (1985) BA

Facts: The Wisconsin Department of Natural Resources denied the Milwaukee Metropolitan Sewerage District's (District) request for an adjudicatory hearing under the state Administrative Procedure Act (APA). The District had no statutory right to a hearing unless found in the APA.

Issue: Must a party have a pre-existing right to a hearing in order to qualify for an informal adjudication under the state APA?

Rule: Since the state APA does not require a pre-existing right to a hearing, a party must only fulfill the pre-requisites contained within the state APA itself.

Note: The Wisconsin APA closely follows the 1981 Model State Administrative Procedure Act.

American Airlines, Inc. v. Civil Aeronautics Board (1966) BA

Facts: The Civil Aeronautics Board (CAB) issued a regulation restricting "blocked space service" to all-cargo carriers only, and then amended their licenses accordingly. Opponents were given notice and comment, as well as an opportunity for oral argument. The Federal Aviation Act required that CAB give a formal adjudicatory hearing to modify a license.

Issue: Must an agency hold a formal hearing when it promulgates a regulation with the effect of an adjudication?

Rule: Formal rulemaking proceedings are required where expressly mandated by statute, unless the rule promulgated is generic (i.e., affecting the interests of a class in relation to other classes, as opposed to affecting an individual's interest in relation to those of its own class).

Dissent: This case does affect individuals' rights in relation to those of its class. The majority has used an overly limited definition of "class."

Withrow v. Larkin (S.Ct. 1975) BA, BS, GB, S

Facts: The Wisconsin Examining Board held an investigatory hearing regarding a physician's alleged illegal activities. Two months later, the same Board began an adjudicatory hearing to decide whether to suspend the physician's license.

Issue: May an agency member perform both investigatory and adjudicatory functions on the same case?

Rule: (White, J.) The existence of combined agency functions will not in itself overcome the presumption of an adjudicator's integrity. There must be evidence that the risk of unfairness is "intolerably high."

Andrews v. Agricultural Labor Relations Board (1981) BA
Facts: The Agricultural Labor Relations Board appointed Armando Menocal, a private attorney, as a temporary administrative law officer in a case regarding unfair labor practices. Menocal's firm had worked on many racial employment discrimination cases with Mexican-Americans in the past. Several parties in the case were Mexican-American, and some opponents claimed that Menocal was a biased decisionmaker.
Issue: When may an administrative adjudicator be disqualified because of bias?
Rule: The opposing party must concretely demonstrate the actual existence of bias before an adjudicator must be disqualified.
Concurrence: The mere existence of a cultural, racial, or sexual commonality between a decisionmaker and a party does not establish bias.
Dissent: The appearance of bias should serve to disqualify an adjudicator as well.

Professional Air Traffic Controllers Organization (PATCO) v.
Federal Labor Relations Authority (FLRA) (1982) BA, GB
Facts: After PATCO called a strike, the Federal Labor Relations Authority (FLRA) revoked PATCO's certification in a formal hearing under § 557 of the Administrative Procedure Act. The revocation was challenged on the basis of two *ex parte* communications between FLRA decisionmakers and "interested parties."
Issue: When will improper *ex parte* communications invalidate a formal agency hearing?
Rule: Formal agency proceedings are voidable when "blemished" by improper *ex parte* communications that irrevocably taint an agency's decision. In determining whether an agency decision has been "blemished," the court should consider the gravity of the communication, the influence that resulted, whether the interested party benefitted from the communication, whether the communication was disclosed, and whether voiding the agency action would be useful.

Ashbacker Radio Corp. v. FCC (S.Ct. 1945) BS, CD, S
Facts: Two radio stations applied for a license to broadcast at the same frequency. The Federal Communications Commission granted

the second applicant an adjudicatory hearing after granting the license to the first applicant without a hearing.

Issue: May an agency resolve two mutually exclusive claims in separate hearings?

Rule: (Douglas, J.) Where two bona fide applications are mutually exclusive, the grant of one without a hearing to both deprives the loser of a meaningful adjudication.

Dissent: (Frankfurter, J.) The agency exists to ensure the public interest, not to enforce private rights. An agency need only determine that an application will protect the public interest. That a subsequent applicant may be better qualified is irrelevant as long as the first applicant is deemed to be qualified at all.

Central Florida Enterprises Inc. v. FCC (Cowles I) (1978) BS

Facts: In a hearing for renewal of a broadcasting license, a more qualified applicant for the same frequency was turned down in favor of the less qualified broadcaster who currently broadcast on that frequency.

Issue: May the renewal expectancy of a current license holder be a decisive factor in an application for renewal of a license?

Rule: An incumbent's past performance is relevant to a licensing hearing only insofar as it predicts whether future performance will be better or worse than that of its competing applicants. Incumbency per se is not a decisive factor.

Central Florida Enterprises Inc. v. FCC (Cowles II) (1982) BS

Facts: In a hearing for renewal of a broadcasting license, a more qualified applicant for the same frequency was turned down in favor of the less qualified broadcaster who currently broadcast on that frequency.

Issue: Is the renewal expectancy of a current license holder a legitimate factor to be weighed when considering an application for renewal of a license?

Rule: A current license holder's expectation of renewal is a factor that may be given weight due to the public's interest in consistency, the desire to encourage long-term investment, and the uncertainty of a challenger's "paper proposals."

FCC v. WNCN Listeners Guild (S.Ct. 1982) BS

Facts: The Federal Communications Commission promulgated a rule elaborating very lax standards for when a radio station may change its format. The rule contradicted many lower court rulings that had required the Commission to hold a hearing for proposed changes in entertainment formats.

Issue: May the courts require agencies to follow a specific standard not mandated by statute in enforcing its statutory obligations?

Rule: (White, J.) Unless required by statute, an agency has wide discretion in how it is to enforce its obligations.

Wong Yang Sung v. McGrath (S.Ct. 1950) BS, S

Facts: A Chinese citizen was tried as an illegal alien before an immigration inspector. Immigration inspectors performed both investigatory and adjudicatory roles. This combination of functions did not comply with the Administrative Procedure Act (APA).

Issue: When do the APA's rules on administrative adjudications apply?

Rule: (Jackson, J.) The APA strictures on administrative adjudications apply whenever an agency hearing is compelled by statute or by the Constitution.

Hercules, Inc. v. EPA (1978) BS

Facts: The Environmental Protection Agency promulgated a rule applying only to the party in the suit. During the rulemaking proceedings, the presiding rulemaking officer engaged in several *ex parte* communications, normally forbidden in administrative adjudications.

Issue: Will *ex parte* communications invalidate a hybrid rulemaking session that has the effect of an administrative adjudication, in which such communications are prohibited?

Rule: *Ex parte* communications are not always prohibited in hybrid rulemaking sessions, even if the hearings have the effect of an administrative adjudication.

Association of National Advertisers v. FTC (1979) BS, CD, S, MM

Facts: The Federal Trade Commission (FTC) issued a notice of proposed rulemaking regarding a ban on certain types of children's advertising. The Chairman of the FTC had previously written several articles advocating similar legislation.

Issue: In rulemaking, when must an agency member be disqualified due to bias?

Rule: An agency member must recuse himself from rulemaking only where there is a clear and convincing showing that the member has an unalterably closed mind on matters critical to the rulemaking.

Concurrence: No agency rulemaker can be completely unbiased given the long and intimate knowledge that agency members will have regarding the regulated area.

Dissent in Part: The adjudicative aspects of hybrid rulemaking require that a rulemaker be as unbiased and open-minded as any formal adjudicator.

Gibson v. Berryhill (S.Ct. 1973) BS, CD, S

Facts: The Alabama Board of Optometry adjudged the Lee Optometry Company guilty of professional misconduct. Were the company shut down, it business would most likely have gone to the Board members.

Issue: May an administrative adjudication be disqualified if members of the adjudicative body have a pecuniary interest in the outcome of the adjudication?

Rule: (White, J.) In order to ensure an impartial decisionmaker, any adjudicator with a pecuniary interest in the outcome of the adjudication must be disqualified due to bias.

Morgan v. United States (Morgan I) (S.Ct. 1936) BS, GB, S

Facts: The Secretary of Agriculture fixed rates for livestock in Kansas City after the Acting Secretary conducted a formal hearing on the issues involved.

Issue: Has a full hearing been afforded where the resulting order is supported by the findings of the hearing, even if the ultimate decisionmaker did not preside over the hearing?

Rule: (Hughes, C.J.) There is no full hearing unless the person who ultimately decides the issues has presided over the hearing. The person who decides must hear.

National Nutritional Foods Association v. FDA (1974) BS

Facts: After production of over 32,000 pages of testimony in a formal proceeding regarding revisions of regulations, a new Commissioner took over the agency and enacted fourteen new regulations in twelve days.

Issue: May an administrator be questioned as to whether he personally participated in the decisionmaking where there is evidence that he did not have sufficient time to personally review the hearing record?

Rule: Courts may not require administrators to testify about their rulemakking decisions without a stong preliminary showing of bad faith.

Nash v. Califano (1980) GB

Facts: The Director of the Bureau of Hearings and Appeals instituted several reforms designed to cope with the backlog of cases for Administrative Law Judges (ALJs). ALJ Nash sued, but his case was summarily dismissed due to a lack of standing.

Issue 1: Do ALJs have a statutory right to decisional independence?

Rule 1: The Administrative Procedure Act vests ALJs with a limited right be free from interference with their ability to make decisions.

Issue 2: Do ALJs have standing to sue based on infringement of this limited right?

Rule 2: ALJs have a personal interest in their right to non-interferrence in their decisionmaking, giving them standing to sue for infringement of that right.

Grolier, Inc. v. Federal Trade Commission (1980) GB

Facts: A presiding Administrative Law Judge (ALJ) was found to have been an outside adviser to the Federal Trade Commission (FTC) Commissioner, and may have been involved as an attorney in the case before him. Both the ALJ and FTC refused to produce documents regarding allegations of bias.

Issue: When should an ALJ be disqualified due to bias if he is not presently employed by the agency whose dispute he must resolve?

Rule: Congress intended to preclude from decisionmaking in a particular case any persons involved in that case, or a factually related case, who had either *ex parte* information, or had developed a "will to win" regarding that case.

Morgan v. United States (Morgan II) (S.Ct. 1938) GB

Facts: The Secretary of Agriculture fixed rates for livestock in Kansas City after a formal hearing on the issues involved, but never told the companies affected what standard would be used in fixing the rates.

Issue: What information must be given to parties prior to a formal hearing?

Rule: (Hughes, C.J.) Prior to a formal hearing, affected parties must be given enough information such that they may pose meaningful counter-arguments.

Note: In dicta, the Court held that the mental processes of an administrative decisionmaker may not be probed to ensure that the Secretary reviewed the relevant evidence, as required by *Morgan I.*

American Telephone & Telegraph Co. (1976) GB

Facts: The Common Carrier Bureau (CCB) represented the Federal Communication Commission (FCC) in hearings that would revise telephone rates. To reach a decision before a judicially imposed deadline, the FCC consulted the CCB on certain issues necessary to making a final determination.

Issue: May an outside party representing an agency in a quasi-judicial hearing consult with the agency regarding the final determination?

Rule: An agency is not forbidden, by statute or the Constitution, from consulting with outside parties so long as the agency retains responsibility for making the final decision.

Concurrence: Although not required, it is good politics to avoid any appearance of impropriety. In this case, however, the impending deadline makes the retention of new, uninvolved counsel impractical.

Dissent: Although consulting outside parties retained to represent the agency is not expressly prohibited, it is inequitable for agencies to contact those parties once arguments have ended. That a deadline would soon expire is no justification.

Ash Grove Cement Co. v. FTC (1978) GB

Facts: The Federal Trade Commission first investigated, and then adjudicated charges of unfair trade practices in the cement industry.

Issue: When may an agency be disqualified from adjudicating an issue it has investigated?

Rule: Where the presumption of agency integrity is overcome, an agency may be disqualified from adjudicating an issue it investigated.

Pillsbury Co. v. Federal Trade Commission (1966) GB

Facts: The Federal Trade Commission (FTC) investigated Pillsbury for alleged anti-competitive actions. During the adjudication, a Senate subcommittee required the FTC Chairman and other staff members to appear before it. The subcommittee questioned the FTC members at length about the Pillsbury case. Although the FTC Chairman recused himself from the case, others before the subcommittee did not and proceeded to decide the facts and issues involved.

Issue: When does an appearance before a Senate subcommittee invalidate an agency adjudication?

Rule: Where congressional investigation focuses upon the mental decisional processes of a case pending before the agency, parties to the adjudication have been deprived of a full and fair trial.

Sierra Club v. Costle (1981) BA, GB, CD, MM

Facts: The Environmental Protection Agency (EPA) adopted new sulfur dioxide emission rules in a hybrid rulemaking procedure. After notice of the proposed rules, and before enactment, there was a rush of oral *ex parte* communications between EPA administrators, White House officials, and congressmen. Neither the informal rulemaking procedures of the Administrative Procedure Act nor the rulemaking provisions of the Clean Air Act contained any mention of *ex parte* communications, although the Clean Air Act did require agency decisions to be made exclusively on the basis of what was contained in the rulemaking record.

Issue 1: In hybrid rulemaking, when are oral *ex parte* communications prohibited?

Rule 1: *Ex parte* communications with agency officials are prohibited where agency action resembles judicial action (i.e., formal rulemaking, adjudication, or resolution of conflicting claims to a valuable privilege).

Issue 2: In hybrid rulemaking, when are *ex parte* meetings between agency and White House officials prohibited?

Rule 2: Except where prohibited by statute, *ex parte* communications among executive agencies will not invalidate an agency decision, unless the rulemaking agency is considered to be "independent" of the executive branch of government.

Issue 3: In hybrid rulemaking, when are *ex parte* meetings between agency and congressional officials prohibited?

Rule 3: Two conditions must be met to prove undue congressional interference with administrative rulemaking. First, congressional pressure to consider factors not made relevant by the applicable statute must have been applied. Second, the agency must actually be affected by such pressures. In this case, those conditions were not met.

LaSalle National Bank v. County of Lake (1983) GB

Facts: A law firm, representing clients against the state, employed a former state attorney who had limited access to relevant files.

Issue: Is an entire firm disqualified from participating in a case due to the disqualification from the case of one attorney who had been partially screened?

Rule: A law firm is disqualified from participation in a case where any one of its attorneys must be disqualified, unless the firm can rebut the presumption that the attorney's forbidden knowledge has not affected the case.

Thomas v. Union Carbide Agricultural Products Co. (S.Ct. 1985) CD

Facts: Union Carbide provided data to the Environmental Protection Agency (EPA) in support of registration applications for its various pesticides. The Federal Insecticide, Fungicide, and Rodenticide Act permitted companies to seek monetary compensation through binding arbitration if the EPA released this application data to the general public.

Issue: May Congress allocate judicial functions to non-Article III courts?

Rule: (O'Connor, J.) Congress may vest traditional judicial decision-making authority in administrative agencies.

Concurrence: (Brennan, J.) Government participation in the arbitration process makes this case one of "public rights," traditionally within an agency's jurisdiction.

Cinderella Career And Finishing Schools, Inc. v. Federal Trade Commission (1970) CD

Facts: The Federal Trade Commission Chairman refused to disqualify himself from deciding an administrative adjudication, even after making a public speech in which he indirectly referred to the pending case in a manner that indicated that he had decided the case without having been presented evidence on the issues.

Issue: When must administrative adjudicators disqualify themselves from a pending case due to bias?

Rule: Administrative adjudicators must disqualify themselves where a disinterested observer may conclude that the agency has in some measure adjudged the facts as well as the law of a particular case in advance of hearing it.

Friedman v. Rogers (S.Ct. 1979) CD

Facts: An optometrist sought declaratory relief to invalidate the Texas Optometry Board's (TOB) proposed enforcement of the Texas Optometry Act banning commercial optometry. The TOB contained a majority of professional optometrists with a pecuniary interest in seeing commercial optometry banned.

Issue: When may enforcement by adjudicators with pecuniary interests in the outcome of any future litigation be challenged?

Rule: (Powell, J.) As long as the statute to be enforced is constitutional, hearings by adjudicators with pecuniary interests in enforcing the statute may not be challenged until disciplinary proceedings have been instituted.

United States v. Storer Broadcasting Co. (S.Ct. 1956) CD

Facts: The Federal Communications Commission promulgated a rule limiting the number of broadcast stations one individual may own. Storer, who owned more stations than the rule permitted, had his application for an additional television station rejected without a hearing on the basis of the new rules.

Issue: May an agency promulgate rules outlining pre-requisites that applicants must fulfill before being able to obtain a statutorily guaranteed adjudicatory hearing?

Rule: (Reed, J.) An agency may establish threshold guidelines that determine when an application states a valid basis for granting review and may summarily reject applications that do not meet these guidelines.

Office of Communication of the United Church of Christ v. Federal Communications Commission (Church of Christ I) (1966) CD, S

Facts: A petition filed by a coalition of listeners to intervene in a proceeding adjudicating the renewal of a broadcast license was denied because the petitioners did not have an economic interest in the outcome. The Federal Communications Commission had also agreed to assume that the petitioners' statement of facts was true, obviating any need for an adjudication of factual issues.

Issue 1: When may a party intervene in an adjudicatory proceeding?

Rule 1: An intervenor need only show a legitimate interest distinct from the public at large. This interest need not be economic in nature.

Issue 2: When must an evidentiary hearing be held if there are no factual issues to be decided?

Rule 2: An evidentiary hearing must be held, despite the absence of issues of fact, when agency action seems to run counter to the public interest.

Citizens Communications Center v. Federal Communications Commission (1971) CD

Facts: The Federal Communications Commission enacted a policy statement that would limit comparative hearings regarding broadcast license renewals to the issue of whether the incumbent broadcaster had rendered substantial past performance without serious deficiencies. The challenger's relative merits would not be considered unless the incumbent had not substantially performed.

Issue: May a comparative hearing be limited to consideration of only the incumbent's merits?

Rule: A comparative hearing must always consider the merits of all applicants for a license, both incumbent and challenger.

Cowles Florida Broadcasting, Inc. (1976) CD

Facts: In a hearing to renew a broadcasting license, a more qualified applicant for the same frequency was turned down in favor of the less qualified broadcaster who currently broadcast on that frequency.

Issue: May a current broadcaster's expectations of renewal weigh in favor of finding for an incumbent applicant in a comparative hearing for the renewal of a broadcasting license?

Rule: Given the subjective nature of comparative hearings and an agency's administrative "feel" for the situation, a broadcaster's expectations should be considered in a comparative hearing for the renewal of a broadcasting license.

Note: This case was overturned in *Central Florida, Inc. v. FCC (Cowles I)*, above.

Random Selection Lotteries (1984) CD

Facts: In 1981, Congress amended the Federal Communications Act to explicitly permit the use of a lottery system in granting broadcasting licenses.

Issue: When would the granting of broadcasting licenses through the use of a lottery system be in the "public interest"?

Rule: Lotteries that would give some preference to applicants with a greater likelihood of acting in the public interest (e.g., diversity of ownership, or minority participation) may protect the public interest better than time-consuming comparative hearings.

Note: The Federal Communications Commission has used random lotteries to award licenses for low power television stations and cellular radio systems.

RKO General, Inc. (WNAC-TV) (1980) CD

Facts: Contemporaneously with a hearing for the renewal of a broadcast license, RKO's parent company was found guilty of several violations of federal antitrust, SEC and tax laws.

Issue: What criteria may an agency consider when evaluating the impact of an incumbent licensee's misconduct?

Rule: When evaluating an incumbent's license renewal application, an agency should consider the frequency of any misconduct by the incumbent, the relation of the misconduct to the regulated activity, and the recency of the misconduct.

Note: RKO's appeal of this decision appears below.

RKO General, Inc. v. Federal Communications Commission
(1981) CD

Facts: Contemporaneously with a hearing for the renewal of a broadcast license, RKO's parent company was found guilty of several violations of federal antitrust, SEC and tax laws.

Issue: What effect may proven violations of federal law have upon an incumbent's application for renewal of a broadcasting license?

Rule: The detrimental effect of violations of federal law may be tempered by the length of time since the violations, the conduct since the violations, and any ambiguities in the relevant law.

Writers Guild of America, West, Inc. v.
American Broadcasting Cos. (1980) CD

Facts: After several informal meetings with network executives and several public speeches threatening government action, the Federal Communications Commission Chairman convinced television networks to adopt amongst themselves an informal policy restricting sex and violence in shows aired during the first hour of prime time.

Issue: May agency members influence the actions of private citizens without having to resort to rulemaking and adjudicatory procedures?

Rule: Regulation through "raised eyebrow" techniques or so-called "jawboning" is a valid exercise of agency influence.

FTC v. Standard Oil of California (S.Ct. 1981) S

Facts: Standard Oil sought review of the issuance of a complaint against it before an administrative adjudication on the merits.

Issue: Is an agency's filing of a complaint a "final agency action" that is reviewable before administrative adjudication concludes?

Rule: (Powell, J.) An agency complaint is a mere threshold determination that is not reviewable until all administrative remedies have been exhausted.

Kuhn v. CAB (1950) S

Facts: In an administrative proceeding revoking Kuhn's pilot license, Kuhn had actual notice, but not formal notice, that the Civil Aeronautics Board would try the issue of his not keeping a proper lookout.

Issue: May an administrative tribunal try an issue without providing formal notice to the party charged?

Rule: Actual notice is sufficient to maintain an agency adjudication, as long as the parties have opportunity to present evidence on the issues of which they were actually, though not formally, notified.

Herald Co. v. Weisenberg (1983) S

Facts: An administrative law judge closed an adjudicatory hearing to the public without giving members of the press an opportunity to be heard on the issue of closure. The newspaper's subsequent request for a transcript of the hearing was denied.

Issue: When may an administrative law judge exclude the public from what is normally an open hearing?

Rule: Before closing an adjudicatory hearing to the public, and administrative law judge must first give the press an opportunity to be heard on the issue of closure.

Walters v. National Association of Radiation Survivors (S.Ct. 1985) S

Facts: Final authority to determine veterans' benefits rested in the Board of Veterans' Appeals (BVA). According to a statute passed in 1864, a veteran's legal counsel could not charge more than ten dollars per case.

Issue: May Congress restrict the amount an attorney may charge when representing a petitioner of non-financially need-based government benefits at an administrative hearing?

Rule: (Rehnquist, J.) Although restricting access to expert representation, attorney fee limitations, absent a strong showing of probability of error, do not deny due process to claimants in "informal and non-adversarial" proceedings.

Dissent: (Stevens, J.) The right to consult an attorney falls firmly within due process, and should not be destroyed by an outmoded and paternalistic law.

Guerrero v. New Jersey (1981) S

Facts: An administrative law judge (ALJ) made findings of fact and law that the New Jersey State Board of Medical Examiners accepted in its entirety when deciding to find Dr. Guerrero guilty of gross medical malpractice.

Issue: Must an administrative adjudicator personally hear all evidence relevant to a case?

Rule: The *Morgan* cases establish, that in administrative adjudications, deciding officers need not actually hear the witnesses' testimony.

Schweiker v. McClure (S.Ct. 1982) S

Facts: The plaintiffs, who were denied Medicare benefits, received a hearing before a decisionmaker chosen by private insurance carriers, but paid for by the federal government.

Issue: Must a decisionmaker be appointed by the government and have formal legal training?

Rule: (Powell, J.) Where knowledge of the law is not crucial to the decisionmaking process, an agency's decision maker need not have legal training. Furthermore, a decisionmaker must be unbiased, but not necessarily government appointed.

FTC v. Cement Inst. (S.Ct. 1948) S

Facts: The Federal Trade Commission (FTC) refused to disqualify itself from an administrative adjudication regarding unfair trade practices. Members of the FTC had already expressed their opinion that the alleged practices were illegal. Only the FTC could adjudicate the case.

Issue: When must a decisionmaking body be disqualified from an adjudication due to bias?

Rule: (Black, J.) A decisionmaking body should be disqualified from an adjudication due to bias where it is shown that the minds of the members are irrevocably closed on the issues involved.

New England Telephone & Telegraph Co. v. Public Utilities Commn. (1982) S

Facts: Only eight days after a hearing examiner's report rejected a proposal on revised telephone rates, the Public Utilities Commission enacted an order nearly identical to the hearing examiner's.

Issue: Must administrative agencies review the entire adjudicatory record before enacting an order?

Rule: Due process does not require that decisionmakers hear and read all of the testimony on which their decision is based.

Mazza v. Cavicchia (1954) S

Facts: In a state proceeding to revoke a liquor license, the Division of Alcoholic Beverage Control (ABC) hearer sent a copy of his report to the ABC Director, but not to the holder of the revoked license.

Issue: Must parties receive all information used by the decisionmaker to decide the case?

Rule: Parties must receive all information used by the decisionmaker to decide the case, so that they may have an opportunity to refute erroneous allegations.

FCC v. Allentown Broadcasting Corp. (S.Ct. 1955) S

Facts: The hearing examiner awarded a broadcasting license to Allentown Broadcasting rather than to Easton Publishing. The Federal Communications Commission (FCC) overruled the examiner and awarded the license to Easton. The Court of Appeals reversed the FCC on the grounds that the FCC had not proven that the examiner's decision was "clearly erroneous."

Issue: When may an agency overrule an administrative adjudicator?

Rule: (Reed, J.) Agencies may overrule hearing examiners (now administrative law judges), if, upon a preponderance of the evidence, the agency determines that the examiner's decision was incorrect.

Northeastern Broadcasting, Inc. v. FCC (1968) S

Facts: The Federal Communications Commission refused to review the decision of an agency review board that authorized a change in status for a broadcasting station. One of the station's competitors claimed that denial of review was "arbitrary and capricious" and, thus, invalid.

Issue: When may an agency refuse to review an administrative adjudicatory decision?

Rule: Agencies have broad discretion in deciding when to review decisions of administrative adjudications, which will only be overturned in cases of clear abuse.

KFC National Management Corp. v. NLRB (1974) S

Facts: National Labor Relations Board members allowed their vote deciding whether to conduct an administrative hearing to be cast by their assistants. The members did not consider the case, or tell their assistants how to vote. The National Labor Relations Act instructs Board members to decide whether to hear a case.

Issue: When will delegation of decisionmaking authority not comport with due process?

Rule: Where a statute makes specific administrators legally responsible for a vote, those members may delegate the actual voting to subordinates, but must instruct those subordinates on how to vote.

Citizens Bank v. Board of Banking (1977) S

Facts: The Board of Banking granted a banking license to a petitioner in a contested hearing. The agency's statement of facts and law supporting the decision merely restated the facts in favor of the decision and the applicable law, without addressing either facts that may be contrary to the case or how the facts stated relate to the applicable law.

Issue: What must an administrative adjudicatory decision contain?

Rule: An administrative adjudicatory decision must set forth the underlying evidentiary facts that lead to the agency's conclusion, along with an explanation of the methodology by which complex evidence was considered.

Citizens to Preserve Overton Park v. Volpe (S.Ct. 1971) S

Facts: The Department of Transportation Act required that the Secretary of Transportation not approve federal funds for highway projects that extend through public parks if a "feasible and prudent" alternative existed. In an administrative adjudication, petitioners contended that proposed highway I-40 could have been routed around Overton Park and that the plan for the project did not include "all possible" methods of reducing harm to the park, as required by statute. Respondents argued that the Secretary of Transportation's plan was sufficient and the decision was not reviewable.

Issue: In reviewing agency discretion, what standard of review applies?

Rule: (Marshall, J.) In reviewing agency discretion, a court must decide if the action was within the agency's scope of authority; if the action was "arbitrary, capricious, an abuse of discretion, or otherwise not in accordance with law"; and if the agency followed procedural requirements.

Concurrence: (Black, J.) Since it is clear that the Secretary did not comply with the necessary procedure, the whole case should be remanded to the Department of Transportation, as opposed to the District Court, as the majority decided.

National Petroleum Refiners Association v. Federal Trade Commission (1974) MM

Facts: The Trade Commission Act, which created the Federal Trade Commission, explicitly authorized the use of adjudicatory means of enforcement, as well as general rulemaking powers.

Issue: Is an agency's rulemaking power limited to procedural pronouncements?

Rule: An agency may promulgate binding substantive rules, as well as rules of procedure regarding the conduct of adjudicatory hearings.

Hynson, Westcott and Dunning, Inc. v. Richardson (1972) MM

Facts: The Food, Drug and Cosmetic Act required the Food and Drug Administration (FDA) to withdraw approval of any drug for which "substantial evidence" of the drug's efficacy was lacking. The FDA had also promulgated a rule requiring a drug manufacturer to prove that a "genuine and substantial issue of fact" exists before a hearing would be held on the issue of the drug's efficacy. The FDA summarily determined that the manufacturer's tests were inadequate, thus not providing any "genuine and substantial issues of fact."

Issue: Where there is conflicting evidence regarding the existence of a "genuine and substantial issue of fact," may an agency refuse to hold a hearing?

Rule: Where there is conflicting evidence regarding the existence of a "genuine and substantial issue of fact," a hearing must be held. At the very least, the conflicting evidence is itself a "genuine and substantial issue of fact" that requires a hearing.

Weinberger v. Hynson, Westcott and Dunning, Inc. (S.Ct. 1973) MM

Facts: The Food, Drug and Cosmetic Act required the Food and Drug Administration (FDA) to withdraw approval of any drug for which "substantial evidence" of the drug's efficacy was lacking. The

FDA had also promulgated a rule requiring a drug manufacturer to prove that a "genuine and substantial issue of fact" exists before a hearing would be held on the issue of the drug's efficacy. The FDA summarily determined that the manufacturer's tests were inadequate, thus not providing any "genuine and substantial issues of fact."

Issue: May an agency create standards by which it may summarily dismiss a request for a hearing?

Rule: (Douglas, J.) To maintain a manageable agency, agencies may create threshold tests by which it may summarily dismiss a request for a hearing.

Concurrence: (Powell, J.) Since the issue of whether an agency may create standards for summarily dismissing adjudicatory hearings is not germane to this case, it should not be decided here.

Weinberger v. Bentex Pharmaceuticals, Inc. (S.Ct. 1973) MM

Facts: The Food, Drug and Cosmetics Act (FDCA) required the Food and Drug Administration to withhold approval of any "new drug" for which "substantial evidence" of its efficacy is lacking. The FDCA defines a "new drug" as a drug that qualified experts consider safe and effective.

Issue: When will a court defer to an agency's interpretation of a statute as applied to a specific applicant?

Rule: (Douglas, J.) When the matter is of technical nature, courts should defer to agency expertise when interpreting relevant statutes applied to specific applicants.

Chapter 3

ADJUDICATORY PROCEDURE

I. INVESTIGATIONS AND DISCOVERY

A. Defined

Agencies have broad powers to force regulated industries to reveal information, either for investigations of possible regulatory violations or during the pre-hearing phase of an agency adjudication. This can be a very pervasive power for the agency. In providing limitations, courts have held that in order for an allegedly investigatory action to be valid, it must be:

1. Authorized by a law other than the APA;

2. Relevant to the agency's general purpose; or

3. Not unduly burdensome.

B. Administrative Procedure Act

Section 555(c) of the Administrative Procedure Act (APA) exempts investigative action from its general procedural requirements. There is a presumption that any challenged agency action is actually investigatory in nature.

C. Required Record-Keeping

1. Defined
   Agencies' may promulgate any record-keeping requirements that are reasonable and have a rational relationship to the area regulated by the agency. Challenges to agency requirements are rarely successful.

2. Fifth Amendment Defense

   a. Self-Incrimination
      No right against self-incrimination exists to justify non-compliance with record-keeping requirements. Corporations, partnerships and unincorporated associations, like unions, may never claim a Fifth Amendment defense.

      The only exception to this rule was noted in *Marchetti v. United States*, where the Supreme Court allowed a Fifth Amendment defense where the required records were not of the sort "customarily kept," and were required of "a selective group inherently suspect of criminal activities."

   b. Property Rights
      The Fifth Amendment protects privileged information that constitutes property interests (such as trade secrets) from public disclosure. But the information must still be divulged to the agency.

C. Inspections

   1. With a Warrant
      Without the permission of the owner, agencies generally need a warrant to inspect privately owned property. However, to gain a warrant, the agency need only show that the property to be inspected was chosen on the basis of reasonable or neutral standards.

   2. Without a Warrant
      To justify warrantless inspections, an agency must satisfy four criteria:

      Mnemonic: <u>LENS</u>
      a. The searches must be <u>l</u>imited in time, place and scope, thus providing a constitutionally adequate substitute for a warrant;

      b. There must be a low <u>e</u>xpectation of privacy, either because:

    i. The statute insures that inspections will be certain and regular; or

    ii. The industry is pervasively regulated;

  c. Unannounced inspections must be <u>n</u>ecessary to further a regulatory scheme; and

  d. There must be a <u>s</u>ubstantial government interest.

D. Subpoenas

  1. Defined
  Subpoenas compel testimony from relevant witnesses and experts. *Subpoenas duces tecum* require subpoenaed parties to appear with requested documents.

  Although an agency may only issue subpoenas where expressly authorized by statute, almost every enabling statute includes such authorization.

  2. Scope
  Agencies are given broad leeway in determining the scope of their own subpoenas. Although the subpoenas must be reasonable, relevant and related to areas where the agency has jurisdiction, since the 1940's courts have consistently held that almost any request is valid. Corporations are not entitled to as much privacy as individuals.

  3. Enforcement
  Agencies may not enforce their own subpoenas via administrative contempt proceedings.

  4. Defenses

  Mnemonic: <u>PULP</u>
  a. <u>P</u>rocedural Irregularities
    A subpoena is invalid when issued by an agency that failed to follow its own rules or relevant statutes.

b. Unreasonably Broad
Subpoenas that are vague and indefinite, or unreasonably broad or burdensome are invalid. This defense is rarely successful.

c. Lack of Jurisdiction
An agency may not issue a subpoena that would reveal information that the agency may not regulate, although the party served with the subpoena need not fall under the agency's jurisdiction.

d. Privileged Information
Privileges (such as lawyer-client or doctor-patient) that are recognized in civil trials are also recognized in agency adjudications. Privileges are generally defined by the discovery practices of the relevant rules of civil procedure.

The Fifth and First Amendments (right against self-incrimination and right to freedom of expression, respectively) also prevent information from being subpoenaed.

II.   EVIDENCE

A. Admissibility

1. Generally
Evidence that is normally excluded from civil trials may be admissible in administrative hearings. Although § 556 of the APA excludes "irrelevant, immaterial or unduly repetitious evidence," evidence is rarely excluded from administrative proceedings.

2. The Residuum Rule
Where a substantial right is at stake, administrative hearings may not rely exclusively on evidence inadmissible in civil trials; a residuum of admissible evidence must be used in the decision, except where:

    a. The inadmissible evidence is substantial, and

    b. Admissible evidence was available, but not properly requested by the parties.

3. Illegally Obtained Evidence

    a. Federal Court
    Illegally obtained evidence is admissible in federal administrative adjudications when the costs of excluding the evidence outweigh the benefits.

    b. State Courts
    State courts have not yet been bound to the federal rule. Most states exclude illegally obtained evidence.

B. Standard of Proof

Generally, courts have interpreted § 556 of the APA as requiring litigants to sustain any burden of proof with the preponderance of the evidence standard. Other statutes may require different burdens of proof. Where no burden of proof is found in the statute or legislative intent, courts are generally free to prescribe whatever burden they find proper.

C. Official Notice

Official notice allows agency decisionmakers to assume facts of that they have expert knowledge or that are common knowledge, when making decisions. Official notice is essentially the administrative version of judicial notice.

Section 556(e) requires administrative adjudicators to give parties an opportunity to rebut officially noticed evidence, except where:

1. The evidence is not beyond a lay person's comprehension; or

2. The parties have already introduced evidence bearing on the same facts that are officially noticed.

III.   PRECLUSION AND PRECEDENT

The doctrines of *res judicata* and collateral estoppel prevent parties from relitigating claims or legal issues that have already been fully litigated.   Once a legal claim is lost, there is no second chance.

Equitable estoppel prevents a party from raising a defense or a claim, even if it has never been litigated previously.   Once it is proven that a litigant has reasonably relied to her detriment on information given by an opposing party, that party is estopped from claiming that it is not responsible for the consequences of the litigant's reasonable reliance.

A. Preclusion in Administrative Adjudications

Agencies must abide by the factual findings of federal and state civil and criminal courts.

B. Preclusion by Administrative Adjudications

1. Findings of Fact
An agency's findings of fact cannot be subsequently relitigated, unless Congress has indicated, expressly or by implication, that it did not intend to give an agency hearing preclusive effect.

2. Declaratory Judgments
Section 554 of the APA allows agencies to make declaratory judgments with the same binding effect as administrative adjudications.

C. Preclusion Against the Government

1. No Offensive Non-Mutual Collateral Estoppel
The government is not precluded from relitigating a claim when a second suit on the same issue is brought by a different party. The government is precluded where it reasserts a defense

against the same party or where it brings a claim, previously lost, in two suits. See *United States v. Mendoza.*

2. Equitable Estoppel

The Supreme Court has yet to apply equitable estoppel (reasonably relying upon misinformation to one's detriment) against the government. The Court held that were equitable estoppel to apply, the government would be subject to enormous liabilities due to inadvertent mistakes by minor government agents. See *Schweiker v. Hansen.*

But some lower federal courts have been more receptive to the claim. A handful of states have also recognized equitable estoppel against the government.

D. Administrative Consistency

Agencies need not follow previous administrative decisions. But an agency decisionmaker who breaks from precedent must furnish the reasons for doing so in the decisionmaking record.

However, an agency adjudicator must abide by the agency's own promulgated rules. Even considerations of equity and fairness do not entitle an administrative law judge to violate agency regulations. Regulations bind the agency just as they bind those regulated.

IV. SANCTIONS

A. First Amendment Limitations

Commercial speech is not always free from regulation. Courts look at four factors to determine a regulation's validity:

1. If the regulated speech is misleading or concerns an unlawful activity, it may always be regulated.

2. If not, the government must have a substantial interest in regulating the contested speech.

3. If a substantial interest exists, the regulation must directly advance that interest.

4. The government interest must not be more extensive than necessary to serve that interest.

B. Affirmative Sanctions

An agency can always order parties over which it has jurisdiction to cease violating regulations. Such negative sanctions are almost always within agency power. However, an agency encounters some difficulty when applying affirmative sanctions to compel corrective action from parties who have been found to violate the law.

An agency may not apply affirmative sanctions where:

1. The sanctions are designed to apply retroactively; or

2. The sanctions are punitive, as opposed to corrective, in nature.

C. Pre-Judgment Action

Agencies may act in a way that harms parties before they have been found guilty of any violations, as long as their action does not act as a punishment against a party. Although this seems to violate the concept of presumed innocence, agencies have some leeway in their pre-judgment actions. See *FTC v. Cinderella*.

CASE CLIPS

Appeal of FTC Line of Business Report Litigation
(1978) BA

Facts: The Federal Trade Commission (FTC) required 450 of the nation's largest manufacturers to complete lengthy and expensive forms to be used to identify monopolistic activity. Some manufacturers refused, claiming the forms were not developed pursuant to proper rulemaking procedure. The FTC claimed that the form was investigatory in nature and thus exempt from rulemaking under the Administrative Procedure Act (APA).

Issue: When is agency action investigatory in nature and thus exempt from the rulemaking procedures of the APA?

Rule: Agency action is investigatory in nature and thus exempt from the rulemaking procedures of the APA where the action is authorized by law other than the APA, is relevant to the agency's general purpose, and is not unduly burdensome. The party opposing the rule must overcome presumptions that the action is neither unreasonable nor burdensome.

Trujillo v. Employment Security Commission (1980) BA

Facts: In a state administrative adjudication, the Employment Security Commission based its decision to reject Trujillo's application for unemployment compensation exclusively upon hearsay testimony that would not have been admissible in civil court.

Issue: When is an administrative order, based exclusively on evidence that would be inadmissible in civil court, invalid?

Rule: Where, as here, a substantial right is at stake, there must be at least a residuum of evidence that would be admissible in civil court to uphold an agency decision.

Note: Many states, and possibly the federal courts, do not follow the "residuum rule."

Franz v. Board of Medical Quality Assurance (1982) BA

Facts: The California Board of Medical Quality Assurance, in finding a doctor guilty of gross negligence, took official notice (i.e., assumed facts that had not been introduced into evidence) of the community's standard of medical negligence regarding certain of the doctor's actions. Some of these factual determinations required expert knowledge. The Board did not give the doctor an opportunity to refute the officially noticed facts.

Issue: According to state law, when must new opportunity to submit evidence be granted when administrative decisionmakers take official notice?

Rule: When an agency takes official notice of legislative and factual issues in an adjudication, due process requires the agency to notify the parties and provide opportunity for rebuttal, unless the significance of underlying facts is within lay comprehension.

Matlovich v. Secretary of the Air Force (1978) BA
Facts: The Air Force dismissed a homosexual employee without explaining why he did not fall under an exemption, used to retain some homosexuals, for "most unusual circumstances." The Air Force had never defined "most unusual circumstances."
Issue: Must an agency's statement of findings and reasons contain an explanation of the applicable standards and how they were applied?
Rule: To allow reviewing courts to judge whether agency action was arbitrary, capricious, or otherwise illegal, a statement of findings and reasons must explain why exemptions were inapplicable to the case.

University of Tennessee v. Elliott (S.Ct. 1986) BA
Facts: A state administrative agency found that an employee's discharge was not the result of racial discrimination. The employee then brought suit in federal court under Title VII of the Civil Rights Act of 1964 and 42 U.S.C. § 1983. Petitioner claimed the agency's rulings had preclusive effect.
Issue: When do a state administrative agency's findings of fact preclude relitigation of those issues in federal court?
Rule: (White, J.) When a state agency properly resolves disputed issues of fact in an administrative adjudication, federal courts must give the agency decision preclusive effect, unless Congress intended otherwise, as in the Civil Rights Act of 1964, but not in 42 U.S.C. § 1983.
Dissent: (Stevens, J.) Nothing in the 1871 Civil Rights Act (42 U.S.C. § 1983) indicates that Congress intended to give state agency decisions preclusive effect.

International Union, United Automobile Workers of America v. NLRB (1986) BA
Facts: The National Labor Relations Board found an implied waiver of the right to union negotiations, despite consistent previous agency decisions that held that a waiver of the right to union negotiations must be clear and unmistakable.
Issue: When may an agency cease to follow its own precedents?

Rule: Although not bound by *stare decisis*, whenever an agency breaks away from its established holdings, it must furnish an adequate explanation for the basis of the new interpretation.

Foote's Dixie Dandy, Inc. v. McHenry (1980) BA

Facts: A certified public accountant for Arkansas's Employment Security Division gave erroneous advice to the owner of two grocery stores regarding whether to file certain transfer forms. Because of this oversight, the State of Arkansas claimed that the owner owed $20,000 in back taxes.

Issue: When a party's reliance on erroneous advice from a government agent causes him to break the law, may that party estop the government from bringing suit?

Rule: The government is estopped from adjudicating a claim involving a routine measure where an agent clothed with considerable authority gave erroneous advice upon which the claimant relied to his detriment, and where there exists not even a scintilla of evidence of bad faith by the accused.

Note: Only a handful of states recognize estoppel against the government, federal court decisions are unclear whether estoppel exists, and although the Supreme Court has so far refused to allow estoppel against the government, recent cases have been more receptive to estoppel claims.

Arizona Grocery Co. v. Atchison, Topeka & Santa Fe Ry. (S.Ct. 1932) BS

Facts: The Interstate Commerce Act of 1887 authorized the Interstate Commerce Commission (ICC) to determine whether a rate charged by a carrier was reasonable. The Hepburn Act and the Transportation Act gave ICC power to establish minimum and maximum rates. ICC had established, through rulemaking, a maximum, but not a minimum, shipping rate. In a subsequent adjudicatory action, the ICC invalidated a shipper's rate that fell below the ICC's maximum rate and then forced carriers to pay damages.

Issue: In an adjudication, may a ratemaking agency declare a rate that falls within its own standards to be unreasonable and void?

Rule: (Roberts, J.) An agency must follow its own rules. When an agency establishes rates, they must, by law, be reasonable, and they may only be changed through subsequent rulemaking, not by adjudication.

Dissent: (Holmes and Brandeis, JJ.) When an agency only sets an upper limit, above which no rate may be charged, whether a rate below the limit is reasonable should be determined in an adjudication.

United States v. Caceres (S.Ct. 1979) BS

Facts: A defendant in a criminal prosecution attempted to exclude evidence that had been obtained by the Internal Revenue Service agents in violation of its own regulations, although not in violation of the Constitution or any statute.

Issue: May evidence obtained by an agency in violation of its own rule be excluded from a criminal proceeding?

Rule: (Stevens, J.) In a criminal proceeding, violation of an agency's own regulation should not result in excluding evidence, but should mandate the requisite agency sanctions for violation of the regulation.

Dissent: (Marshall, J.) Agencies must follow their own regulations. If an agency breaks its own rules, courts may impose appropriate remedies; courts should not depend on the enforcement of agency rules by the agency.

Schweiker v. Hansen (S.Ct. 1981) BS

Facts: A Social Security Administration field representative erroneously told a potential applicant that she was ineligible for benefits. As a result, she lost a year's worth of benefits. She sued for the lost benefits, and the government denied the claim.

Issue: Does erroneous advice from a government agent estop the government from denying a claim for benefits?

Rule: (Per curiam) A government agent's misrepresentations will not estop the government. The government may not be put at risk of enormous liability due to the alleged failure of a government agent.

United States v. Abilene & Southern Ry. (S.Ct. 1924) BS

Facts: The Interstate Commerce Commission (ICC) set railroad rates based in part on annual reports filed with the ICC, but never formally introduced into evidence.

Issue: May agencies make adjudicative decisions based on facts not introduced into evidence?

Rule: (Brandeis, J.) Agencies may not base decisions on facts that have not been introduced into evidence, unless agencies reveal those facts and allow parties an opportunity to rebut.

Ohio Bell Tel. Co. v. Public Utilities Commn. (S.Ct. 1937)
BS, GB

Facts: The Public Utilities Commission (PUC) set utility rates based on predictions of price trends that had not been introduced into evidence and whose source had never been revealed.

Issue: May agencies make adjudicative decisions based on predictions that had not been introduced into evidence?

Rule: (Cardozo, J.) Agencies may not base decisions on predictions that have not been introduced into evidence, unless agencies reveal their source and allow parties an opportunity to rebut.

Market Street Ry. v. Railroad Commn. (S.Ct. 1945) BS, S

Facts: The Railroad Commission set railroad rates based in part on monthly reports filed by the Market Street Railway. The reports were never entered into evidence, but Market Street Railway did enter in evidence expert testimony bearing on the same issue for which the Railroad Commission used the monthly records.

Issue 1: May agencies decide issues in a manner inconsistent with all testimony before it?

Rule 1: (Jackson, J.) Agency decisionmakers may disregard testimony and evidence before them as they see fit.

Issue 2: When may agencies make adjudicative decisions based on facts not introduced into the record?

Rule 2: Where parties have not been prejudiced by agency reliance on facts outside the decisionmaking record, agencies may use facts not introduced into the record.

Charles of the Ritz Distributors Corp. v. FTC (1944) BS

Facts: The Federal Trade Commission instructed the distributor of a moisturizing cream to cease advertising its product as a "Rejuvenescence Cream." The distributor claimed that the false advertising provisions of the Federal Trade Commission Act should not apply to it, since no "straight-thinking" person would believe that the cream actually rejuvenates.

Issue: How broadly may the false advertising provisions of the Federal Trade Commission Act be applied?

Rule: Since the Federal Trade Commission Act was enacted to protect the foolish as well as the wise, all deceptive advertising may be regulated.

Central Hudson Gas & Electric Corp. v. Public Service Commission of New York (S.Ct. 1980) BS

Facts: The Public Service Commission of New York banned almost all advertising by electric companies.

Issue: When may commercial speech be regulated?

Rule: (Blackmun, J.) To determine whether commercial speech is protected by the First Amendment against agency action, a four-part test is necessary. First, the speech regulated must concern lawful activity and not be misleading. Second, the government interest must be substantial. If both of the first two criteria are met, the regulation must also be in proportion to the government interest. Finally, the regulation must not be more extensive than necessary to serve that interest.

Note: The Supreme Court struck down the New York regulation as more extensive than necessary to protect the state's interest.

In re Firestone Tire & Rubber Co. (1972) BS

Facts: The Federal Trade Commission found that Firestone had used deceptive advertising and ordered it to cease such advertising. Intervenor Students Opposing Unfair Practices argued that Firestone should be required to publicize the fact it had used false claims.

Issue: May an agency impose corrective measures on those who have violated agency regulations?

Rule: Where corrective measures are warranted to prevent continuing public injury, it is neither punitive nor retrospective to order such relief.

Note: Although the agency could require corrective advertising, it decided that such a measure was unnecessary in this case.

FTC v. Cinderella Career and Finishing School (1968) BS

Facts: The Federal Trade Commission (FTC) had a policy of issuing press releases regarding upcoming adjudications. The Cinderella

School unsuccessfully petitioned the FTC not to publicize their case and then sought an injunction against future press releases.

Issue: May an agency issue press releases regarding a case pending before it?

Rule: As long as a press release acts as a warning to the public, rather than a punishment against the alleged wrongdoer, administrative agencies may publicize upcoming administrative adjudications.

In re Pfizer, Inc. (1972) BS

Facts: The Federal Trade Commission heard a complaint against Pfizer that its Un-Burn Skin Lotion used unsubstantiated claims in its advertising. Although the manufacturer had made no scientific studies, medical literature did substantiate the manufacturer's claims of efficiency.

Issue: Must a regulated industry always produce its own scientific studies to substantiate its advertised claims?

Rule: Where sufficient studies already exist, regulated industries need not produce their own studies to back up individual product claims.

FTC v. American Tobacco Co. (S.Ct. 1924) BS, S

Facts: As part of an investigation of cigarette price-fixing, the Federal Trade Commission requested virtually all documents generated by the American Tobacco Company in 1921.

Issue: When may an agency make sweeping demands for documents?

Rule: (Holmes, J.) An agency must produce evidence of the materiality of requested documents to comply with statutory and constitutional requirements.

Oklahoma Press Publishing Co. v. Walling (S.Ct. 1946) BS, S

Facts: The Fair Labor Standards Act authorized the issuance of subpoenas without lodging a complaint.

Issue: Where a statute explicitly authorizes the issuance of administrative subpoenas, what limitations are there on an agency's demand for documents?

Rule: (Rutledge, J.) To authorize subpoenas, an agency must show that the investigation is properly authorized by Congress, the subpoena is seeking relevant documents, and the subpoena is reasonable in its specificity of time, place, and manner. There need not be a complaint pending.

United States v. Morton Salt Co. (S.Ct. 1950) BS

Facts: The Federal Trade Commission required the Morton Salt Company to produce a series of special reports to ensure that it complied with an administrative order.

Issue: May an agency demand documents to ensure corporate compliance with an administrative adjudicatory order?

Rule: (Jackson, J.) An agency's demand for documents comports with the Fourth Amendment when it is reasonably relevant, within the authority of the agency, and not too indefinite. Corporations are not entitled to as much privacy as individual citizens.

Red Lion Broadcasting Co. v. FTC (S.Ct. 1969) BS

Facts: The Federal Communications Commission, under its fairness doctrine, required broadcasters to give time to reply to personal attacks and political editorials sponsored by the broadcaster.

Issue: Does a rule requiring licensed broadcasters to give the public time to reply to a broadcaster's editorials abridge the First Amendment's freedoms of speech and press?

Rule: (White, J.) A government-issued broadcasting license is subject to greater restrictions than those allowed for other media. These restrictions may constitutionally include required programming and response time to give fair coverage to both sides of public issues, political editorials or personal attacks.

Miami Herald Publishing Co. v. Tornillo (S.Ct. 1974) BS

Facts: A Florida statute required newspapers to give free reply space to political candidates attacked in editorial columns.

Issue: Is a statute requiring newspapers to provide free reply space an unconstitutional abridgment of freedom of the press?

Rule: (Burger, C.J.) Since the right of newspaper editors to choose what they wish to print cannot be abridged, a statute requiring them to provide free reply space is unconstitutional.

Columbia Broadcasting Systems, Inc. v. Democratic National Committee (S.Ct. 1973) BS

Facts: Columbia Broadcasting Systems denied air access to two groups who wished to advertise their disapproval of the Vietnam War.

Issue: Is there a constitutional right under the First Amendment to purchase broadcast time for the presentation of personal views?

Rule: (Burger, C.J.) The First Amendment does not require the sale of radio or television air time, even if state action controlling the use of broadcast time is involved.

Banzhaf v. FCC (1968) BS

Facts: The Federal Communications Commission required broadcasters to allot air time for anti-smoking advertising.

Issue: What factors are relevant when determining whether a broadcasting regulation comports with the First Amendment?

Rule: To determine whether a broadcasting regulation violates the First Amendment, courts must consider whether any speech will be banned, whether any other speech affected is constitutionally protected, the risk of substantially affecting protected speech, and whether the benefits of such regulation outweigh the loss of First Amendment freedoms.

Marshall v. Barlow's Inc. (S.Ct. 1978) GB, CD, MM

Facts: Section 8(a) of the Occupational Safety and Health Act of 1970 (OSHA) authorized agents of the Secretary of Labor to inspect businesses without a warrant.

Issue: When does the Fourth Amendment require an agency to obtain a warrant before gaining entrance to a place of business?

Rule: (White, J.) The Fourth Amendment always requires an agency to obtain a warrant before gaining entrance to a place of business, except in cases of pervasively regulated businesses long subject to close supervision and inspection.

Dissent: (Stevens, J.) The Fourth Amendment bans only unreasonable warrantless searches. OSHA's statutory procedures ensure that all warrantless searches will be reasonable.

Donovan v. Dewey (S.Ct. 1981) GB

Facts: The Federal Mine Safety and Health Act expressly authorized the Labor Department to inspect underground mines without a warrant.

Issue: When may an agency conduct warrantless searches of places of business?

Rule: (Marshall, J.) Agencies may conduct warrantless searches of businesses where Congress has determined that a warrant would impede a regulatory scheme, and where regulation of the industry is pervasive.

Concurrence 1: (Stevens, J.) Although not necessary to decide in this case, the Fourth Amendment's protections should not automatically cover commercial property.

Concurrence 2: (Rehnquist, J) Had this been a criminal case against private citizens, the Court would not hesitate to strike down the statute. Commercial property is held to a lesser standard.

Dissent: (Stewart, J.) The Court has dropped the requirement that the industry be not only pervasively regulated, but that there be a long history of such regulation. No long history of regulation exists here.

Hunter v. Zenith Dredge Co. (1945) GB

Facts: Hunter sought compensation for injuries sustained in the course of employment. The industrial commission responsible for determining eligibility was required by statute to adhere to the factual findings of a medical board. However, the medical board was not required to reveal its evidence and testimony so its decision could be reviewed by a court.

Issue: Must factual evidence on which an agency bases its findings be ascertainable?

Rule: Due process requires that the evidence on which an agency bases it findings be ascertainable. Where a subsidiary board is delegated the power to determine facts, those factual findings must be available to a reviewing court to protect the due process rights of the claimant.

Richardson v. Perales (S.Ct. 1971) GB, S

Facts: In an administrative hearing rejecting Perales's application for disability benefits, the Social Security Administration based its decision solely on physicians' written reports. Perales' lawyers did not request cross-examination of the physicians until after the agency deadline. The physicians' reports would be inadmissible in civil court.

Issue: When may a federal agency base an adjudicatory decision solely on evidence that, though admissible in agency hearings, would have been inadmissible in civil court?

Rule: (Blackmun, J.) Federal agency decisions may be based solely on evidence inadmissible in civil court where such evidence is substantial, and where admissible evidence was available yet not properly requested by opposing parties.

Banks v. Schweiker (1981) GB

Facts: Relying on statements made by a Social Security Administration (SSA) official, Banks kept Social Security checks sent to him in amounts greater than his entitlement. After he spent the extra money, the Social Security Administration insisted that he owed them the excess money as an overpayment. Banks sought an administrative hearing to contest the overpayment charge. The Administrative Law Judge (ALJ) ruled against Banks based on personal knowledge of Social Security offices and his belief that Banks' testimony was not credible. Banks appealed, charging the ALJ had improperly taken official notice of the practices and customs of SSA offices.

Issue: What is the permissible scope of official notice to be taken be administrative law judges?

Rule: An administrative law judge may take official notice of adjudicative facts whenever he knows of information that will be useful in making the decision; however, the claimant must be afforded an opportunity to show that notice should not be taken or is erroneous.

Ruckelshaus v. Monsanto Co. (S.Ct. 1984) CD

Facts: The Federal Insecticide, Fungicide, and Rodenticide Act (FIFRA) authorized the Environmental Protection Agency to reveal registration data submitted to the agency to competitors registering similar pesticides, as long as the competitors compensate the original applicant for the data used. Compensation was determined through binding, non-reviewable arbitration. The statute exempted trade secrets from disclosure for ten years.

Issue 1: Do trade secrets constitute a property interest protected by the Fifth Amendment?

Rule 1: (Blackmun, J.) Both Missouri law and FIFRA indicate that trade secrets are protected property interests.

Issue 2: What factors will a court consider in determining whether agency action constitutes a "taking" of property that violates the Fifth Amendment?

Rule 2: In determining whether agency action constitutes a taking of property in violation of the Fifth Amendment, courts will consider any interference with reasonable investment-backed expectations, the character of the administrative action, and the economic impact of the administrative action.

Issue 3: What constitutes an agency "taking for public use," which requires just compensation, rather than for private use, which is unconstitutional?

Rule 3: An agency "taking" occurs for public use, requiring just compensation, where Congress has determined that the action is beneficial to the public good.

New York v. Burger (S.Ct. 1987) S

Facts: A New York statute authorized the police to make warrantless searches of automobile junkyards. In conducting warrantless searches, the police occasionally found evidence of other crimes. The automobile junkyard industry was pervasively regulated.

Issue 1: When may an agency make a warrantless search of a place of business?

Rule 1: (Blackmun, J.) To make a warrantless search of a place of business, four criteria must be met. First, the industry inspected must be heavily regulated. Second, there must be a substantial government interest. Third, the warrantless inspections must be necessary to further a regulatory scheme. Finally, the statute's regulatory scheme must provide, in terms of the certainty and regularity of its application, a constitutionally adequate substitute for a warrant.

Issue 2: Is a statute that properly authorizes warrantless searches valid where a police officer locates evidence used in a criminal proceeding during a warrantless search?

Rule 2: That a police officer may locate evidence to be used in a criminal trial while performing a properly authorized warrantless search does not invalidate a statute authorizing such searches.

California Restaurant Assn. v. Henning (1985) S

Facts: A California statute authorized the Department of Industrial Relations to serve subpoenas without prior judicial review. Failure to comply with a subpoena constituted a misdemeanor.
Issue: When will a statute authorizing administrative subpoenas satisfy the Fourth Amendment?
Rule: A statute authorizing administrative subpoenas meets Fourth Amendment requirements where the administrative subpoena relates to an inquiry that the administrative agency is authorized to make, seeks information reasonably relevant to that inquiry, and is not too indefinite.

Endicott Johnson Corp. v. Perkins (S.Ct. 1943) S

Facts: The Walsh-Healey Act authorized the Secretary of Labor to investigate violations of minimum wage laws by government contractors.
Issue: May agencies authorized to investigate violations of law both define the scope of, and issue, investigatory subpoenas without first getting judicial approval?
Rule: (Jackson, J.)   As long as a statute directs investigation of limited violations of law, an agency may define the scope of, and issue, legally enforceable subpoenas without first receiving judicial approval.

Belle Fourche Pipeline Co. v. United States (1983) S

Facts: The Belle Fourche Pipeline Company refused to admit the Federal Energy Regulatory Commission (FERC) onto its premises, after FERC photocopied over 13,000 of Belle's documents, causing great disruption. FERC then sought to enforce a subpoena requesting all documents produced by the company in the last five years. Many of the documents requested did not directly involve matters that FERC regulated.
Issue: What is the proper scope of an agency subpoena?
Rule: An agency may only subpoena records that may reasonably relate to matters that are properly the subject of agency action,

reasonably relevant, within the agency's authority, not unreasonably burdensome, and sufficiently definite.

Consumer Protection Div. v. Consumer Publishing Co. (1985) S

Facts: On the same day the Attorney General filed charges against the Consumer Publishing Company, he also released a press statement that the company alleged was "inflammatory."
Issue: When may a government agent issue press releases about pending agency action?
Rule: Government agents (and agencies) may issue press releases regarding pending agency action as long as Congress has authorized their use, even if the press release damages the reputation of an affected party.

Young v. Board of Pharmacy (1969) S

Facts: The Board of Pharmacy for the State of New Mexico based its decision to revoke Young's license to practice pharmacology on evidence that, although legally admissible in administrative adjudications, would not have been admissible in a civil suit.
Issue: When may a state agency base an adjudicatory decision on evidence that would have been inadmissible in civil court?
Rule: State agency decisions must be based upon at least a residuum of evidence competent under the exclusionary rules in civil court.

Steadman v. SEC (S.Ct. 1981) S

Facts: The Securities Exchange Commission (SEC) applied a "preponderance of the evidence" standard of proof in formal adjudications to determine whether federal securities laws had been violated. The Administrative Procedure Act (APA) required that agency decisions be "in accordance with . . . substantial evidence." Steadman contended that the SEC had to use the stricter "clear and convincing" standard.
Issue: What standard of proof should apply to agency adjudications under the APA?
Rule: (Brennan, J.) Courts may generally prescribe a standard of proof in the absence of contrary congressional intent. But here, the

language of the APA indicates that Congress intended a "preponderance of the evidence" standard to be applied.

INS v. Lopez-Mendoza (S.Ct. 1984) S

Facts: Lopez-Mendoza, a citizen of Mexico, was detained, confessed to being an illegal alien, and was convicted. Since the detention contravened the Fourth Amendment and the confession was improperly introduced into the criminal proceeding, his conviction was reversed under the exclusionary rule. Lopez-Mendoza then sought to exclude the same evidence in a civil deportation hearing.

Issue: When may evidence illegally obtained and inadmissible in a criminal trial be admitted in a federal civil suit?

Rule: (O'Connor, J.) Illegally obtained evidence is admissible in a federal civil suit where the costs of excluding the evidence outweigh the benefits, despite its inadmissibility in criminal proceedings.

Dissent 1: (Brennan, J.) Since the exclusionary rule is derived from the Fourth Amendment, any evidence gained while infringing on a subject's Fourth Amendment rights must be excluded from civil, as well as criminal, trials.

Dissent 2: (White, J.) A proper application of the balancing test used incorrectly by the majority, and first set forth in *United States v. Janis*, reveals that the exclusionary rule should always apply to civil proceedings.

Turner v. City of Lawton (1986) S

Facts: A firefighter's discharge was based on illegally obtained evidence.

Issue: When is illegally obtained evidence admissible in state civil suits?

Rule: Illegally obtained evidence is never admissible in state civil suits.

Note: The court decided this case solely on the basis of state law. What is important is that cases like *US v. Janis*, *Tirado v. Commissioner*, and *INS v. Lopez-Mendoza*, above, which sometimes allow illegally obtained evidence in civil trials, do not necessarily apply to the states.

Air Products & Chemicals, Inc. v. Federal
Energy Regulatory Commn. (1981) S

Facts: In a hearing conducted under the formal adjudicatory procedures of the Administrative Procedure Act, the Federal Energy Regulatory Commission (FERC) denied applications for certificates to transport producer-reserved offshore federal domain natural gas. In reaching its decision, the FERC took official notice (i.e., assumed facts that had not been introduced into evidence) of the current market. The FERC neither gave applicants an opportunity to rebut the noticed information nor recorded the information in the decision. Section 556(e) of the APA required agencies whose decisions rest "on official notice of a material fact not appearing in the evidence in the record . . . [to allow a party] . . . an opportunity to show the contrary."

Issue: When must an agency using the formal adjudicatory procedures of the APA give opponents of a decision an opportunity to rebut officially noticed information?

Rule: An agency using the formal adjudicatory proceedings of the APA must give opponents of a decision an opportunity to rebut officially noticed information that is necessary to the decision and not included in the agency record.

Heckler v. Campbell (S.Ct. 1983) S

Facts: Campbell was denied Social Security disability benefits because of the Administrative Law Judge's reliance on medical-vocational guidelines.

Issue: May an agency base a decision regarding eligibility for benefits on general guidelines?

Rule: (Powell, J.) General guidelines may be used to determine benefit eligibility.

Chapter 4

POLICY FORMATION

I. THE DISTINCTION BETWEEN RULEMAKING AND ADJUDICATION

Administrative agencies implement their policies through the enactment of rules and the proclamation of adjudicative orders.

A. Definitions

1. Rulemaking
   The final product of the rulemaking process is a rule. According to the Federal Administrative Procedure Act § 551(4), a rule is an agency policy statement of general or particular applicability and future effect.

   a. Applicability
   Rules usually set standards of conduct for groups of people in general situations. However, a rule may be applied to a class presently consisting of a single person if the membership may expand in the future.

   b. Temporal Constraints
   A rule is a pronouncement of agency policy that affects future behavior—it is not an evaluation of an actor's past conduct. Thus, rules that have a retroactive effect are usually struck down by the courts.

   c. Quasi-Legislative
   The rulemaking powers of an administrative agency are very similar to the legislative powers of the government.

2. Adjudication
   The final product of the adjudicatory process is an order. According to the APA § 551(6), an order is an agency's final

disposition in a matter other than rulemaking. The authority to issue orders is a "residual power" often used to fill in policy gaps left by the agency's rulemaking procedures.

    a. Applicability
    Usually, an administrative agency will issue an order following an adjudicatory hearing. The order is applicable only to the particular situation and parties before the tribunal, but as a precedent, may serve to enunciate general agency policy much like a rule.

    b. Temporal Constraints
    Administrative orders are only binding retroactively. Following the Supreme Court's decision in *National Labor Relations Board v. Wyman-Gordon Co.*, orders may no longer have an explicit prospective effect. However, they may implicitly guide future behavior as precedents.

    c. Quasi-Judicial
    The ability of an administrative agency to issue binding orders through adjudication is very similar to the judicial power of the government.

B. Rulemaking Versus Adjudication

Both rulemaking and adjudication have distinct characteristics that would warrant the application of one over the other in certain situations.

1. Advantages of Rulemaking

    Mnemonic: PEACUP

    a. Active Public Participation
    Rulemaking procedures usually require that an agency conduct public hearings before the promulgation of a generally applicable rule. All interested parties may submit comments.

b. Efficiency

Policymaking by adjudication requires the collection of many decisions for a sufficient body of precedent. Rulemaking, in contrast, allows an agency to state its policy in one administrative action. Furthermore, administrative orders may often conflict with each other, leaving the true state of agency policy in doubt.

c. Availability

The APA requires that administrative agencies publish their rules in the Federal Register. Rules are therefore easily collected and located by interested parties, whereas administrative decisions are often not published.

d. Agency Control

When an agency decides to create policy through adjudication, it must wait for suitable cases to arise before announcing new standards. Through rulemaking, however, an agency may determine policy according to its own timetable.

e. Uniformity

Administrative rules have the same effect on all people within a class. In contrast, since orders only bind the particular parties to an adjudication, the policies expressed by them may be safely ignored by others.

f. Prospectivity

The prospective effect of rules reduces the chance that reliance interests may be negatively affected by a change in agency policy.

2. Advantages of Adjudication

a. Flexibility

For rulemaking to be effective, an agency must plan for numerous contingencies. Adjudication allows the selective application of agency policy to specific factual situations that may not have been contemplated when the policy was formed.

b. Enforcement
For administrative policy to be effective, an agency must have a means of enforcement. Adjudication allows an agency to review public compliance with its policies on a case-by-case basis—a retrospective application not available through rulemaking.

c. Policy Evolution
An agency may not have enough experience in an area to formulate a comprehensive policy. Adjudication allows the agency to develop its ideas over time.

II. LIMITS ON AGENCY DISCRETION TO CHOOSE A LAWMAKING PROCEDURE

While both rulemaking and adjudication are viable means of expressing administrative policy, an agency may not always be free to utilize the method of its choice. Limits may be imposed on the agency's freedom to choose between rulemaking and adjudication, as well as the procedures that drive each process.

A. Constitutional Requirements

1. Due Process

a. Rulemaking
An agency is not required to grant each citizen an opportunity to be heard before the enactment of a generally applicable rule. See *Bi-Metallic Investment Co. v. State Bd. of Equalization of Colorado*.

b. Adjudication
If the enactment of a rule will particularly affect certain members of a class, these people must be given an opportunity to voice their objections in an adjudicatory hearing. See *Londoner v. Denver*.

2. Other Constitutional Requirements
In *Minnesota State Board for Community Colleges v. Knight*, the Supreme Court refused to recognize a general constitutional right to participate directly in government policymaking. Thus, the due process constraint on adjudication is the only one imposed by the Constitution.

B. Choosing Between Rulemaking and Adjudication

1. Generally
The Supreme Court has generally given administrative agencies wide latitude to use rulemaking or adjudication in a particular situation. See *Securities & Exchange Comm. v. Chenery Corp. (Chenery II)* and *NLRB v. Bell Aerospace Co.*

2. The Decision to Use Rulemaking
Once an agency decides to formulate a rule, it must follow the rulemaking procedures prescribed by law. While the Constitution does not require formal notice and comment proceedings, the administrative procedure acts of many states and the federal government do. Therefore, an attempt to promulgate a rule without complying with the applicable rulemaking procedures might not be upheld. This is detailed in Chapter 6. Also see *National Labor Relations Board v. Wyman-Gordon Co.* and *Morton v. Ruiz*.

3. The Decision to Use Adjudication
Once an agency decides to issue an order through adjudication, it must base that order upon the "relevant and proper standards," regardless of whether those standards had been previously articulated in a formal rule. See *Chenery II*. An agency thus has considerable freedom to shape individual decisions into a general policy.

CASE CLIPS

Anaconda Co. v. Ruckelshaus (1973) BA

Facts: Anaconda demanded an adjudicatory hearing to protest a proposed emission-control regulation by the Environmental Protection Agency (EPA). The EPA held that the hearing was to be legislative and informational, rather than adjudicatory, and thus would not be conducted as a trial.

Issue: Is it a violation of due process for an agency to refuse an adjudicatory hearing when issuing an emissions standard?

Rule: Unless expressly provided by statute, an adjudicatory hearing is not required during rulemaking procedures.

NLRB v. Bell Aerospace Co., Division of Textron, Inc. (S.Ct. 1974) BA, BS, GB, CD

Facts: The United Automobile, Aerospace and Agricultural Implement Workers of America wished to represent employees of Bell Aerospace's purchasing and procurement department in collective bargaining proceedings. Bell opposed the union's petition to the NLRB, claiming that the workers in this department were "managerial employees," and thus not eligible for union representation.

Issue: Must an agency invoke its rulemaking procedures if a new standard is being applied for the first time?

Rule: (Powell, J.) An agency's decision to announce a new principle in an adjudicative proceeding will only be overturned if the agency abused its discretion or rulemaking is expressly required by statute.

Dissent: (White, J.) Managerial employees are "employees" within the meaning of the National Labor Relations Act.

Megdal v. Oregon State Board of Dental Examiners (1980) BA

Facts: Megdal, a dentist licensed in Oregon and California, fraudulently obtained malpractice insurance coverage for his California employees by claiming that they were employed in Oregon. Upon learning this, the Oregon State Board of Dental Examiners revoked his Oregon license on the ground of "unprofessional conduct."

Issue: May an agency hold someone to a broad standard of "professional conduct" in an adjudicatory hearing without first defining that standard through the rulemaking process?

Rule: When the legislature explicitly provides an agency with rulemaking powers, the agency should clarify vague legislative commands through rulemaking rather than ad hoc adjudication.

National Labor Relations Board v. Wyman-Gordon Co.
(S.Ct. 1969) BA, BS, CD, S, MM

Facts: The National Labor Relations Board (NLRB) ordered Wyman-Gordon to provide a list of its employees to several competing unions. The agency based its order on a previous adjudicatory decision that purported to announce a new prospective only rule requiring such a list.

Issue: May an agency promulgate rules of general application through adjudicatory proceedings?

Rule: (Fortas, J.) An agency may not replace the statutory rulemaking provisions with a procedure of its own invention. Adjudicated cases may announce agency policies and serve as precedents, but need not be obeyed as generally applicable rules without further legal action. In this case, however, the NLRB's request should be upheld because it was issued as an order in the process of an adjudicatory hearing.

Concurrence: (Black, J.) An agency may promulgate prospective rules through adjudication, as well as rulemaking. To require otherwise would force the agency to determine the temporal effect of its holding prior to the adjudication/rulemaking decision.

Dissent 1: (Douglas, J.) When choosing to exercise its quasi-legislative powers, an agency should be bound to follow the statutory requirements for rulemaking.

Dissent 2: (Harlan, J.) If an agency's adjudicative order purports to take effect in the future, it falls within the Act's definition of a rule and must satisfy its rulemaking requirements.

The Permian Basin Area Rate Cases (S.Ct. 1968) BS

Facts: In an effort to control rising prices in the natural gas industry, the Federal Power Commission (FPC) enacted rate control regulations. Due to the large number of producers in the industry, the agency found it impossible to determine maximum rates on an ad hoc basis. Instead, the FPC determined maximum rates for all the producers in a given area based upon an average of cost figures for individual units.

Issue: May an agency regulate producers' sales by the prescription of maximum area rates, rather than by proceedings conducted on an individual producer basis?

Rule: (Harlan, J.) Administrative agencies may calculate rates for a regulated class without first evaluating the separate financial position of each member of the class.

Dissent: (Douglas, J.) Even where the rates fixed will recover the average operating expenses, the individual producer's right to a minimum of its operating expenses and capital charges should be protected.

Phillips Petroleum Co. v. Wisconsin (S.Ct. 1954) BS

Facts: The Federal Power Commission (FPC) wished to regulate the prices charged by Phillips Petroleum, a natural gas producer without any interstate pipeline ownership.

Issue: Does the jurisdiction of the FPC extend to those companies that produce natural gas but do not transport it?

Rule: (Minton, J.) A natural gas producer is a "natural gas company" as defined by the Natural Gas Act. The Act covers the sale of gas produced by the entire industry, whether before, during, or after transmission by an interstate pipeline company. Thus, FPC jurisdiction extends to producers who do not engage in interstate transport.

National Petroleum Refiners Association
v. Federal Trade Commission (1973) BS, CD

Facts: The FTC promulgated a rule requiring the posting of octane ratings on gasoline pumps.

Issue: Is an agency's rulemaking power limited to procedural pronouncements?

Rule: An agency may promulgate binding substantive rules, as well as rules of procedure regarding the conduct of adjudicatory hearings.

Morton v. Ruiz (S.Ct. 1974) BS, CD, MM

Facts: The Bureau of Indian Affairs' internal operations manual required applicants to live on a reservation to be eligible for federal benefits. The BIA rejected Ruiz' application because he lived near, but not on, a reservation. The rule in question was not published in the Federal Register.

Issue: May an agency make ad hoc decisions based upon a rule that has not been promulgated in accordance with the formal rulemaking procedures of the Administrative Procedure Act?

Rule: (Blackmun, J.) Before an agency may distinguish among applicants, it must first promulgate eligibility requirements according to established procedures.

Securities & Exchange Comm. v. Chenery Corp. I (S.Ct. 1947) GB, BS

Facts: Chenery filed a voluntary reorganization plan with the SEC. The agency did not allow officers of the corporation to purchase preferred stock, but based its decision on controversial judicial precedents. After reconsidering the case, the SEC reached the same conclusion based on proper statutory standards and its accumulated expertise in the area.

Issue 1: May an agency's pronouncement in an adjudication have both prospective and retroactive effect?

Rule 1: (Murphy, J.) Although an agency may possess rulemaking powers, it may often be forced to formulate new standards of conduct through adjudication.

Issue 2: Must an agency's order in an adjudicatory hearing be based upon the standards of a general rule or regulation?

Rule 2: (Murphy, J.) An order in an adjudicatory hearing must be based upon the relevant and proper standards, regardless of whether those standards previously had been articulated in a general rule or regulation.

Dissent: (Jackson, J.) Before an order may be issued banning a previously legal activity, standards of conduct must be prescribed by the agency.

Ford Motor Company v. Federal Trade Commission (1981) GB

Facts: The FTC questioned Ford's practice of undervaluing repossessed automobiles. After an adjudicatory hearing, Ford was ordered to credit the debtor with the retail, rather than wholesale, value for his vehicle.

Issue: Is the adjudicatory process appropriate for enacting rules of widespread application?

Rule: If the change of an existing law would be limited in scope, an agency may proceed by adjudication. Otherwise, rules of general application should be enacted through the rulemaking process. Since the FTC's new interpretation of the statute will apply throughout the car dealership industry, the agency should proceed through rulemaking.

Dissent: Barring an abuse of discretion, an agency is free to choose between rulemaking and adjudication.

Heckler, Secretary of Health and Human Services v. Campbell (S.Ct. 1983) GB

Facts: Campbell applied for disability benefits under the Social Security Act. After her application was denied, she requested a hearing de novo before an Administrative Law Judge. The ALJ found that Campbell could still perform certain jobs within the national economy and thus was not disabled under the terms of the Act.

Issue: May an agency rely upon published guidelines to determine an applicant's eligibility for benefits?

Rule: (Powell, J.) Even when individualized hearings are mandated by statute, an agency may rely on properly enacted rules to resolve certain issues in the adjudication.

Concurrence: (Brennan, J.) When a claimant's special characteristics hamper the proper resolution of issues in a hearing, the ALJ's duty of inquiry takes on a special urgency.

Allison v. Block (1983) GB

Facts: Allison defaulted on governmental farm loans issued under the Consolidated Farm and Rural Development Act. The United States Department of Agriculture rejected his application for a deferral and began foreclosure proceedings.

Issue: May an agency decide individual cases solely upon the basis of its discretion, without using formal rulemaking procedures?

Rule: An agency must choose to develop a set of standards, either through rulemaking or adjudication, with which to decide cases. However, if the agency decides to proceed through adjudication, the decisionmaker must clearly articulate the reasons behind each determination in a manner susceptible to judicial review.

Trebesch v. Employment Div. (1985) S

Facts: The Employment Division denied unemployment benefits to Trebesch on the ground that he had not undertaken a "systematic and sustained effort to obtain work."

Issue: Must an agency promulgate rules in advance of adjudication?

Rule: In the absence of a statutory command to elaborate a standard through rulemaking, an agency may issue orders based upon rules or prior adjudicatory decisions.

Chapter 5

RULEMAKING PROCEDURE

I. INTRODUCTION

A. Administrative Procedure Acts (APAs)

1. Federal APA
   In 1946, Congress adopted the APA. The APA standardized procedures for all federal administrative agencies. The APA established two kinds of rulemaking procedures. First, where a statute requires rules to be "made on the record after opportunity for an agency hearing," the formal rulemaking procedures of §§ 556 and 557 apply. Otherwise, the informal rulemaking procedures of § 553 of the APA apply, subject to certain exemptions outlined below.

2. State APAs
   Each state has adopted its own APA to standardize state agencies. Most state APAs are modeled on the federal APA, or have adopted the Model State Administrative Procedure Act (MSAPA). In general, states require agencies to provide only informal rulemaking procedures.

B. Providing More than the APA Requires

1. Legislative Action
   Occasionally, statutes require more than the minimum requirements of § 553, without invoking the formal requirements of §§ 556 and 557. This is known as hybrid rulemaking.

2. Agency Action
   An agency may provide more rulemaking procedures than mandated by the APA, as long as the extra procedures are not arbitrary and capricious.

3. Judicial Action

Generally, a court will not compel an agency to provide more process than required by statute (see *Vermont Yankee*), except in cases of:

a. Insufficient Procedures

A court may impose more procedures to compel satisfaction of due process and any applicable statutes.

b. Extremely Compelling Circumstances

Although suggested as a possible exception in *Vermont Yankee*, no court has ever defined "extremely compelling circumstances." The Supreme Court has even held that disposal of nuclear waste is not an extremely compelling circumstance, so it is doubtful that the exception really exists.

c. Denied Rulemaking Petitions

A court may force an agency to institute rulemaking procedures only where:

i. A significant reason that had previously been given to deny the petition no longer exists, and

ii. The agency has only qualified discretion as to when it may deny a rulemaking petition (i.e., "for cause").

d. Insufficient Rulemaking Records

Courts have mandated more procedure to ensure a reviewable record, but this practice has been on shaky legal ground since *Vermont Yankee.*

C. Goals of Rulemaking Procedures

1. Encourage informed rulemaking.

2. Increase agency efficiency.

3. Make agencies responsive to the public.

4. Provide adequate notice of new rules.

5. Prevent overregulation.

6. Ensure fair and equitable rules.

7. Heighten public satisfaction with agency operations.

8. Keep agencies from overstepping the limits of their authority.

II. INFORMAL RULEMAKING

Section 553 of the APA outlines the minimum requirements of informal rulemaking, also known as "notice and comment" rulemaking.

A. Notice and Comment

  1. Notice

    a. An agency must either announce in the Federal Register that it is proposing a new regulation, or give all affected parties actual notice.

    b. The notice must include the time, place and nature of the rulemaking proceedings.

    c. The notice must include reference to the legal authority under which the rule is proposed.

    d. The notice must describe the subjects and issues involved, so that interested persons may adequately criticize and comment upon the proposed rule.

2. Comment

 a. Opportunity to Participate
 The agency must let interested parties submit their opinions of the proposed rules. This opportunity need not be oral or judicial in nature.

 The APA contains no minimum time to begin comment proceedings, or a minimum duration. But courts have determined that agency action be "reasonable," based upon the complexity and the scope of the proposed rule.

 b. Subsequent Opportunity to Comment
 An agency must afford a new opportunity to comment whenever a proposed rule is "significantly" altered, unless the alterations are "logical outgrowths" of the preceding proposal.

3. Statement of Basis and Purpose
 The agency must submit an opinion that provides appellants a base for their appeal, and appellate courts a base for their decision.

 The statement should contain:

 a. The factual, legal, and policy foundations for the new rule. Post hoc reasoning cannot be included.

 b. All materials used to draft and support the new rule.
 Note: The APA does not provide an exception for confidential documents.

 c. Responses to major policy issues, both for and against the adopted rule, which are brought before the agency.

 d. The relation between the new rule and the appropriate statute.

e. The agency's definition of "good cause," if a good cause exception has been invoked.

4. Exceptions to "Notice and Comment"

These exceptions apply equally to informal, hybrid, and formal rulemaking procedures. However, these exceptions do not exempt agencies from the publication requirement (see below) or from allowing interested parties to participate.

a. Interpretive Rules and Policy Statements
Interpretive rules merely clarify language or remind others of preexisting duties. Policy statements serve as a guide to agency members on how to act in discharging their duties. Neither affects the legal rights of the public nor requires a pre-enactment hearing of any sort.

In determining when an agency's statement is an interpretation or policy, as opposed to a rule, courts generally apply one of two tests:

i. Majority: Legal Effect Test
The court considers the following factors to determine if the public's rights have been affected:

(1) The language of the statement.

(2) The circumstances of the statement's promulgation.

(3) Courts also give some deference to what the agency claims its statement is, but it is not conclusive.

ii. Minority: Substantial Impact Test
If the court determines that the statement will have a substantial and practical effect on the public, the statement is a substantive rule, not a statement of policy or interpretation.

b. Procedural Rules

A procedural rule governs only the internal operations of an agency. Courts apply the substantial impact test, above, to determine whether an agency rule is procedural.

c. Good Cause

An agency claiming a "good cause" exception should do so when issuing a proposed rule, if possible. Also, agencies should always make a good faith attempt to comply with the APA. Courts will take these factors into account when deciding whether good cause exists.

The APA defines good cause as areas where usual rule making procedure is "unnecessary, impracticable, or contrary to the public interest."

i. Unnecessary

Rules and amendments that cause only a minor change in either the existing legal framework or in the legal rights and duties of the regulated parties do not require rule-making proceedings. This exemption is very limited and hardly ever invoked.

ii. Impracticability

Good cause exists when the execution of the agency's function would be unavoidably prevented by its undertaking rulemaking procedures.

iii. Contrary to the Public Interest

Good cause exists where advance notice of the rule and the delay of an informal procedure would demonstrably worsen the problem the agency is trying to combat. This exemption is rarely, if ever, invoked, except in conjunction with one of the other two good faith exemptions.

Courts will generally defer to the agency's public interest claim where the action reduces the danger of imminent public harm, but will scrutinize closely any action that may increase the risk of direct public harm.

B. Publication of the Rule

If an agency neither publishes the final version of the new or revised rule in the Federal Register nor gives actual notice to all affected parties, the new rule has been improperly adopted and is invalid.

Publication must occur within thirty days of the effective date of the rule, except in cases of:

1. Interpretive rules and policy statements.

2. Good cause.

3. Rules that grant or recognize exemptions or relieve restrictions.

C. Regulatory Analysis

Although not mentioned in the federal APA, some state APAs require agencies to produce a detailed analysis of the potential impact of the proposed rule. Regulatory analysis ensures that the rule is properly enacted and best suited to produce the desired results in the most efficient manner for both the government and society at large.

D. Exemptions From All Rulemaking Procedures

Courts limit all exemptions to situations where the rule "clearly and directly" involves the exempted activity. Of course, some exemptions are so broad that even narrowly construed exemptions may include many prospective rules.

1. Military or Foreign Affairs

2. Agency Matters and Personnel
   This exemption does not apply where the rule substantially affects persons outside the national government.

3. Proprietary Matters

   a. Public property
   Includes public domain, mineral rights and leases.

   b. Loans
   Includes federal loan programs and loans to state and local governments.

   c. Grants
   Includes federal subsidies to states, municipalities and private citizens.

   d. Benefits
   Includes pensions, social security, and some welfare programs. Rules that encompass both recipients and providers of benefits are exempted.

   e. Contracts
   Includes employment, purchases of goods, services and land, as well as the issuance of government bonds and securities.

III.   HYBRID PROCEEDINGS

A. Rulemaking Record

Since § 553 of the APA does not require a written record of informal rulemaking procedures, courts and agencies have had to use a variety of measures to ensure that a written record is available for judicial review.

1. Paper Hearing
Paper hearings are the most common way for an agency to keep a record of their proceedings. Courts will rarely dictate to the agency exactly what a rulemaking record should include, so the completeness of a paper hearing will vary from agency to agency and case to case, depending upon the requirements of the appropriate statutes and the complexity of the proposed rule.

But a paper hearing must be so complete that a court cannot call agency actions "arbitrary and capricious." The paper hearing should contain all substantial evidence for and against the agency's findings. A paper hearing may contain:

a. All written documents submitted to the agency regarding the proposed rule.

b. Memoranda of disclosed *ex parte* communications (see below).

c. Transcripts of oral testimony given during comment proceedings.

d. Data that, without disclosure, would impede the presentation of relevant comment.

e. The statement of basis and fact.

2. Subpoenaed Testimony
   Courts may require agency decisionmakers to state all the factual reasons used to formulate the rule and then allow opposing parties to contest the agency's versions of the facts. However, this allows agencies to submit post hoc rationales, and comes very close to a *de novo* review of the case.

3. Remand to Agency
   Reviewing courts may remand the proceeding to the agency for assembly of the relevant evidence.

4. *De Novo* Review
   A court will hold a fresh evidentiary hearing only where the agency hearing was "wholly inadequate" or where new factual issues are raised in judicial enforcement of agency decisions. *De novo* review is infrequently, if ever, used.

B. *Ex Parte* Communications

To ensure an unbiased result and that the rulemaking record is complete, courts have held that some *ex parte* communications between rulemakers and interested parties invalidate a rulemaking procedure.

Not all *ex parte* communications are prohibited, though, and some may be legitimized through disclosure — an action that places an "off the record" communication onto the agency rulemaking record.

1. Conflicting Claims
   Ex parte communications are always improper where the rule-making involves resolution of conflicting private claims to a valuable privilege.

2. Government Communications

   a. Internal Communications
      Agencies may retain in-house or outside consultants who may advise agency decisionmakers.

   b. Intra-Executive Communications
      Unless one of the agencies is "independent" of the executive branch (i.e., the Federal Reserve Board), communications among executive agencies are not prohibited and must be disclosed only where required by statute.

   c. Congressional Communications
      Communications with Congress are improper where:

      i. The legislative agent applies pressure to consider factors not made relevant by the applicable statute, and

      ii. That pressure affects the rulemaking process.

C. Bias

Where an agency member has been shown, clearly and convincingly, to have an "unalterably closed mind" on the issues involved, that member may not participate in that rulemaking action.

IV. FORMAL PROCEEDINGS

Formal hearings contain almost all the requirements of informal hearings. But in lieu of the informal "comment" proceedings, formal rulemaking requires "on the record" hearings outlined in APA §§ 556 and 557.

Formal hearings and formal administrative adjudications follow the same procedures. In fact, formal rulemaking is often described as quasi-adjudicative rulemaking. Of course, an enabling statute may require more than what is contained in the formal rulemaking procedures of the APA.

A. Elements

Mnemonic: <u>PONDER</u>

1. <u>P</u>ublication of the Final Rule
   The Federal Register publication requirement is identical to that of informal rulemaking, above.

2. <u>O</u>ral Proceedings
   The proceedings will be oral, with opportunities for interested parties to submit evidence and cross-examine witnesses.

   But, where the parties will not be prejudiced, an agency or administrative law judge (ALJ) may decide to limit the proceedings to written submissions only.

3. <u>N</u>otice
   The notice requirement is identical to that of informal rulemaking, above.

4. Unbiased Decisionmaker
   The decisionmaker is biased where a disinterested observer may conclude that the decisionmaker has in some measure adjudged the facts as well as the law of a particular case in advance of a hearing. A biased decisionmaker must recuse himself.

5. *Ex Parte* Ban
   No *ex parte* communications are allowed once notice of the proceedings has been issued. This is a much stricter standard than that of hybrid rulemaking.

   The decisionmaker can choose not to censure the parties involved where:

   a. There is disclosure of the banned communications, and

   b. "Cause" may be shown as to why the offender's interest should not be adversely affected.

   In determining "cause", courts will consider:

   i.   The gravity of the communication.

   ii. The influence that resulted, if any.

   iii. The benefit accrued by the violator, if any.

   iv. Any disclosure of the communication to adverse parties.

   v.   The utility of voiding the proceedings.

6. Record of the Proceedings
   A full, written transcript of the proceedings must be kept, including disclosed *ex parte* communications, the statement of findings and conclusions, and the final version of the rule.

B. When Required

According to § 553 of the APA, a formal hearing is required when the enabling statute requires a decision to be "on the record after an opportunity to be heard." The courts are relatively strict regarding when a statute requires a formal hearing. A mere "hearing" requirement is not sufficient. The statute must require some sort of adjudicatory hearing. See *U.S. v. Florida East Railway Co.* Only about fifteen statutes fulfill such a requirement.

Where an informal rule would have the effect of a rule that normally requires formal rulemaking, informal and hybrid rule-making procedures are insufficient.

C. Pros and Cons of Formal Hearings

1. Pros

   a. Aids agency gathering of information.

   b. Creates a record that facilitates judicial review.

   c. Affords a genuine opportunity to question agency policies.

   d. Oral presentations are more effective for conveying arguments.

2. Cons

   a. Expensive.

   b. Time-consuming.

   c. Inefficient.

   d. May encourage agencies to abandon programs rather than go through a formal rulemaking procedure.

    e. Encourages agencies to evade decisionmaking procedures altogether.

    f. Instead of formulating the most effective regulations, agencies compromise to prevent costly hearings.

V. PUBLIC PARTICIPATION

A. Petitions

Section 553(e) of the APA allows interested persons to petition agencies to adopt, amend, review or repeal a rule. Denial of a petition requires a statement of reasons.

The definition of "interested persons" is commonly understood to mean anybody whose interests may be affected by the proposed rule. Since this definition is very broad, courts will rarely, if ever, find that a petitioner is not an interested person.

B. Intervention

Unless Congress excludes a party, agencies must allow intervention by third parties whose specific interests will be affected.

Representatives of public advocacy groups may also intervene in rulemaking procedures involving private interests that provide a public benefit (such as a television station).

C. Negotiation

The use of judicial style hearings in hybrid and formal rulemaking has increased the cost and length of those proceedings. One proposed remedy is negotiated rulemaking, where all interested parties would come together to comment upon or devise a new rule.

Professor Harter has identified several factors that increase the likelihood of successful negotiations.

1. Opposing parties should have comparable clout.

2. Opposing parties should be few in number to retain a manageable negotiation.

3. Disputed issues should be sufficiently crystallized to permit resolution.

4. The need for resolution of the issues should be apparent to all involved.

5. The potential for resolution should appeal to all parties.

6. The dispute should not involve the "fundamental values" of any party.

7. The agency's standards should allow for compromise.

8. The dispute should be multi-faceted to allow for trade-offs.

9. The agency should be able to implement a negotiated solution.

10. The agency should take an active role in negotiations.

11. An impartial negotiator should preside.

CASE CLIPS

United States v. Florida East Coast Railway Co.
(S.Ct. 1973) BA, BS, GB, S, MM
Facts: When the Interstate Commerce Commission was required to raise certain fixed rates, it rejected the railroads' requests for an oral

hearing, but gave them sixty days to reply in writing. Section 1(14)(a) of the Interstate Commerce Act limited agency action until "after a hearing." The Administrative Procedure Act (APA) mandated formal procedures — including oral presentations and cross-examinations — where the applicable statute required rules to be "made on the record after opportunity for a hearing."

Issue: Does the phrase "after a hearing" in a statute automatically trigger the application of the APA's formal rulemaking requirements?

Rule: (Rehnquist, J.) The formal procedures of the APA are not always invoked when "after a hearing" is found in a statute, because the term "hearing" may, as here, be satisfied by only an informal, written opportunity to be heard.

Dissent: (Douglas, J.) Ratemaking, because it involves factual determinations, is an exercise in administrative rulemaking that requires a formal APA hearing complete with arguments and cross-examinations.

Vermont Yankee Nuclear Power Corp. v. Natural Resources Defense Council, Inc. (NRDC)
(S.Ct. 1978) BA, BS, GB, CD, S, MM

Facts: While considering the licensing of several nuclear power plants, the Atomic Energy Commission (AEC) also considered a rule about nuclear waste storage. Although the AEC had complied with the informal rulemaking procedures of § 553 of the Administrative Procedure Act (APA), the Court of Appeals invalidated the rule for insufficient procedures. The National Environmental Policy Act also required the agency to publish a detailed statement of findings, including alternatives to the proposed action. The AEC's statement did not include energy conservation, because that alternative had not been brought to the agency's attention until after the rule had been promulgated.

Issue 1: May a court compel an agency to provide more procedure than the APA requires?

Rule 1: (Rehnquist, J.) Agencies are free to devise their own rulemaking procedures as long as agency procedures are constitutionally and statutorily sufficient, and extremely compelling circumstances do not exist.

Issue 2: Which alternatives must an agency discuss in a detailed statement of findings?

Rule 2: A detailed statement of findings need not include alternatives not available to the agency at the time the rule was considered.
Note: The second issue and rule is included in the Cass & Diver textbook only.

Home Box Office, Inc. v. FCC (1977) BA, BS, GB, CD
Facts: The Federal Communications Commission had *ex parte* communications with many members of the cable, broadcast, motion picture and sports industries before and after issuing notice of a proposed rule.
Issue 1: When are *ex parte* communications allowed in informal rulemaking procedures?
Rule 1: With informal rulemaking, no communication should occur between the agency and interested parties after the issuance of a notice of a proposed rule.
Issue 2: In what manner must private *ex parte* communications between the agency and interested parties be made public?
Rule 2: Communications made before issuance of a notice of proposed rulemaking do not have to be made public, unless it forms the basis for agency action. Any communication that occurs after the issuance of a formal notice of proposed rulemaking must be disclosed so interested parties may respond.
Concurrence: The decision bans only *ex parte* communications during informal rulemaking sessions that involve competing interests to a limited resource (television viewers). The rest is dictum.

Sierra Club v. Costle (1981) BA, GB, CD, MM
Facts: The Environmental Protection Agency (EPA) adopted new sulfur dioxide emission rules in a hybrid rulemaking procedure. After notice of the proposed rules, and before enactment, there was a rush of oral *ex parte* communications between EPA administrators, White House officials, and congressmen. Neither the informal rulemaking procedures of the Administrative Procedure Act nor the rulemaking provisions of the Clean Air Act contained any mention of *ex parte* communications, although the Clean Air Act did require agency decisions to be made exclusively on the basis of what was contained in the rulemaking record.

Issue 1:   In hybrid rulemaking, when are oral *ex parte* communications prohibited?

Rule 1:   *Ex parte* communications with agency officials are prohibited where agency action resembles judicial action (i.e., formal rulemaking, adjudication, or resolution of conflicting claims to a valuable privilege).

Issue 2:   In hybrid rulemaking, when are *ex parte* meetings between agency and White House officials prohibited?

Rule 2:   Except where prohibited by statute, *ex parte* communications among executive agencies will not invalidate an agency decision, unless the rulemaking agency is considered to be "independent" of the executive branch of government.

Issue 3:   In hybrid rulemaking, when are *ex parte* meetings between agency and congressional officials prohibited?

Rule 3:   Two conditions must be met to prove undue congressional interference with administrative rulemaking.   First, congressional pressure to consider factors not made relevant by the applicable statute must have been applied.   Second, the agency must actually be affected by such pressures.   In this case, those conditions were not met.

Association of National Advertisers v. FTC
(1979) BA, CD, S, MM

Facts: The Federal Trade Commission (FTC) issued a notice of proposed hybrid rulemaking regarding a ban on certain types of children's advertising.   The Chairman of the FTC had previously written several articles advocating similar legislation.

Issue: In informal and hybrid rulemaking, may an agency member be disqualified from participating in a rulemaking proceeding due to bias?

Rule: An agency member must recuse himself from informal and hybrid rulemaking only where there is a clear and convincing showing that the member has an unalterably closed mind on matters critical to the disposition of the rulemaking.

Concurrence: No agency rulemaker can be completely unbiased given the long and intimate knowledge that agency members have regarding the area the agency regulates.

Dissent in Part: The adjudicative aspects of hybrid rulemaking require that a rulemaker be as unbiased and open as an adjudicative decisionmaker.   A "preponderance of the evidence" standard is more appropriate than the unnecessarily strict "unalterably closed mind" standard.

California Hotel & Motel Ass'n v. Industrial Welfare Comm'n (1979) BA

Facts: The Commission was required to publish a statement as to the basis upon which a rule was created. The Commission's statement of basis did not explain its refusal of certain exemptions, was not published, and was not sent to affected employers.

Issue: Under state law, what must a statement of basis contain?

Rule: A statement of basis must show the factual, legal, and policy foundations for the action taken, that the order is supported by the agency's materials, and that it is reasonably related to the appropriate statute.

Iowa Bankers Ass'n v. Iowa Credit Union Dept. (1983) BA

Facts: Iowa had adopted the 1961 Model State Administrative Procedure Act (MSAPA), which required publication of a statement of basis upon request. Although a statement was requested before adoption of a new rule, none was issued until after the rule's adoption, six months after the request. The MSAPA requires "substantial compliance" with the publication requirement.

Issue: What factors will determine whether an agency has "substantially complied" with the MSAPA's requirement of publication of a concise statement of basis?

Rule: Factors indicating substantial compliance with the requirement to publish a concise statement of basis include the harm suffered by parties and non-parties, the interest in strict compliance with the MSAPA, whether non-compliance was purposeful, and whether parties were prevented from participation in, or reaction to, the rulemaking process.

United States v. Gavrilovic (1977) BA

Facts: The Drug Enforcement Agency (DEA) illegalized mecloqualone two days after publishing notice in the Federal Register. The Administrative Procedure Act (APA) required thirty-day notice unless "good cause" may be shown. The DEA claimed that health and public welfare concerns created by the defendants' operations constituted "good cause."

Issue: Where an agency promulgates a rule imposing criminal sanctions, what constitutes a "good cause" exception to the APA's thirty-day notice requirement?

Rule: An agency claiming a "good cause" exception to the APA's thirty-day notice requirement, after promulgating a rule imposing criminal sanctions, must sustain a heavy burden of showing that the necessity for immediate implementation of the new rule outweighs any considerations of fundamental fairness that would allow affected persons a reasonable time to prepare for the effective date of its ruling.

WWHT, Inc. v. FCC (1981) BA, GB

Facts: The Federal Communications Commission denied WWHT's request for rulemaking proceedings under APA § 553.

Issue: When may a court require an agency to institute rulemaking proceedings?

Rule: An agency may be forced to institute rulemaking proceedings only where required by law, or where a significant factual reason that had previously been given to deny a petition to institute rulemaking procedures has been removed.

Humana of South Carolina v. Califano (1978) BA

Facts: The Department of Health, Education and Welfare (HEW) issued a new regulation without providing the required notice and comment. HEW claimed that the rule fell under the exemption from the APA for rules relating to benefits.

Issue: Does the "benefits" exemption from informal rulemaking procedures apply to providers as well as recipients of benefits?

Rule: The "benefits" exemption to informal rulemaking encompasses not only recipients of benefits, but everyone who is clearly and directly affected by a rule's promulgation.

United States Department of Labor v. Kast Metals Corp. (1984) BA

Facts: Without providing notice and comment, the Occupational Health and Safety Administration (OSHA) changed its method of selecting companies to inspect. OSHA claimed that its new policy fell under the Administrative Procedure Act's exemption from informal rulemaking's notice-and-comment requirements for procedural rules. **Issue:** When is a rule procedural and thereby exempted from the notice-and-comment requirements of informal rulemaking? **Rule:** If the rule departs from existing practice and has a substantial impact upon the rights of those affected by the rule, a rule is only nominally procedural, and not within the APA's procedural exemption to the notice-and-comment requirements of informal rulemaking.

Chamber of Commerce v. OSHA (1980) BA

Facts: Without providing notice and comment, the Occupational Safety and Health Administration (OSHA) implemented a new rule requiring employers to pay employees for time they spend with OSHA inspectors conducting inspections. The Occupational Safety and Health Act prohibited discrimination against these employees, and OSHA claimed that the new policy was merely an "interpretive rule," which was exempted from informal rulemaking's notice-and-comment requirements.

Issue: When is a statement interpretive and thereby exempted from the notice-and-comment requirements of informal rulemaking?

Rule: A statement is interpretive, and thereby exempted from the notice-and-comment requirements of informal rulemaking, where the agency has not been delegated rulemaking power in that area of the law, or where the agency intends the rule to be no more than an expression of its construction of a statute or rule.

Mada-Luna v. Fitzpatrick (1987) BA

Facts: The Immigration and Naturalization Service (INS) denied Mada-Luna "deferred action" status that would delay his deportation. In 1978 and 1981, without providing notice and comment, or publication in the Federal Register, the INS had developed priorities to determine when "deferred action" status would be granted. The INS claimed that its priorities fit under the "policy" exception to informal rulemaking's notice-and-comment requirements.

Issue: What constitutes a policy statement, which is exempted from informal rulemaking's notice-and-comment requirements?

Rule: To qualify as a general statement of policy and thus be exempt from informal rulemaking's notice-and-comment requirements, a statement must satisfy two requirements. First, the statement must only apply prospectively. Second, the statement must not be binding or determinative on the issues to which it is addressed, but must instead leave the agency official free to consider the individual facts of the various cases that arise.

Pacific States Box & Basket Co. v. White (S.Ct. 1935) BS

Facts: An administrative order regulated the size of raspberry and strawberry containers, without a record of the rulemaking procedure.
Issue: When may a court remand a rulemaking proceeding in order to create a reviewable record?
Rule: (Brandeis, J.)   Unless an opposing party proves that an agency's action is arbitrary and capricious, in the absence of a rule-making record, a court must presume that a state of facts exists to justify the agency action.
Note: The agency must disprove any allegations that it overstepped its legislatively delegated bounds.

FPC v. Texaco, Inc. (S.Ct. 1964) BS

Facts: Utilizing the informal rulemaking procedures of the Administrative Procedure Act, the Federal Power Commission (FPC) required independent producers of natural gas to file contract rate schedules. The FPC denied Texaco's application for a certificate allowing gas sales, under § 7 of the Natural Gas Act (NGA), without a hearing, because of violation of these regulations.   Section 7 of the NGA requires the FPC to set a hearing for every application.
Issue: May an agency develop, through rulemaking, standards to be met before an applicant qualifies for a statutorily required hearing?
Rule: (Douglas, J.)   An agency may refuse to hold a statutorily required hearing because of an applicant's failure to meet threshold standards created through rulemaking.

American Airlines, Inc. v. CAB (1966) BS

Facts: The Civil Aeronautics Board (CAB) issued a regulation restricting "blocked space service" to all-cargo carriers only.   Opponents were given notice and an opportunity for oral argument.   The Federal Aviation Act required that the CAB give "notice and hearing," which the petitioners interpreted to mean a formal hearing.

Issue: If not expressly required, when must an agency afford formal proceedings when rulemaking?
Rule: Formal rulemaking proceedings are required where expressly mandated by statute, and where the proceeding is quasi-adjudicatory, rather than quasi-legislative, in nature.

United States v. Nova Scotia Food Products Corp.
(1977) BS, MM

Facts: The Food and Drug Administration used informal rulemaking proceedings to regulate the smoked fish industry without revealing the scientific data upon which it relied. Nova Scotia contended that criticism and comment was meaningless without release of the data used.
Issue: When must an agency disclose data used in informal rulemaking proceedings?
Rule: In informal rulemaking, an agency must disclose data whose omission would impede the presentation of relevant comment and prevent compilation of an adequate record of the proceedings.

Weyerhauser Co. v. Costle (1978) BS

Facts: In an informal rulemaking procedure, the Environmental Protection Agency regulated production of paper waste without giving opponents of the rule a new opportunity to comment on erroneous figures that substantially affected the rule's outcome.
Issue: In informal rulemaking, when must a new opportunity for comment be afforded due to alterations in the facts upon which the final rule was based?
Rule: In informal rulemaking, new opportunity to comment upon a proposed rule must be afforded whenever "significant" information is added to or altered in the agency's final published explanation of an adopted rule, unless the new information is a "logical outgrowth" of the preceding notice and comment proceedings.

Professional Air Traffic Controllers Organization (PATCO) v.
Federal Labor Relations Authority (FLRA) (1982) BS, GB

Facts: After PATCO called a strike, the Federal Labor Relations Authority (FLRA) revoked PATCO's certification in a formal hearing under § 557 of the Administrative Procedure Act. The revocation was challenged on the basis of two *ex parte* communications by FLRA officials with "interested parties."

Issue: When will improper *ex parte* communications invalidate a formal agency hearing?

Rule: Formal agency proceedings are voidable when "blemished" by improper *ex parte* communications that irrevocably taint an agency's decision. In determining whether an agency decision has been "blemished," a court should consider the gravity of the communication, the influence that resulted, whether the interested party benefitted from the communication, whether the communication was disclosed, and whether voiding the agency action would be useful.

Concurrence 1: Agency officials should endeavor to avoid all contact with interested parties who may try to engage in prohibited communications, even if they are friends, neighbors or even family. Although the prohibited *ex parte* communications in this case are appalling, they do not blemish the proceedings.

Concurrence 2: Sometimes invalidation is not enough. Criminal sanctions (18 U.S.C. § 1505) may be imposed as well.

Sangamon Valley Television Corp. v. United States (1959) BS

Facts: After informal rulemaking proceedings, the Federal Communications Commission (FCC) moved a television station license from Springfield, Ill., to St. Louis, Mo. During consideration of the rule, a St. Louis television executive had many informal *ex parte* conversations with FCC Commissioners and sent each of them a Thanksgiving turkey.

Issue: In informal rulemaking, when will *ex parte* communications invalidate an agency decision?

Rule: Any *ex parte* attempts to influence an agency member invalidate an administrative rulemaking proceeding.

Action for Children's Television v. FCC (1977) BS

Facts: Action for Children's Television requested the Federal Communications Commission (FCC) to create a rule regarding children's programming. The FCC rejected these proposals after a private meeting with officials of the broadcasting industry who agreed to self-imposed standards.

Issue: In informal rulemaking, when will *ex parte* communications invalidate an agency rulemaking decision?

Rule: *Ex parte* communications will only invalidate a rule where informal rulemaking involves resolution of conflicting private claims to a valuable privilege.

Note: This holding limits *Home Box Office v. FCC* and *Sangamon Valley Television Corp. v. United States*, above.

Moss v. CAB (1970) BS

Facts: The Civil Aeronautics Board (CAB), in an order suspending an airline-proposed rate hike, proposed its own rate scheme, which was accepted by the airlines. CAB completely excluded the public from meetings between airlines and the agency during this informal rulemaking procedure. CAB ratemaking normally required a formal rulemaking hearing.

Issue: Where an agency's informal rulemaking decision has the effect of a decision usually requiring a formal hearing, must formal rulemaking proceedings be held?

Rule: A formal rulemaking hearing must be held whenever an agency action would have the effect of a decision requiring a formal rulemaking hearing.

Seacoast Anti-Pollution League v. Costle (1978) GB

Facts: The Environmental Protection Agency granted the Public Service Company of New Hampshire permission to discharge heated water "after opportunity for public hearing," as required by the Federal Water Pollution Control Act. The agency did not follow the formal hearing requirements of the Administrative Procedure Act (APA), although the APA must be used whenever a statute requires an adjudication "on the record after a hearing."

Issue: If the applicable statute does not use the term "on the record after a hearing," when must an agency use the formal rulemaking procedures of the APA?

Rule: A formal APA hearing is required whenever the applicable statute specifically provides for administrative adjudication after an opportunity for an agency hearing, unless the pertinent statute indicates a contrary congressional intent.

Pacific Gas & Electric Co. v. Federal Power Comm.
(1974) GB

Facts: Without complying with the rulemaking requirements of the Administrative Procedure Act (APA) § 553, the Federal Power Commission set forth an order that constituted a "statement of policy" declaring when natural gas rationing would become necessary due to shortages. Statements of policy were usually exempt from the APA rulemaking procedures. The Pacific Gas and Electric Company contended that the order was effectively a substantive rule, rather than a policy statement, and should have followed § 553 of the APA.

Issue: When is an agency order exempted from APA rulemaking procedures as a "policy statement"?

Rule: An agency order fits under the APA exemption for "policy statements" when the agency indicates that it will allow reconsideration of the policy in an adjudication over agency actions that the policy affects. Some deference will be given to the agency's classification of the statement.

In the Matter of Edlow International Co. (1976) GB

Facts: The United States agreed to supply fuel to a nuclear power plant in India. Three political organizations applied to intervene in the rulemaking proceeding, under the Administrative Procedure Act (APA), regarding export licensing applications for the nuclear fuel.

Issue: When may a third party intervene in an APA rulemaking proceeding?

Rule: An agency using APA rulemaking procedures must always allow third party intervention, unless the party's interests are no different from those of the nation at large.

Wirtz v. Baldor Electric Co. (1964) GB, MM

Facts: The Secretary of Labor relied on confidential documents to make factual determinations at a rulemaking hearing. Opponents were not allowed to see the confidential documents, but the hearing was otherwise procedurally sufficient.

Issue: Must an agency reveal documents received under a pledge of confidentiality if those documents were used in rulemaking?

Rule: The Administrative Procedure Act affords no exceptions for pledges of confidentiality, so failure to disclose documents will result in invalidation of the rulemaking process.

United Steelworkers of America, AFL-CIO-CLC v. Marshall
(1981) GB

Facts: Following the hearing requirements of the Occupational Health and Safety Act, the Administrative Procedure Act and due process, the Occupational Safety and Health Administration (OSHA) issued new rules regarding airborne lead in the workplace. OSHA used both in-house staff advocates, as well as outside consultants in setting the standard. The outside consultants acted both as evaluators of testimony and expert witnesses.

Issue 1: May staff advocates and agency decisionmakers have *ex parte* communications in hybrid rulemaking proceedings?

Rule 1: Unless specifically barred by statute, nothing prevents *ex parte* communications between agency decisionmakers and staff advocates in hybrid rulemaking proceedings.

Issue 2: May outside consultants and agency decisionmakers have *ex parte* communications in hybrid rulemaking proceedings?

Rule 2: In hybrid rulemaking proceedings, unless specifically barred by statute, nothing prevents *ex parte* communications between agency decisionmakers and outside consultants, who are considered to be identical to in-house consultants.

Dissent: Outside consultants must be unbiased and neutral in their evaluation of the record.

Chocolate Manufacturers Association v. Block (1985) CD

Facts: Following informal rulemaking procedures, the Food and Nutrition Service (FNS) promulgated a rule excluding several foods, including chocolate milk, from a federally funded food program. In the notice of the proposed rule, no mention had been made of any alteration in the status of chocolate milk.

Issue: In informal rulemaking, when must an agency provide new notice and opportunity to comment when it strays from its original proposal for a new rule?

Rule: In informal rulemaking, new notice and comment is not required unless changes in the original rule proposal are neither in character with, nor a logical outgrowth of, the proposed rule as stated in the original notice.

Natural Resources Defense Council, Inc. (NRDC) v. Nuclear Regulatory Commission (NRC) (1976) CD

Facts: While creating a rule regarding the licensing of several nuclear power plants, the NRC (previously the Atomic Energy Commission) also considered a rule about nuclear waste storage. Although the NRC did comply with all of the informal rulemaking procedures of § 553 of the Administrative Procedure Act (APA), opponents of the rule were not allowed to cross-examine a key expert witness.

Issue: When may a court find that an agency's compliance with all statutorily mandated informal rulemaking procedures is insufficient?

Rule: Informal rulemaking procedures that are not arbitrary and capricious may still be insufficient if they do not create a fully developed evidentiary record.

Note: The Supreme Court reversed this decision in *Vermont Yankee*, above.

Stryker's Bay Neighborhood Council v. Karlen (S.Ct. 1980) CD

Facts: As required by the National Environmental Policy Act (NEPA), the Department of Housing and Urban Development (HUD) published a report regarding its plan for low income housing. The neighborhood council opposed the plan on the grounds that all alternative plans were not considered, as required by NEPA. The lower court held that HUD had incorrectly weighed different factors detailed in the statement.

Issue: May the courts use a required report to analyze the agency's reasoning?

Rule: (Per curiam) Since a report is required only to insure that an agency has considered proper alternatives, a court may not criticize its reasoning. The reporting requirement is essentially a procedural, not a substantive requirement.

Dissent: (Marshall, J.) The statement should be used to determine whether a "hard look" arbitrary and capricious standard has been satisfied.

State Bd. of Equalization v. Sierra Pacific Power Co. (1981) S

Facts: The Nevada State Board of Equalization published a formula used to assess the property tax on Sierra Pacific Power Company's

property, without following the state's Administrative Procedure Act (APA). The Board claimed that the formula was not a rule, and thus not subject to the rulemaking requirements of the state APA.
Issue: What constitutes a regulation or a rule governed by an Administrative Procedure Act?
Rule: A rule is any agency statement about how it proposes to administer a statutory provision.

In re Permanent Surface Mining Regulation Litigation (1981) S
Facts: The Secretary of the Interior passed regulations regarding minimum requirements for permit applications submitted to state agencies.
Issue: May a federal agency enact regulations affecting state agencies?
Rule: As long as Congress has properly delegated rulemaking power to a federal agency, its regulations affecting state agencies are valid.

Reuters Ltd. v. FCC (1986) S
Facts: Reuters was awarded licenses for thirteen microwave stations. Associated, a competitor, applied for the same stations five days late due to a procedural error, but claimed that the Federal Communication Commission (FCC) had impliedly extended the deadline thirty days. In an administrative adjudication, the FCC rejected Associated's claim regarding deadline extensions, but rescinded Reuters's licenses anyway, claiming principles of fairness.
Issue: In an administrative adjudication, may an agency modify its express regulations to consider elements of equity and fairness in applying its own regulations?
Rule: An agency must abide by its own rules and regulations, regardless of the equities of the situation.

American Textile Manufacturers Inst. v. Donovan (The Cotton Dust Case) (S.Ct. 1981) S
Facts: The Occupational Safety and Health Administration (OSHA) set the permissible standard for cotton dust, known to cause "brown lung disease," by using the "most protective standard that was technologically and economically feasible." Manufacturers brought suit

claiming the procedures required to reduce dust were not economically feasible in proportion to the benefits proposed.

Issue: Must an agency use cost-benefit analysis to determine the feasibility of a proposed rule?

Rule: (Brennan, J.) Cost-benefit analysis need not be used to determine a proposed rule's feasibility.

Federal Crop Insurance Corp. v. Merrill (S.Ct. 1947) S

Facts: The Wheat Crop Insurance Regulations, which were properly promulgated and recorded in the Federal Register, did not cover reseeded wheat fields. But an agent of the Federal Crop Insurance Corporation (FCIC) incorrectly told Merrill that his reseeded wheat fields were insured by the government. Merrill was unaware of these regulations. When Merrill's reseeded wheat crops were destroyed, the FCIC refused to pay, as per the regulations.

Issue 1: Where an agency publishes notice in the Federal Register, but does not provide actual notice, are affected parties bound by the published rules?

Rule 1: (Frankfurter, J.) Unless statutorily required to do more, public agencies need only publish their rules in the Federal Register to bind affected parties.

Issue 2: May a litigant estop the government due to misrepresentations of a government agent from raising a defense?

Rule 2: Equitable estoppel does not apply against the government. "Men must turn square corners when they deal with the government."

Schweiker v. Hansen (S.Ct. 1981) S

Facts: A Social Security Administration field representative erroneously told a potential applicant that she was ineligible for benefits. As a result, she lost a year's worth of benefits.

Issue: May a litigant estop the government from raising a claim due to misrepresentations of a government agent?

Rule: (Per curiam) A government agent's misrepresentations will not estop the government. The government may not be put at risk of enormous liability due to the alleged failure of a government agent.

Note: Equitable estoppel is discussed in the Chapter 3 outline, section III.D.

Sharp v. Department of Public Welfare (1973) S

Facts: The Department ordered Sharp to make certain improvements or cease operating his nursing home. Sharp did not comply and was ordered to close after an administrative hearing. Sharp claimed that the incomplete record of the hearing violated the state administrative procedure law requiring a "full and complete" rulemaking record.

Issue: When is a rulemaking record "full and complete?"

Rule: A rulemaking record that gives an appellant a base from which to appeal and a reviewing court a basis for its decision is full and complete.

Banegas v. Heckler (1984) S

Facts: After an administrative hearing in which conclusive evidence was submitted in favor of reinstating terminated disability benefits, the Administrative Law Judge (ALJ) observed the petitioner outside of the courtroom exhibiting no disabilities. Based on this observation, the ALJ denied benefits.

Issue: May an ALJ use evidence not on the record before him?

Rule: An ALJ may only use information gained from the record and in the capacity of a judge, not as a witness.

Chapter 6

GOVERNMENTAL CONTROL OF AGENCY ACTION

I. THE DELEGATION OF GOVERNMENTAL POWER

As early as 1825, Chief Justice Marshall realized that the federal government could not adequately administer its myriad activities without delegating some of its responsibilities to others. While the importance of administrative agencies has long been recognized, constitutionally imposed limits to their authority remain. Furthermore, these limits often differ at the federal and state levels.

A. The Delegation of Legislative Power

1. The Non-Delegation Doctrine
   Article I of the Constitution vests all legislative power in the Congress of the United States. While the separation of powers doctrine would seem to prevent the delegation of legislative authority, the Supreme Court has generally taken a more permissive approach. Throughout the first 150 years of the nation's existence, the Supreme Court routinely rejected "non-delegation" challenges to congressional statutes. In most of these cases, the Court ruled that Congress had retained its discretionary lawmaking power; the enabling statute merely empowered the agency to "ascertain a fact" or "determine a contingency." To reach this conclusion the Court searched for (and usually found) congressionally set standards to guide the agency's decisions. Only when a statute that lacked meaningful standards was it viewed as an unrestrained grant of policy-making authority in violation of Article I.

   The non-delegation doctrine remained oft-quoted and little-used until the Great Depression. In what has been viewed by many scholars as a politically motivated exercise of judicial authority, the Supreme Court utilized the long dormant doctrine to strike down two provisions of President Roosevelt's National Industrial Recovery Act. The 1935 case of *Panama Refining Co. v. Ryan* provided the Court with an opportunity to curb the executive's growing power over the national economy. A majority felt that the standards contained within the NIRA were not detailed enough to govern the president's decisionmaking, thus effectively granting him unlimited power to create legislative policy. Similar considerations led to an identical result in the case of *A.L.A. Schechter Poultry Corp. v. United States,* decided the same year.

2. Chief Justice Rehnquist and the Non-Delegation Doctrine
The non-delegation doctrine generally fell into disfavor following the *Panama* and *Schechter* decisions. During the past fifty years, the Court has been reluctant to recognize non-delegation challenges, construing enabling statutes narrowly to avoid the constitutional problem. However, recent minority opinions by Chief Justice Rehnquist indicate that the Court is not yet willing to discard the doctrine completely. His dissent in *Industrial Union Dept., AFL/CIO v. American Petroleum Institute* (The Benzene Case) expressed the belief that the Court had been delinquent in its constitutional duty to restrain the congressional delegation of power. In the Chief Justice's view, the non-delegation doctrine serves three important functions: it ensures that policy decisions are made by Congress, provides the executive with an "intelligible principle" to guide the exercise of discretion, and ensures meaningful judicial review by setting standards against which agency action may be measured. As of yet, the Chief Justice's views have not received the support of a majority of the Court.

B. The Delegation of Executive Power

Congress may delegate executive powers to administrative agencies. However, an attempted delegation of executive authority to a member of the legislative or judicial branch is a violation of the separation of powers doctrine and therefore unconstitutional. See *Bowsher v. Synar.*

C. The Delegation of Adjudicatory Power

1. Generally

Congress may delegate limited judicial power to administrative agencies (non-Article III courts). Early cases recognized different constitutional requirements for the adjudication of disputes between private parties (private rights) and disputes between a private party and the government (public rights). The Supreme Court has since rejected the doctrine that the traditional "private right/public right" distinction is dispositive, holding that the identity of the parties alone does not determine whether adjudicatory power may be delegated under Article III. Furthermore, the Court has ruled that the provisions of Article III providing federal judges with lifetime tenure and fixed compensation do not bar Congress from vesting adjudicatory power in tribunals that lack these qualities. Thus, a congressional delegation of judicial power will be valid so long as the transfer does not undermine the power of the federal judiciary in violation of the separation of powers doctrine. Among the factors the Supreme Court has considered in this area are the extent to which the administrative tribunal exercises powers normally vested only in Article III courts, the origins and importance of the right to be adjudicated, and the congressional concerns that led to the delegation. See *Commodity Futures Trading Commission v. Schor.*

2. Authority to Decide Whether to Penalize or Fine

A congressional delegation of adjudicatory authority does not include the power to decide what is criminal; that power remains firmly lodged in Congress. However, administrative agencies may impose penalties or fines for rule violations. The source of this penal power is not an affirmative grant from Congress. Rather, the authority is derived from a congressional statute making the violation of a properly enacted agency regulation unlawful. This subtle yet important distinction has also been embraced by most of the state court systems.

II. SUBSEQUENT CONTROL OF DELEGATED POWER

Following a proper delegation of authority to an administrative agency, the legislative, judicial, and executive branches of government often try to influence the direction of agency policymaking.

A. Legislative Control

Mnemonic: NASAL

1. Narrow Enabling Statutes
   Congress may restrict an agency's autonomy by confining the original delegation of power within narrow limits.

2. Appropriations
   Congress may influence agency decisions through its control of administrative funding. Fiscal power allows Congress to promote certain administrative programs while hampering the implementation of others.

3. Sunset Review
   Sunset legislation restricts the lifetime of an administrative agency. By making an agency's mandate conditional upon periodic review, Congress may effectively force the agency to become politically accountable.

4. Administrative Rules Review Committees (ARRC)
   State legislatures often establish Administrative Rules Review Committees to review the legality of agency rules. The committees may hold public hearings and submit proposals for revised legislation to the lawmaking body. Some legislative oversight committees also have the power to temporarily suspend the operation of agency regulations pending review.

5. Legislative Veto
   Until 1983, the predominant form of legislative control over administrative agencies was the legislative veto. This device enabled Congress to review individual agency actions before

they became effective. If Congress disapproved of the agency's decision, it could nullify the act through a majority vote in one of the two houses. However, the landmark decision of *Immigration and Naturalization Service v. Chadha* removed this arrow from the congressional quiver. The Supreme Court reasoned that, as an exercise of legislative power, the legislative veto must fulfill the bicameralism and presentment requirements of the Constitution. Except in specific circumstances outlined in Article I of the Constitution, the actions of one congressional house cannot have the force of law. The Model State Administrative Procedure Act of 1981 expressly rejected the use of the legislative veto, as have many state supreme courts.

B. Executive Control

Mnemonic: EAR

1. Executive Orders
   As chief executive officer, the president may issue instructions to executive officials in the form of executive orders. Through this device, the president may effectively control the conduct and organization of the federal bureaucracy.

2. Appointments
   The president has virtually unlimited authority to appoint administrative officials within the executive branch. Congressional attempts to reserve this power for itself have been found to violate the separation of powers doctrine and, hence, unconstitutional. The president's freedom to appoint officials is somewhat restricted when staffing those departments that are not located within the executive branch. These independent agencies often perform quasi-legislative and quasi-judicial functions and thus require a certain degree of autonomy from executive control. Accordingly, Congress has carefully prescribed political affiliation quotas and staggered terms for independent agency officials.

3. Removal

The president enjoys broad constitutional removal power over administrative officials within the executive branch. However, his removal power over independent agency officials may be limited by Congress. In *Humphrey's Executor v. United States*, the Supreme Court ruled that the separation of powers doctrine prevents the president from exercising unlimited removal authority over agency officials acting in quasi-legislative or quasi-judicial capacities.

C. Judicial Control

Once an administrative agency's enabling statute has passed the muster of a non-delegation inquiry (see above), judicial control over the agency is limited to *ultra vires* review. An ultra vires exercise of power is an attempt by an agency to transcend the boundaries of its jurisdiction as defined by its enabling statute. While a non-delegation challenge seeks to undermine the foundation of the entire agency, an ultra vires challenge merely seeks the invalidation of a particular administrative action. Although not as powerful a device as the non-delegation doctrine, ultra vires review enables the judiciary to curb the expansion of administrative power into unauthorized areas.

Courts often consider many factors when deciding whether an agency has acted beyond the scope of its delegated powers. Professors Bonfield and Asimow have identified the following important factors.

1. Should the statute be construed broadly or narrowly?

2. Does the actual language authorize the agency action?

3. Is the agency action consistent with the legislative intent?

4. Does the express grant of authority in one area imply the denial of authority in another?

5. Does the express grant of authority in one area imply other grants of authority?

6. Does legislative inaction during agency exercise of authority constitute legislative permission?

7. Does an agency lose authority to act through a long period of inaction?

8. Is the statute unconstitutional?

CASE CLIPS

Kent v. Dulles (S.Ct. 1958) BA

Facts: The Secretary of State refused to issue a passport to Kent, citing a State Department regulation prohibiting the issuance of passports to members of the Communist party. The Secretary's authority was derived from an 1856 congressional statute that allowed him to issue passports "under such rules as the President shall designate."

Issue: How broadly may Congress delegate authority to regulate a constitutionally protected activity?

Rule: (Douglas, J.) A court will narrowly construe all delegated powers that curtail or dilute activities that are natural and often necessary to the well-being of an American citizen.

Boreali v. Axelrod (1987) BA

Facts: The Public Health Council (PHC) of New York promulgated an extensive set of regulations prohibiting smoking in a wide variety of public areas. The regulations were enacted under the Public Health Law, which authorized the PHC to "deal with any matters affecting the . . . public health."

Issue: How much authority may a state legislature delegate to an agency?

Rule: A legislative grant of authority is constrained by the separation of powers doctrine and the language of the statutory mandate.

Dissent: A broad construction is often necessary in order to provide an agency with the flexibility that expert problem-solving requires.

Amalgamated Meat Cutters and Butcher Workmen v. Connally (1971) BA, BS, MM

Facts: The Economic Stabilization Act of 1970 allowed the President "to issue such orders and regulations as he may deem appropriate to stabilize prices, rents, wages, and salaries." Amalgamated Meat Cutters asserted that the Act "vested unbridled legislative power in the President."

Issue: When does a broad grant of price-fixing authority violate the non-delegation doctrine?

Rule: The delegation of legislative power is forbidden where Congress fails to lay down an intelligible principle to which the agency must conform.

Industrial Union Dept., AFL/CIO v. American Petroleum Institute (The Benzene Case) (S.Ct. 1980) BA, BS, GB, CD, S

Facts: The Occupational Safety and Health Act of 1970 (OSHA) gives the Occupational Safety and Health Administration authority to set standards for toxic chemical use in the work place. In 1977, the agency, without first making appropriate findings, tried to reduce its standard for benzene from 10ppm to 1ppm.

Issue: Does OSHA require the agency to prove a "significant risk of harm" before issuing stricter standards?

Rule: (Stevens, J.) The statute put the burden on the agency to prove that new standards were necessary to prevent significant risk of harm. Statutes should be construed with a presumption that appropriate standards exist to constrain the quasi-legislative authority delegated to an agency.

Concurrence 1: (Powell, J.) Congress intended administrative agencies to use cost-benefit analysis before issuing standards under OSHA.

Concurrence 2: (Rehnquist, J.) Congress has improperly delegated its legislative authority to the Secretary of Labor. The language of OSHA does not provide the Secretary with any criteria to guide his determination of a "safe" benzene level, and the broad standard of "feasibility" renders meaningful judicial review impossible. Congress itself must make the critical policy decisions.

Dissent: (Marshall, J.) A court is not permitted to distort a statute's meaning in order to make it conform with a judge's own views of sound social policy. In this case, the agency's decision under the statute was reasonable and supported by evidence.

Note: The Rehnquist concurrence, which advocates a more rigorous application of the non-delegation doctrine, bears most directly on this chapter. A more detailed discussion of *Benzene* is located in Chapter 8.

Thygesen v. Callahan (1979) BA

Facts: Under the Illinois currency exchange act, the Director of Financial Institutions had the authority to regulate the maximum rates that could be charged for check cashing and money order services.

Issue: May the legislature delegate its powers to an administrative agency without providing statutory guidelines?

Rule: Intelligible standards or guidelines must accompany legislative delegations of power. To be valid, a legislative delegation should include the persons and activities subject to regulation, the harm sought to be prevented, and the general means available to the administrator to prevent the harm.

Warren v. Marion County (1960) BA

Facts: Warren challenged the promulgation of a building code, charging that the legislature unconstitutionally delegated its powers to the administrative agency.

Issue: May the legislature delegate its powers to an administrative agency without providing statutory guidelines?

Rule: A statute need not express standards limiting delegated powers, but the procedure established must furnish adequate safe-guards to those who are affected by the state administrative action; thus, the legislature may, in abstract terms, delegate its power.

Commodity Futures Trading Commission
v. Schor (S.Ct. 1986) BA, GB, S

Facts: The Commodity Futures Trading Commission (CFTC) was created as an independent agency to enforce the provisions of the Commodity Exchange Act. The Act provided that, in the case of broker misconduct, customers could submit their damage claims to the CFTC for adjudication. If a broker wished to assert a common law counterclaim, the CFTC had the authority to decide that issue as well.

Issue: When may Congress delegate the initial adjudication of common law counterclaims to an administrative agency?

Rule: (O'Connor, J.) Congress may delegate limited jurisdiction in non-Article III courts over a narrow class of common law claims when the delegation does not create a substantial threat to the separation of powers.

Dissent: (Brennan, J.) The provisions of Article III that provide federal judges with lifetime tenure and a fixed salary help maintain the independence of the judiciary. The delegation of adjudicatory power over traditional common law claims will destroy this independence.

United States v. Grimaud (S.Ct. 1911) BA

Facts: Grimaud was indicted for grazing sheep without a permit in violation of Department of Agriculture regulations.

Issue: When may an agency independently impose criminal sanctions?

Rule: (Lamar, J.) Although an agency may not create criminal codes, where Congress has made the violation of a properly enacted agency regulation unlawful, criminal penalties may be imposed for such a violation. The power to penalize belongs to Congress, not the agency.

Waukegan v. Pollution Control Board (1974) BA

Facts: The Illinois Environmental Protection Agency imposed a monetary fine on the City of Waukegan for violations of the Environmental Protection Act.

Issue: When may the state legislature delegate the authority to impose monetary penalties to an administrative agency?

Rule: The state legislature may grant an agency the power to impose discretionary civil penalties where this power is necessary to accomplish the agency's goals.

Immigration and Naturalization Service v. Chadha (S.Ct. 1983) BA, BS, GB, CD, S, MM

Facts: Chadha successfully sought a suspension of deportation from the INS and the Attorney General. Congress had delegated the power to suspend deportation orders to the Attorney General, reserving the right of either the Senate or House of Representatives to veto suspensions. The House of Representatives vetoed Chadha's suspension.

Issue: Are statutory clauses that reserve to Congress legislative veto power violative of the separation of powers doctrine?

Rule: (Burger, C.J.) The legislative veto is an exercise of legislative power. Under Article I of the Constitution, all legislation must pass through both houses of Congress and receive the president's signature in order to become law. By circumventing these requirements, the legislative veto denies the president his constitutional right to participate in the lawmaking process, and thus violates the separation of powers doctrine.

Concurrence: (Powell, J.) Congress, by deciding the merits of an individual case, has assumed a judicial function in violation of the separation of powers doctrine.

Dissent: (White, J.) Without the legislative veto, Congress may refrain from delegating necessary authority, leaving major national problems unresolved. In the alternative, Congress may abdicate its lawmaking function to the executive branch and independent agencies, risking unaccountable policymaking by those not elected to fill that role.

Dissent: (Rehnquist, J.) The legislative history shows that Congress has been unwilling to grant the executive branch the unlimited power to suspend deportations. Furthermore, one cannot nullify the legislative veto clause without nullifying the entire statute, including the Attorney General's ability to suspend deportations.

Morrison v. Olson (S.Ct. 1988) BA, MM

Facts: The 1978 Ethics in Government Act created a special court to investigate and prosecute violations of federal law by high ranking government officials. In certain circumstances, the court was authorized to appoint an independent counsel to assist in the investigation. To avoid conflicts of interest, the statute only permitted the counsel to be removed for "good cause."

Issue: When may Congress restrict the president's power to remove an executive officer consistent with the separation of powers doctrine?

Rule: (Rehnquist, C.J.) Congress may restrict the president's power to remove government officials except where the removal restrictions impede the president's ability to perform his constitutional duty.

Dissent: (Scalia, J.) The Constitution vests all of the executive power in the president. Therefore, where agency action is the exercise of purely executive power, any statute that deprives the president of exclusive control over this power must be unconstitutional.

State ex rel. Railroad & Warehouse Commn. v. Chicago, M. & St. P. Ry. (1888) BS

Facts: The Minnesota Railroad Commission set rate ceilings for milk carried on passenger trains.

Issue: May the legislature delegate discretionary power to administer a law to an agency?

Rule: The power to carry into effect a law already passed may be delegated, but the power to say what the law shall be may not. Agencies may promulgate rules to administer the law.

Crowell v. Benson (S.Ct. 1932) BS

Facts: The Longshoremen's and Harbor Workers' Compensation Act provided disability benefits to injured longshoremen. In order to qualify, the employee must have been injured while employed on the navigable waters of the United States. Congress authorized the United States Employees' Compensation Commission to decide claims under the Act.

Issue: When may Congress grant adjudicative power to an administrative agency?

Rule: (Hughes, C.J.) Congress may establish administrative tribunals to decide disputes between the government and private parties (public rights). Congress may also grant an agency the power to make factual determinations in disputes between private parties (private rights). Administrative adjudications must be subject to *de novo* judicial review, however, because the courts possess complete authority to insure the proper application of the law.

Dissent: (Brandeis, J.) Article III does not require a *de novo* review of facts determined in an administrative proceeding. Such a review would hamper the speedy administration of an act.

A.L.A. Schechter Poultry Corp.
v. United States (S.Ct. 1935) BS, S

Facts: Schechter was convicted for violating the Live Poultry Code, a regulation promulgated by the President under section 3 of the National Industrial Recovery Act (NIRA).

Issue: May Congress delegate unhampered authority to initiate law to the president?

Rule: (Hughes, C.J.) When delegating legislative authority, Congress must also provide the limits to that authority.

Concurrence: (Cardozo, J.) Section 3, unlike § 9(c), is an attempted delegation not confined to any single act nor described by reference to a standard.

Myers v. United States (S.Ct. 1926) BS

Facts: Acting pursuant to a statute providing that postmasters "shall be appointed and may be removed by the President and with the advice and consent of the Senate," President Wilson appointed Myers to a four-year term as postmaster. Subsequently, the President dismissed Myers without consulting the Senate.

Issue: May Congress limit the president's power to remove an executive official by requiring the Senate's approval?

Rule: (Taft, C.J.) Because Article II of the Constitution vests general executive power in the president alone, the decision to remove an important executive official must lie completely within the president's discretion to insure the uniform execution of the laws contemplated by the Constitution.

Dissent 1: (Holmes, J.) Congress may transfer or limit the president's power to appoint and remove executive officials. The duty of the president to see that the laws be executed does not go beyond that which Congress sees fit to leave within his power.

Dissent 2: (Brandeis, J.) In order to prevent arbitrary executive action, the Constitution provided that presidential appointments be made with the consent of the Senate. Supreme Court precedents and the writings of the Founding Fathers have extended this requirement to presidential removals, as well.

Humphrey's Executor v. United States (S.Ct. 1935) BS, MM

Facts: In an attempt to force the Federal Trade Commission to implement New Deal policies, President Roosevelt sought Humphrey's removal as commissioner of the independent agency.

Issue: May Congress limit the president's authority to dismiss an officer who occupies no place in the executive department and who exercises no part of the executive power vested by the Constitution?

Rule: (Sutherland, J.) Congress may restrict the president's removal power over officers acting in a quasi-legislative or quasi-judicial capacity, as opposed to purely executive officers.

Weiner v. United States (S.Ct. 1958) BS

Facts: President Eisenhower removed Weiner from his position as Commissioner of the War Claims Commission, which had jurisdiction to adjudicate claims arising from World War II. The statute creating the Commission, the War Claims Act of 1948, did not explicitly require Senate approval of presidential dismissal decisions.

Issue: Does the president have unlimited authority to dismiss administrative officials if the enabling statute does not explicitly reserve to the Senate a right of approval?

Rule: Where an agency's function is wholly adjudicative, the president has no power to remove its commissioner, even if the enabling statute does not explicitly limit the president's discretion.

Boyce Motor Lines, Inc. v. United States (S.Ct. 1952) BS

Facts: An Interstate Commerce Commission (ICC) regulation, promulgated under the ICC enabling statute, required drivers carrying explosive or flammable materials to avoid congested thoroughfares and tunnels "so far as practicable and where feasible by prearrangement of routes." Boyce's truck exploded in the Holland Tunnel injuring sixty people. The statute subjected "knowing" violators to heavy sanctions. Boyce contended that the regulation was unconstitutionally vague.

Issue: Where an agency regulation promulgated under a statute punishes only those who intend to commit a violation, is it unconstitutionally vague?

Rule: (Clark, J.) While only legislatures may authorize criminal sanctions, an agency regulation promulgated under a statute requiring intent to violate is not unconstitutionally vague.

Dissent: (Jackson, J.) Where the federal crime-making power is delegated to an agency, courts should require considerable precision in its exercise.

Soglin v. Kauffman (1969) BS

Facts: Plaintiff students obstructed access to a university building and were disciplined for "misconduct." They contended that "misconduct" was an unduly vague standard that violated due process.

Issue: What constitutes an unduly vague standard for applying university conduct rules?

Rule: Disciplinary action may not be taken against university students without reference to a specific preexisting rule to guide acceptable behavior.

Hornsby v. Allen (1964) BS

Facts: Hornsby was an unsuccessful applicant for a license to operate a retail liquor store. She claimed that she met the licensing requirements but was denied a license without notification of the reason, in violation of due process requirements.

Issue: Must a license applicant be afforded an opportunity to know the objective standards governing licensing?

Rule: Due process is violated where an agency fails to promulgate reasonable regulations indicating the objective standards governing licensing and to provide an opportunity for a hearing to denied applicants.

Holmes v. New York City Housing Authority (1968) BS

Facts: A class action was brought against the New York City Housing Authority, challenging the procedures used to admit tenants to low-rent public housing projects. Plaintiffs alleged that numerous deficiencies in the application process denied them due process.

Issue: Does a failure to publish ascertainable standards violate due process?

Rule: The existence of absolute and uncontrolled discretion by an agency is intolerable and, for this reason alone, due process requires that decisions be made according to ascertainable standards.

Fook Hong Mak v. Immigration and
Naturalization Service (1970) BS

Facts: Mak, an alien, obtained an "in transit" visa permitting him to travel through, but not remain in, the United States. The Immigration and Naturalization Service (INS) sought to deport him after he outstayed the length of his visa. The Attorney General adopted a regulation, pursuant to the Immigration and Nationality Act, that precluded Mak's class of visa applicants from applying for relief from deportation. Mak contended that the regulation was illegal, since it categorically denied him relief without opportunity for a case-by-case adjudication.

Issue: May an agency, pursuant to a statute, make regulations affecting categories of cases rather than undertaking individual adjudications?

Rule: There is no rule barring administrators from making regulations rather adjudicating case by case.

Asimakopoulos v. Immigration and
Naturalization Service (1971) BS

Facts: Petitioners applied for suspension of deportation after overstaying their "protected status" visas. The Board of Immigration Appeals denied their petition based on a categorical rule refusing to exercise discretion in favor of "protected status" aliens who could not show "particularly strong equities" in their favor.

Issue: May an agency refuse to exercise discretion in reviewing a petition for relief?

Rule: Where a party is eligible for relief, the right to the exercise of discretion is triggered, though granting of the relief is not compelled.

Securities & Exchange Comm.
v. Chenery Corp. I (S.Ct. 1947) BS

Facts: Chenery filed a voluntary reorganization plan with the SEC. The agency did not allow officers of the corporation to purchase preferred stock, but based its decision on controversial judicial precedents. After reconsidering the case, the SEC reached the same conclusion based on proper statutory standards and its expertise in the area.

Issue 1: May an agency's pronouncement in an adjudication have both prospective and retroactive effect?
Rule 1: (Murphy, J.) Although an agency may possess rulemaking powers, it may often be forced to formulate new standards of conduct through adjudication.
Issue 2: Must an agency's order in an adjudicatory hearing be based upon the standards of a general rule or regulation?
Rule 2: (Murphy, J.) An order in an adjudicatory hearing must be based upon the relevant and proper standards, regardless of whether those standards had been previously articulated in a general rule or regulation.
Dissent: (Jackson, J.) Before an order may be issued banning a previously legal activity, standards of conduct must be prescribed by the agency.

Securities & Exchange Comm. v. Chenery Corp. II
(S.Ct. 1947) BS

Facts: See *Chenery I* above. Chenery argued that the Commission was required to proceed by rulemaking rather than by specific order against Chenery.
Issue: May an agency use its discretion to determine whether to proceed by rulemaking or adjudication?
Rule: (Murphy, J.) Agencies alone can determine the best method for enforcement of regulations; courts may not preclude agencies from using case-by-case adjudication rather than rulemaking.

Contractors Transport Corp. v. United States (1976) BS

Facts: The Motor Carrier Act left determinations of "certificates of convenience and necessity" to the discretion of the Interstate Commerce Commission (ICC). Contractors Transport had its application denied, while another company similarly situated had its application approved. The ICC denied accusations of inconsistency, claiming the decision was totally within its discretion.
Issue: Where an agency has discretion in applying standards, must it supply adequate reasons for its decisions?
Rule: Patently inconsistent application of agency standards to similar situations lacks rationality and is arbitrary. The grounds for an agency decision must be reasonably discernible from its report and order; a reviewing court will not supply post-hoc rationalization.

Brennan v. Gilles & Cotting, Inc. (1974) BS

Facts: The OSHA Review Commission overturned a fine imposed on a general contractor for violations by a subcontractor, claiming that no employees of the general contractor were present at the site. The Commission ignored prior decisions holding that potential access to the site by the general contractor was sufficient for the imposition of fines.

Issue: May an agency ignore its prior holdings in issuing a decision?

Rule: While agencies may change previously announced policies, and fashion exceptions and qualifications, they must explain departures from agency policies or rules apparently dispositive of a case.

People v. Tibbitts (1973) GB

Facts: The Illinois legislature empowered the Commission on Human Relations to compile lists of residential property owners who did not wish to sell their homes. Any real estate agent that knowingly solicited a listed owner was charged with a criminal offense.

Issue: In the absence of statutory standards, may a state agency exercise its discretion to determine what the law means and to whom it shall apply?

Rule: A law vesting discretionary power in a state administrative officer, without properly defining the terms under which his discretion is to be exercised, is void as an unlawful delegation of legislative power.

Allen v. California Bd. of Barber Examiners (1972) GB

Facts: Four barbers had their licenses revoked by the Board of Barber Examiners for furnishing barbering services at prices below those prescribed in the minimum price schedule for the county. The Board, consisting of four barbers and one member of the public, had been authorized to create the price schedule by the California legislature.

Issue: When may the legislature delegate power to an administrative board composed of interested members of an industry?

Rule: When attempting to delegate power to an administrative board made up of interested members of an industry, the legislature must provide strict standards to prevent an abuse of the delegated power.

Lincoln Dairy Co. v. Finigan (1960) GB

Facts: The Nebraska Grade A Milk Control Act authorized the director of the Department of Agriculture and Inspection to promulgate quality standards for milk. The statute provided that any person violating the regulations was guilty of a misdemeanor.

Issue: May a legislature empower an administrative official to promulgate regulations, the violation of which is criminal?

Rule: The legislature may not delegate its power to create criminal offenses and prescribe penalties to an administrative or executive authority.

Note: Compare this case with *United States v. Grimaud* above.

Bowsher v. Synar (S.Ct. 1986) GB, CD, S, MM

Facts: In an attempt to limit the growth of the federal budget deficit, Congress passed the Balanced Budget and Emergency Deficit Control Act of 1985. Commonly known as the "Gramm-Rudman-Hollings Act," the statute required the Comptroller General, a legislative branch official, to independently calculate the size of the federal deficit for a given fiscal year as well as the program cuts that would be necessary to balance the budget. The president was then required to issue an order mandating the recommended cuts. The Budget and Accounting Act of 1921 provided that Congress could remove the Comptroller General through impeachment or joint resolution.

Issue: Does Congress violate the separation of powers doctrine when it grants executive powers to legislative officials?

Rule: (Burger, C.J.) By placing executive responsibility in the hands of an officer who is subject to removal only by the legislature, Congress has retained control over the execution of legislation, unconstitutionally intruding into the executive function.

Concurrence: (Stevens, J.) Congress may not exercise its fundamental power to formulate national policy by delegating that power to one of its two houses, to a legislative committee, or to an individual agent of the Congress.

Dissent 1: (White, J.) The Budget and Accounting Act satisfies the requirements of bicameralism and presentment laid down in *Chadha*. Congress may only remove the Comptroller General for one of five specified reasons. In addition, the congressional removal provision requires the passage of a joint resolution, which by definition must be passed by both Houses and signed by the president. Furthermore,

Congress has never exercised or threatened to exercise its removal power since 1921. Any pressure Congress could exercise over the Comptroller is minimal at best.

Dissent 2: (Blackmun, J.) Any incompatibility between the Budget and Accounting Act and the Deficit Control Act should be cured by invalidating the antiquated congressional removal process, and not by striking down the important central provisions of Gramm-Rudman.

Note: See the District Court's opinion in *Synar v. United States* below.

Buckley v. Valeo (S.Ct. 1975) CD, MM

Facts: A federal statute authorized a Federal Election Commission, composed of congressional appointees, to make investigations and keep records regarding federal elections. The Commission had the power to devise federal election rules and penalize those who violated the statute or commission regulations.

Issue: May Congress enact a law that reserves to itself the power to appoint those who will execute and administer a statute?

Rule: (Per Curiam) Since only "officers of the United States" (i.e., appointed by the president or by a department head) have power to execute law, congressional appointees may not administer or enforce the law.

FTC v. American National Cellular, Inc. (1987) S

Facts: The Federal Trade Commission charged the defendants with intentionally misleading investors with false and deceptive statements in violation of the Federal Trade Commission Act. American National contended that the Act violated Article 2 of the Constitution by authorizing the FTC, which is not part of the executive branch, to enforce federal law. The District Court held the FTC's enforcement authority constitutional.

Issue: Does a statute delegating enforcement authority to an agency outside the executive branch violate separation of powers?

Rule: Officers of the United States who are appointed by the President with the advice and consent of the Senate, and are subject to congressional removal only by impeachment, may engage in the enforcement of federal law without violating separation of powers.

Mulhearn v. Federal Shipbuilding & Dry Dock Co. (1949) S

Facts: Mulhearn sought an appeal from a Workmen's Compensation Bureau decision. Respondent claimed that Mulhearn's injuries were only compensable under a more limited statute and the Workmen's Compensation Division did not have jurisdiction for the appeal. The Division overruled this defense and the respondent below sought certification to determine the jurisdiction question.

Issue: Is a state agency an "inferior court," within the meaning of the Constitution, whose judgments may be reviewed directly by certification to the state supreme court?

Rule: Under Article III of the Constitution, a state agency located in the executive branch cannot be an "inferior court" without violating the separation of powers. Therefore, certification must be denied.

United Farm Workers v. Agricultural Employment Relations Bd. (1984) S

Facts: United Farm Workers (UFW) charged that the Arizona Agricultural Employment Relations Board, a tripartite committee with balanced interests, was unconstitutional on its face. The Board had two members who were agricultural employers, and the UFW claimed their presence deprived UFW members of an impartial tribunal before which its rights were determined.

Issue: Does a legislative effort to balance the composition of an appointed board by selecting partisan members inherently violate adjudicatory impartiality?

Rule: A consciously balanced tripartite board does not violate the impartiality required for adjudication. The only constitutionally prohibited violation of impartiality is the appointment of an adjudicator who has a distinct financial or personal stake in the outcome.

Panama Refining Co. v. Ryan (S.Ct. 1935) S

Facts: President Roosevelt issued an executive order prohibiting the interstate transportation of petroleum in excess of statutory quotas. The plaintiff challenged the President's authority to issue the order, which was based upon a congressional delegation in section 9(c) of the National Industrial Recovery Act.

Issue: When may Congress delegate its legislative powers?

Rule: (Hughes, C.J.) Congress is permitted to transfer the essential legislative functions with which it has been vested when the delegation is accompanied by defining standards to prevent unhindered discretion.

Dissent: (Cardozo, J.) The policies behind the NIRA have been debated and clearly stated by Congress. The statute does not delegate Congress' lawmaking duty, but creates a standard to limit and guide the president's actions.

Synar v. United States (1986) S

Facts: In an attempt to limit the growth of the federal budget deficit, Congress passed the Balanced Budget and Emergency Deficit Control Act of 1985. Commonly known as the "Gramm-Rudman-Hollings Act," the statute required the Comptroller General, a legislative official, to independently calculate the size of the federal deficit for a given fiscal year as well as the program cuts that would be necessary to balance the budget. The president was then required to issue an order mandating the recommended cuts. The Budget and Accounting Act of 1921 provided that Congress could remove the Comptroller General through impeachment or joint resolution.

Issue: May Congress delegate the power to make economic budgetary decisions to administrative officials?

Rule: The constitutionality of a legislative delegation rests upon the scope of the power granted and the specificity of the standards governing its exercise. In this case, the Comptroller General's discretional power is limited to factual decisions. Furthermore, the totality of the Deficit Control Act's standards, definitions, context, and reference to past administrative practice provide an adequate "intelligible principle" confining the exercise of administrative discretion. Hence, delegating economic budgetary decisions is constitutional.

Note: This statute was ultimately found to be unconstitutional on separation of powers grounds.

Reid v. Engen (1985) S

Facts: The National Transportation Safety Board (NTSB) suspended Reid's pilot license for 120 days. The NTSB found that her un-airworthy aircraft and incomplete repair records threatened "safety in air commerce or air transportation and the public interest."

Issue: Is a standard of "public interest" unconstitutionally vague?

Rule: A "public interest" standard is sufficiently definite to guide an agency's investigations and decisions.

Commissioner of Agriculture v.
Plaquemines Commission Council (1983) S

Facts: A Louisiana statute provided that all parish pesticide ordinances be reviewed in a public hearing before the Commissioner of Agriculture. The Commissioner had the authority to restrict the use of a pesticide at the hearing if he found that it was a hazard under specific conditions.

Issue: May a state legislature grant an agency the power to approve or disapprove use restrictions without elaborating standards of guidance?

Rule: There is an unconstitutional delegation of legislative authority to the executive branch of the government where a statute vests arbitrary discretion in a board or an official without prescribing standards of guidance.

Thomas v. Union Carbide Agricultural Products Co. (S.Ct. 1985) S

Facts: Union Carbide provided data to the Environmental Protection Agency (EPA) in support of registration applications for its various pesticides. The Federal Insecticide, Fungicide, and Rodenticide Act permitted companies to seek monetary compensation through binding arbitration if the EPA released this application data to the general public.

Issue: May Congress allocate judicial functions to non-Article III courts?

Rule: (O'Connor, J.) Congress may vest traditional judicial decision-making authority in administrative agencies.

Rosenthal v. Hartnett (1975) S

Facts: A Department of Motor Vehicles hearing officer found petitioner guilty of speeding.

Issue: May the state legislature constitutionally authorize administrative rather than judicial adjudication of traffic infractions?

Rule: The adjudication of traffic violations may be transferred to an administrative agency, provided that conviction can result only in the imposition of fines with no imprisonment. The legislature is presumed to have adequately investigated the need for this particular delegation of power.

State v. Broom (1983) S
Facts: Criminal laws regulating the handling and storage of explosives were promulgated by the director of public safety in the exercise of his statutory duty to protect the public's "health, welfare, and safety."
Issue: May the legislature delegate the authority to define felonies to an administrative official?
Rule: Constitutional separation of powers principles prevent the legislature from delegating the right to define felony offenses to administrative bodies or department heads.

Wright v. Plaza Ford (1978) S
Facts: An administrative law judge held an attorney in contempt and sentenced him to a three-day jail term.
Issue: May a state administrative officer in an adjudicatory proceeding punish a party for criminal contempt of court?
Rule: The separation of powers doctrine prevents the state legislature from granting the contempt power to an administrative agency or any member of the executive branch.

Green v. United States Coast Guard (1986) S
Facts: The Coast Guard fined Green $1,000 for the negligent operation of his pleasure boat.
Issue: If a federal administrative agency wishes to assess a civil penalty, must it conduct the proceeding in a federal district court and follow criminal trial procedures?
Rule: An administrative assessment of a civil penalty requires neither an adjudication in district court, nor the protections of a criminal trial.

Abel v. United States (S.Ct. 1960) S
Facts: Abel was an alien residing illegally in the United States. Acting on information provided by the Federal Bureau of Investigation, the United States Immigration and Naturalization Service (INS) arrested and detained Abel pending deportation proceedings.
Issue 1: May the government use an administrative warrant for the purpose of gathering evidence in a criminal case?

Rule 1: (Frankfurter, J.) Since a criminal prosecution must be pursued in strict obedience to the safeguards and restrictions of the Constitution and laws of the United States, the use of an administrative warrant to circumvent the procedural protections of the Constitution is prohibited.

Issue 2: May agencies conduct administrative arrests and detentions as preliminaries to deportation?

Rule 2: Since statutes authorizing administrative arrest to achieve detention pending deportation proceedings have been used throughout the nation's history, they are constitutional.

Sun Ray Drive-In Dairy, Inc.
v. Oregon Liquor Control Commission (1973) MM

Facts: Sun Ray's application for a liquor license was denied on the grounds that there were "sufficient licensed premises in the locality," and "local objections to the license." In addition, the Liquor Control Commission did not believe that Sun Ray possessed sufficient inventories to qualify as a grocery store under the governing statute.

Issue: Must an agency establish written standards to apply a broad legislative delegation of power?

Rule: Written, published standards equally applicable to all applicants must be established by an agency when it exercises a broad delegation of power.

Youngstown Sheet & Tube Co. v. Sawyer (S.Ct. 1952) MM

Facts: Responding to a proposed work stoppage in the steel industry, President Truman issued an executive order directing the Secretary of Commerce to seize and operate most of the nation's steel mills.

Issue: Do presidential orders have the force of law when they are not based on either congressional statute or constitutional grants of executive power?

Rule: (Black, J.) Lawmaking power is entrusted solely to Congress; hence, the president's power to issue and enforce an order must stem from either an act of Congress or the Constitution itself. The Constitution limits the president's role in the lawmaking process to recommending and vetoing legislation.

Concurrence: (Jackson, J.) Presidential authority is greatest when acting pursuant to an express or implied authorization from Congress. In contrast, the president's power is lowest when acting contrary to the congressional will. When congressional intent is unknown, the president's authority depends upon the imperatives of events rather than abstract theories of law. In this instance, Congress has not left seizure of private property an open field but has covered it by three statutory policies inconsistent with presidential action in this area.

Dissent: (Vinson, C.J.) History shows that presidents have taken prompt action to enforce laws and protect the country whether or not Congress provided a method of execution in advance. The energetic executive office envisioned by the Founding Fathers requires that the president have power under the Constitution to meet a critical situation even in the absence of express statutory authorization.

Environmental Defense Fund v. Thomas (1986) MM

Facts: The Hazardous and Solid Waste Amendments to the Resource Conservation and Recovery Act required the Environmental Protection Agency to issue new standards for underground holding tanks by March 1, 1985. Extensive review by the Office of Management and Budget delayed the promulgation of the regulations until after the statutory deadline had passed.

Issue: May the executive branch delay the enactment of an agency's regulations by using its regulatory review power?

Rule: The executive branch has no authority to use its regulatory review to delay promulgation of administrative regulations beyond the date of a statutory deadline.

Chapter 7

OPEN GOVERNMENT

I. FREEDOM OF INFORMATION ACT (FOIA)

A. Goals

The Freedom of Information Act, 5 U.S.C. § 552, located in the Administrative Procedure Act (APA), was enacted in 1966 to open government to public inspection. Providing access to agency information permits the public to evaluate the quality of government programs and policies. Opening up government to public scrutiny may deter misconduct and allow interested citizens to demand more effective representation. The Freedom of Information Act has been successful in these goals, but there have been costs as well as benefits.

B. Problems

   1. Resources
   Disclosure requests under the FOIA cost money and valuable staff resources that might be used elsewhere.

   2. Conflicts with Other Public Interests
   Disclosure may conflict with other public interests, such as national security or private business trade secrets.

   3. Competitive Advantage
   Businesses often try to use the FOIA to gain competitive advantages through disclosure of trade secrets or other vital information.

   4. Timeliness
   Contested FOIA actions may take years to resolve with appeals for judicial review, and the information requested may have lost its value by then.

C. Structure

1. Publication

   The first section of the FOIA requires government agencies to publish certain important information. Anyone who does not have actual timely knowledge of this information cannot be adversely affected by it.

2. Available for Inspection

   Under this section, agencies must index and make available for inspection and copying specified additional information, such as final opinions and staff manuals.

3. Disclosure

   This section has generated the most litigation. Agencies must disclose any reasonably described record requested by any person for any reason. If an agency refuses, a person can obtain *de novo* review in federal district court to compel disclosure. If the agency invokes one of the nine exemptions listed in § 552(b), it must justify use of the exemption.

4. Exemptions

   There are nine categories of information that are exempt from disclosure in FOIA. These exemptions only permit withholding of information when disclosure would harm an important government or individual privacy interest. They have been construed narrowly by reviewing courts. The exemptions to the FOIA are not mandatory, and "reverse FOIA" actions cannot compel an agency to withhold information it chooses to disclose. However, disclosure is a final agency action subject to judicial review. See *Chrysler Corp. v. Brown.*

   a. Exemption 1: National Security Secrets

      When an Executive Order classifies certain information as a national security secret, that information is exempt from disclosure unless a court, in a closed chamber review known as *in camera* inspection, decides it was improperly classified See *EPA v. Mink.*

b. Exemption 2: Internal Personnel Rules
This exemption exists to relieve agencies of the burden of assembling and maintaining records relating solely to internal policy matters in which the public could not reasonably be expected to have an interest. Where matters are the subject of genuine and significant public interest, they are not exempt. See *Department of the Air Force v. Rose.*

c. Exemption 3: Statutes That Direct Nondisclosure
Where another statute specifically prevents agency disclosure of certain information, then the information is exempt from FOIA requests. See *Central Intelligence Agency v. Sims.*

d. Exemption 4: Private Business Information
One potential problem with the Freedom of Information Act is the ability of corporations to discover damaging information about their competitors through agency records. To solve this problem and protect proprietary information, Exemption 4 allows agencies to withhold commercial secrets "obtained from a person and privileged or confidential." "Confidential" refers to information that, if disclosed, would impair the government's ability to obtain information in the future or cause "substantial harm to the competitive position of the person from whom the information was obtained." See *National Parks & Conservation Ass'n v. Morton.*

e. Exemption 5: Internal Agency Memoranda
This exemption permits agency withholding of information that "would not be available by law to a private party...in litigation with the agency." Evidentiary privileges such as the attorney-client privilege and the executive privilege are preserved. The executive privilege only protects predecisional documents, not final decisions. See *NLRB v. Sears.*

f. Exemption 6: Personal Privacy Protection
Exemption 6 seeks to prevent a "clearly unwarranted" invasion of personal privacy through release of agency information. This exemption is a balancing test of an individual's right to privacy and the need for public scrutiny

of agency procedures. See *Department of the Air Force v. Rose.*

g. Exemption 7: Investigatory Records for Law Enforcement
An agency cannot be forced to disclose information "compiled for law enforcement purposes" where disclosure could reasonably be expected to reveal the identity of a confidential source or interfere with enforcement proceedings. See *NLRB v. Robbins Tire & Rubber Co.*

h. Exemption 8: Financial Institutions
This exemption seeks to secure the stability of financial institutions by exempting release of documents from agencies responsible for the regulation or supervision of financial institutions.

i. Exemption 9: Natural Resources
Agencies are exempt from disclosing "geological and geophysical information and data concerning wells."

5. Defining "Agency Records"

a. "Agency"
Agencies are defined as governmental bodies with regulatory or grant-making powers, as oppcsed to purely advisory groups. The Office of the President is not an "agency" within the Act, so documents from that office are not subject to disclosure. See *Kissinger v. Reporters Committee for Freedom of the Press.*

b. "Records"
The FOIA applies only to "agency records," but does not define this term. Courts have held that documents created for the purpose of facilitating daily activities are "agency records," but documents for personal use by an agency member are not. See *Bureau of National Affairs v. United States Dept. of Justice.* In addition, physical presence in an agency office does not make a document an "agency record."

II. THE GOVERNMENT IN SUNSHINE ACT

A. Goals

The Government in Sunshine Act, 5 U.S.C. § 552b, located in the APA, was designed to open agency meetings to the public to lessen corruption. Meetings must be announced at least a week in advance, and any closed meetings must be carefully recorded in the event a court later rules it should have been held in the open, though a court may not invalidate agency action due to a closed meeting that should have been open. The Sunshine Act applies only to official sessions where decisions on specific policies are made, not to unofficial meetings where background matters are discussed. Gatherings of agency members with outside groups are generally not covered. See *FCC v. ITT World Communications, Inc.*

B. Problems

While the idea of open meetings is appealing, the results of the Sunshine Act are controversial. The law may be easily circumvented by passing memoranda around to staff members instead of holding a meeting, with each member voting for or against a proposal on paper. Agency meetings may then become farces with the outcome already known and the decision just a public confirmation of policies hashed out in private. Even if all decision making could be forced into public, the question remains whether the best policy decisions would be developed under such scrutiny. Agency members might be hesitant to propose novel solutions or debate the true merits of proposals.

C. Exemptions

The Act has a list of exemptions similar to those in the Freedom of Information Act. However, there is no exemption for internal memoranda or natural resources, and there are exemptions for criminal accusations, sanctions, subpoenas, and civil suits, to prevent frustration of agency actions not yet disclosed. See Hanau Chart 7.1. Courts have been wary of agency attempts to hold closed meetings, construing exemptions to the Sunshine Act narrowly to serve the purposes of the Act.

III. PARTICIPATION IN AGENCY PROCEEDINGS

A. Generally

Parties must have standing to participate in agency proceedings. As in civil suits, standing to participate in agency adjudications has expanded in recent years. While a party once had to demonstrate economic injury, now many non-economic injuries suffice, especially in public interest actions. An "interest representation" model of agency action has developed, expanding access to agency adjudications to those acting in the public interest.

B. Interest Representation View

1. Standing to Intervene
   Parties that assert a personal injury, economic or non-economic, have standing to intervene in an agency adjudication. This standing requirement has permitted groups representing the public interest to intervene where no great injury occurs to an individual, but injury to its members collectively and the public interest is severe. Standing to intervene has the same requirements as standing to obtain judicial review.

2. Compelling Agency Enforcement
   A public interest group, or any other party meeting standing requirements, may bring suit to compel an agency to take enforcement action against a party in violation of agency rules. Where an agency is not rigorously enforcing its rules, perhaps due to industry pressure, actions to compel enforcement serve as a check on government and as a way for public interest groups to ensure that agency discretion is equitably exercised.

3. Attorneys' Fees
   One barrier to suits in the public interest is the cost of litigation. The award of attorneys' fees encourages public interest

groups to battle large corporations when often they are the only people concerned enough to pursue legal action.

a. Traditional American Rule
The American rule in litigation has traditionally prohibited the award of attorneys' fees to the prevailing party. A few statutory exceptions to the rule have been made.

b. No Common Law Exceptions
A court's attempt to fashion its own exception to the American rule was overturned on appeal. In *Wilderness Society v. Morton*, the court awarded attorneys' fees to a plaintiff bringing suit in the public interest. In *Alyeska Pipeline Service Co. v. Wilderness Society*, the Supreme Court ruled that only Congress may determine when attorneys' fees may be awarded. No exceptions may be made without a congressional statute.

CASE CLIPS

National Labor Relations Board v.
Sears, Roebuck, & Co. (S.Ct. 1975) BA, GB, CD, MM
Facts: Sears sought disclosure from the General Counsel of the National Labor Relations Board (NLRB) of certain memoranda regarding the filing of unfair labor practice complaints. The General Counsel contended that the memoranda were exempt from Freedom of Information Act disclosure under § 552(b)(5) as "intra-agency communications" made in the course of formulating agency decisions.
Issue: Are all intra-agency documents exempt from disclosure under Exemption 5 of the FOIA?
Rule: (White, J.) Exemption 5 exempts from FOIA disclosure only those documents that would normally be privileged in the civil discovery context, such as attorney work products. Documents that embody the agency's effective law and policy are not exempt from disclosure.

Chrysler Corporation v. Brown (S.Ct. 1979) BA, BS, GB, MM
Facts: Chrysler filed reports on its affirmative action plans in accordance with Office of Federal Contract Compliance Programs (OFCCP) regulations. These OFCCP regulations permitted public inspection of reports filed, with some exemptions. Chrysler sought to enjoin release of its report on the grounds that Exemption 4 of the Freedom of Information Act (FOIA) prevented the disclosure, or alternatively, that the Trade Secrets Act provided a cause of action for injunctive relief against disclosure. The District Court granted the injunction, which was overturned on appeal.
Issue: Does a private cause of action to enjoin disclosure of information submitted to agencies arise from either the FOIA or the Trade Secrets Act?
Rule: (Rehnquist, J.) The FOIA exemptions are not mandatory bars to disclosure. Where an agency chooses to disclose information, neither the FOIA nor the Trade Secrets Act create a cause of action to prevent disclosure. However, disclosure is a final agency action subject to judicial review.

Office of Communication of the United Church
of Christ v. FCC (Church of Christ I) (1966) BS
Facts: The Church of Christ petitioned to intervene in the license renewal proceedings of television station WLBT, claiming they were injured by the station's discriminatory programming. The Federal Communications Commission dismissed the petition for lack of standing and granted the station a one-year probationary license without conducting a hearing.
Issue: Where listeners are offended by a station's programming, do they have standing to intervene in the station's license renewal proceeding?
Rule: To safeguard the public interest, members of the public must be permitted to intervene in formal agency proceedings even where the injury claimed is non-economic and applies to a broad group of people.

Scenic Hudson Preservation Conf. v. FPC (I) (1965) BS

Facts: Respondent contended that petitioners did not have standing to obtain review of an Federal Power Commission licensing decision absent a personal economic injury.

Issue: Must a party show personal economic injury to gain standing to seek judicial review?

Rule: Where a statute protects non-economic as well as economic interests, parties who have shown a special interest in subjects protected by the statute have standing to seek judicial review as aggrieved parties.

National Welfare Rights Organization v. Finch (1970) BS

Facts: The Department of Health, Education, and Welfare (HEW) claimed that certain states were not complying with federal standards in administering grants under the Social Security Act. HEW scheduled an adjudicatory hearing for the state agencies, and the National Welfare Rights Organization sought to intervene. Appellees contended that the Act precluded intervention by outside parties.

Issue: May the beneficiaries of a statutory scheme intervene in a formal agency hearing adjudicating state conformity with the statute?

Rule: Beneficiaries of a statutory scheme who would have standing to obtain judicial review of an agency action also have standing to intervene in formal administrative adjudications.

Environmental Defense Fund, Inc. v. Ruckelshaus (1971) BS

Facts: After making findings on the pesticide DDT, the Secretary of Agriculture refused to suspend its registration or to begin the formal agency procedures used to terminate registration. The Environmental Defense Fund sought judicial review of the order refusing interim relief.

Issue: Where an agency refuses to commence formal proceedings, may a reviewing court compel initiation of enforcement?

Rule: Where, as here, the statutory requirements for commencing agency action have been met, a reviewing court may compel the agency to take enforcement action.

Office of Communication of United Church of Christ
v. FCC (Church of Christ II) (1969) BS

Facts: See *Church of Christ I* above. On remand, the Federal Communications Commission (FCC) put the burden of proof on the intervenors, Church of Christ, to "sustain their serious allegations" against the licensee. Finding the allegations not sustained, the FCC granted the license renewal.

Issue: Where an intervenor alleges a public interest injury in an agency adjudication, must the intervenor carry the burden of proof?

Rule: When an agency action is alleged to be against the public interest, the beneficiary of the action, not the intervenor for the public interest, must carry the burden of proof in agency adjudication.

Wilderness Society v. Morton (1974) BS

Facts: Appellants successfully prosecuted a case to bar construction of the trans-Alaska pipeline and then sought payment of their attorneys' fees as part of their relief. The traditional American rule prohibited the award of attorneys' fees, but a few categories of exceptions were made.

Issue: May attorneys' fees be awarded to a plaintiff suing to enjoin injuries to a broad class of people?

Rule: When a statutory violation causes little injury to any one individual, but great injury to important public interests protected by the statute, attorneys' fees should be awarded to prevailing "private attorney general" plaintiffs who bring suit as a public service.

Alyeska Pipeline Service Co. v.
Wilderness Society (S.Ct. 1975) BS

Facts: Appeal from *Wilderness Society v. Morton,* above.

Issue: Where no congressionally approved exception exists, may the courts award attorneys' fees to deserving parties acting in the public interest?

Rule: (White, J.) Congress, not the courts, determines when attorneys' fees may be awarded to the prevailing party in litigation. Unless specified by statute, Congress may not be presumed to approve the award of attorneys' fees.

Note: This case reversed the award of attorneys's fees in *Wilderness Society v. Morton.*

Mead Data Central, Inc. v. Dept. of the Air Force (1977) BS

Facts: Mead Data sought access to internal memoranda of the Air Force reflecting negotiations with West Publishing Co. for a licensing agreement. The Air Force claimed that some of the documents were subject to Exemption 5 of the Freedom of Information Act (FOIA) as attorney work product or predecisional, advisory memoranda.

Issue: Does Exemption 5 of the FOIA exempt all predecisional materials from disclosure?

Rule: Predecisional materials are not automatically exempt; they must also be part of the deliberative process. Exemption 5 applies to advisory but not factual materials, unless factual materials disclose the deliberative process.

Taxation with Representation Fund v. IRS (1981) BS

Facts: Memoranda at the Internal Revenue Service (IRS) prepared prior to a final policy decision later were used to explain agency policy. The IRS refused to disclose the documents, claiming they were protected by the governmental privilege in Exemption 5 to the Freedom of Information Act.

Issue: Are documents prepared during the deliberative process considered predecisional and protected by the governmental privilege?

Rule: Materials supplying the basis for an agency policy later adopted constitute post-decisional "working law" and are not exempt from disclosure under Exemption 5 of the FOIA.

Arthur Andersen & Co. v. Internal Revenue Service (1982) GB

Facts: Arthur Andersen sought access to Internal Revenue Service documents under the Freedom of Information Act (FOIA), contending that the documents were final decisions not exempt from disclosure. The IRS claimed the documents were written by employees without authority to make final decisions.

Issue: Where a document is written by an employee without authority to draft final decisions, is it exempt under Exemption 5 as predecisional?

Rule: An agency showing that the authors of documents could not make final policy decisions without approval from their superiors meets the burden of proof for predecisional documents under Exemption 5 of the FOIA.

Bureau of National Affairs v.
United States Dept. of Justice (1984) GB

Facts: The Bureau of National Affairs (BNA) filed a Freedom of Information Act (FOIA) request with the Department of Justice (DOJ) for records of all appointments and meetings of an Assistant Attorney General with parties outside the Department. DOJ claimed the materials were not "agency records" subject to disclosure under the FOIA.

Issue: Where an employee claims that documents are personal materials and not "agency records," may the documents be exempt from disclosure?

Rule: Documents created and used solely for personal convenience are not "agency records" and may be exempt from disclosure. But documents created for the purpose of facilitating daily activities at the agency and for distribution to other employees are not exempt from disclosure.

National Parks and Conservation Ass'n v. Morton (1974) GB

Facts: The National Parks and Conservation Association sought agency records from the National Park Service containing audit reports of concessions operating within the national parks. The Service claimed, and the District Court ruled, that Exemption 4 of the Freedom of Information Act (FOIA) prevented disclosure of the park records as "trade secrets and commercial or financial information obtained from a person and privileged or confidential."

Issue: When is commercial or financial information considered "confidential" under Exemption 4 of the FOIA?

Rule: Commercial or financial data about a party is "confidential" for the purposes of Exemption 4 where disclosure of the information would either impair the Government's ability to obtain necessary information in the future or cause substantial harm to the competitive position of the party involved.

Department of the Air Force v. Rose (S.Ct. 1976) GB, CD

Facts: Respondents, student editors at New York University Law Review, sought access to case summaries of honor and ethics hearings maintained by the United States Air Force Academy. The Academy based its refusal to disclose the summaries on Freedom of Information

Act Exemption 2, protecting disclosure of "internal personnel rules" and Exemption 6, protecting "unwarranted invasions of personal privacy."

Issue: Where an agency keeps summaries of personnel actions, are those records exempt from disclosure as either internal matters or invasions of personal privacy?

Rule: (Brennan, J.) Congress did not create a blanket exemption for personnel files. Exemption 2 does not apply to matters subject to genuine and significant public interest. Exemption 6 seeks only to prevent a "clearly unwarranted" invasion of personal privacy, balancing the individual's right to privacy against the need for public scrutiny of agency actions.

Dissent: (Burger, C.J.) The majority frustrates congressional intent by not giving serious weight to the grave consequences of releasing this information, thereby disrupting the balancing of interests. Judicial editing of the documents may reduce the risk of invading personal privacy, but *in camera* inspection is a tremendous burden on district courts, which the FOIA never intended.

Common Cause v. Nuclear Regulatory Commission
(1982) GB, CD

Facts: The Nuclear Regulatory Commission (NRC) refused to open its meetings discussing budget priorities and planning to members of the public interest group Common Cause. The NRC claimed the meetings were exempt under Exemption 9B of the Sunshine Act protecting "premature disclosure" of agency matters.

Issue: What constitutes "premature disclosure" under Exemption 9B of the Sunshine Act?

Rule: "Premature disclosure" applies only to agency actions that could affect private decisions by non-governmental parties. Exemptions must be construed narrowly to avoid frustrating the purposes of the Sunshine Act.

United States v. Nixon (S.Ct. 1973) CD

Facts: The Special Prosecutor subpoenaed certain tapes and documents recounting meetings between President Nixon and others. The President moved to quash the subpoena on the claim of absolute privilege for confidential conversations between the President and his advisors.

Issue: May confidentiality be asserted to support a claim of executive privilege where documents are subpoenaed for a pending criminal trial?

Rule: (Burger, C.J.) A generalized interest in confidentiality will not prevail over a demonstrated, specific need for subpoenaed evidence in a pending criminal trial.

Kissinger v. Reporters Committee for Freedom of the Press (S.Ct. 1980) CD

Facts: Henry Kissinger, as Assistant to the President, had all his telephone conversations recorded and transcribed. William Safire requested access to those transcripts while Kissinger was Secretary of State, claiming the transcripts were "agency records" of the State Department subject to Freedom of Information Act (FOIA) disclosure requirements. Kissinger removed the transcripts and other papers from his office in the State Department. Other reporters sought disclosure, and the District Court ordered the materials released on grounds that they had been "improperly withheld" by the State Department.

Issue 1: What constitutes a withholding of documents in violation of the FOIA?

Rule 1: An agency has improperly withheld documents where it refuses to release documents within its physical possession at the time of the FOIA request.

Issue 2: Are personal documents compiled by an assistant to the President of the United States "agency records" subject to FOIA disclosure requirements?

Rule 2: (Rehnquist, J.) Under the FOIA, the Office of the President is not considered an agency, so documents from presidential aides are not "agency records" subject to disclosure requirements. Physical location of documents in an agency office does not make them "agency records."

Dissent: (Stevens, J.) The majority decision exempts documents that have wrongfully been removed from an agency's files from FOIA scrutiny, creating an incentive for outgoing agency officials to remove potentially embarrassing documents from their files to frustrate future FOIA requests.

Central Intelligence Agency v. Sims (S.Ct. 1985) CD

Facts: The Central Intelligence Agency (CIA) financed a research project to develop operations to control human behavior. Sims and the Public Citizen Health Research Group filed a Freedom of Information Act (FOIA) inquiry to discover the names of institutions and individuals involved in the project. Exemption 3 of the FOIA exempted from disclosure matters that were specifically exempted by statute. The CIA invoked this exemption claiming the National Security Act gives the Agency discretion to protect its sources.

Issue: Does the FOIA Exemption 3 permit agencies to withhold the identities of their "intelligence sources" and other revealing information?

Rule: (Burger, C.J.) Where, as here, the pertaining statute gives an agency broad discretion to protect its intelligence sources, Exemption 3 permits withholding of any information that might reveal those sources.

Concurrence: (Marshall, J.) The Court stretches Exemption 3 beyond its natural limit where the case could be decided solely on the narrow Exemption 1 for national security.

Federal Bureau of Investigation v. Abramson (S.Ct. 1982) CD

Facts: Abramson, a professional journalist, sought Federal Bureau of Investigation (FBI) documents to determine whether the White House had received derogatory information from the FBI about political opponents. The requested documents were summaries or memoranda containing information originally culled from law enforcement documents. Exemption 7 of the Freedom of Information Act (FOIA) protects against unwarranted invasions of privacy where the information sought was compiled for law enforcement purposes.

Issue: Where information compiled for law enforcement purposes is later used in documents unrelated to law enforcement, does Exemption 7 still protect them from disclosure?

Rule: (White, J.) There is no indication that Congress intended to strip law enforcement information from its exempt status when reproduced in non-law-enforcement documents, since that information continues to meet threshold requirements for Exemption 7.

Dissent: (O'Connor, J.) The documents withheld by the FBI do not fit within the express language of Exemption 7 and must be released. Exemptions to the FOIA must be construed narrowly.

Federal Communications Commission v.
ITT World Communications, Inc. (S.Ct. 1984) CD

Facts: Members of the Federal Communication Commission (FCC) participated in an international conference to facilitate joint planning of facilities and exchange information on regulatory policies. ITT objected to the conference, which would permit the entry of new competitors into the market, and filed a petition charging violation of the Sunshine Act requirements for open meetings.

Issue: What constitutes a "meeting" that must be open to the public under the Government in Sunshine Act?

Rule: (Powell, J.) The Sunshine Act applies to "meetings of an agency," which does not include informal international conferences where a quorum of agency members qualified to conduct agency business is not present and official agency policy is not formulated.

EPA v. Mink (S.Ct. 1973) S

Facts: Congresswoman Mink sought disclosure of agency recommendations to the President regarding underground nuclear testing. The documents had been classified as top secret pursuant to a valid Executive Order. Petitioners moved for summary judgment on the grounds that the information was protected by Exemption 1 of the Freedom of Information Act (FOIA), exempting national security secrets.

Issue: Are documents classified as national defense secrets under Executive Order subject to FOIA disclosure?

Rule: (White, J.) Any documents classified top secret pursuant to an Executive Order are protected from disclosure by Exemption 1 in the interest of national defense. Exemption 1 does not permit *in camera* inspection by the courts to determine "nonsecret components" of classified documents.

Note: The 1974 amendments to FOIA overrule this decision and make Exemption 1 only applicable to documents that are properly classified as top secret pursuant to an executive order, permitting the courts to examine the records *in camera* to make that determination.

NLRB v. Robbins Tire & Rubber Co. (S.Ct. 1978) MM

Facts: The National Labor Relations Board issued an unfair labor practice complaint charging Robbins Tire with violations of the National Labor Relations Act in a representation election. A hearing was scheduled, and Robbins requested copies of all potential witnesses' statements prior to the hearing. The NLRB denied the Freedom of Information Act (FOIA) request, claiming the statements fell under Exemption 7A, which protects "investigatory records compiled for law enforcement purposes, but only to the extent that the production of such records would ... interfere with enforcement proceedings." Robbins contended that this exemption was only available after specific proof that the materials would actually interfere in this case.

Issue: Must an agency prove actual interference with law enforcement in an individual case in order to invoke Exemption 7A?

Rule: (Marshall, J.) Congress did not intend to prevent the federal courts from determining that, with respect to particular kinds of enforcement proceedings, disclosure of certain investigatory records while a case is pending would generally "interfere with enforcement proceedings." No case-by-case proof is needed.

Dissent: (Powell, J.) There is a general presumption of disclosure absent a particularized showing of likely interference. An agency's own discovery rules should not be used to evade the Freedom of Information Act.

Chapter 8

SCOPE OF JUDICIAL REVIEW

I. OVERVIEW

Administrative actions result from a series of agency decisions. First, the agency decides the law by interpreting relevant statutes. Second, the agency engages in a factfinding process. Third, the agency uses discretion in determining when and where to apply the law to the facts. Each of these decisions is subject to judicial review. The scope of judicial review depends on whether the case involves primarily issues of law, fact, or discretion.

A. Questions of Law

1. Generally
   Questions of law are clearly the province of the court and are less likely to be seen as usurping congressionally delegated authority from the agency. The main problem arises in ascertaining what is law and what is fact.

   Since courts will generally classify an issue as one of law if they would like to review it and one of fact if they would not, it often seems like a chicken and egg problem. Is it a question of law because the court reviewed it that way, or did the court review it that way because it was a question of law?

2. Statutory Interpretation
   State courts generally take a less deferential position in reviewing agency interpretations of law than do federal courts. The *Madison* and *Chevron* cases illustrate these two positions. In determining how much deference to give to an agency interpretation of the law, courts might consider the following factors:

    a. Completeness of agency procedures.

    b. Date and duration of construction.

    c. Consistency of agency's position.

    d. Endorsement of interpretation by legislature.

    e. Agency interpretation of its own rule.

    f. Need for technical expertise.

    g. Public reliance on agency interpretation.

B. Questions of Fact

The scope of judicial review for questions of fact is usually measured by the "substantial evidence" standard, where the court may not reverse an agency decision if a reasonable person could have reached the same conclusion. Some states use a "clearly erroneous" standard, permitting reversal only if the judge has a firm conviction that a mistake has been made. Occasionally, a court may exercise its independent judgment on the facts, based on the agency record, but these circumstances are very limited.

C. Agency Discretion: Application of Law to Facts

Cases of application can either be decided as questions of law or fact. This distinction determines whether the court should judge the agency decision by a deferential "reasonableness" standard or on its own decision of "rightness." This is often determined by whether Congress delegated the authority to apply the law to the agency.

The courts may only overturn a discretionary agency decision if it is "arbitrary and capricious." This test applies to the discretionary parts of administrative rules, formal adjudication, and agency factfinding where no hearing is required.

II. QUESTIONS OF LAW

A. Generally

Where the issue is not solely one of fact, a mixed question of fact and law usually exists. These questions span a continuum from a predominance of factual issues, where the agency is given great deference, to a predominance of legal issues, where the court is more comfortable substituting its own judgment. Determining where a case falls on this continuum is a fuzzy business. The appropriate standard for reviewing mixed cases is difficult to determine, and individual judges tend to apply different standards, apparently depending on how they feel about the issue or judicial review. There are no steadfast rules to apply in this area of the law; it is still in the development stage. With that in mind, a two step analysis suggested by Professors Gellhorn and Levin may be a useful approach.

1. Law
   First, examine any pure questions of law. The APA, in § 706 (2)(B) and (2)(C), gives the courts the power to set aside agency action that is "contrary to constitutional right, power, privilege, or immunity" or "in excess of statutory jurisdiction, authority, or limitations, or short of statutory right." If the agency has overstepped its constitutional or statutory bounds, then judges are free to substitute their judgment on the matter.

2. Application
   If an agency's legal interpretations survive a fairly independent review, then their application of the law to the facts should be given a limited examination. The standard for judging application of law to fact should be one of reasonableness. The reviewing court may only set aside the agency findings if there is no rational basis for upholding them. This standard does not preclude judges from taking a "hard look" at the record below, making sure that reasonable explanations have been offered for agency behavior.

B. Statutory Interpretation

1. Strong Deference
    The recent trend has been toward strong deference to agency interpretations of statutes. But even when precedent seems to dictate deference, judges can usually find an interpretation that permits them to substitute their own judgment if they desire. The *Chevron* test has become the standard for federal judicial review of agency actions.

    Chevron v. Natural Resources Defense Council stands for the proposition that a deferential standard should be used for review of agency actions that are not specifically prohibited by Congress. The two part *Chevron* test requires the reviewing court to determine 1) if Congress has spoken on the precise issue and 2) whether the agency's construction of the statute is "permissible." If Congress has addressed the issue, then its intent is dispositive.

    This is a "reasonableness" standard rather than one of "rightness." The judge may not substitute a more appropriate policy choice if the agency's reading of the statute is lawful and reasonable. Where an agency has promulgated regulations under a statute, agency interpretations of that statute are generally granted greater deference. See *Ford Motor Credit Co. v. Milhollin.*

2. Weak Deference
    Agency interpretations may be accorded more or less weight based on factors such as consistency, legislative endorsement, or technical expertise needed. See above, at I(A)(2). Agency rulings on law are not controlling, but courts often follow them if the rulings are reasonable. See *Skidmore v. Swift & Co.* The trend in the last decade has been toward more deferential review, but if the courts disagree strongly with an agency, they can usually find that Congress has addressed the issue at hand, permitting them to interpret the statute themselves.

C. Agency Policymaking

An agency may choose to implement policies through rules. These rules are often challenged, and the courts must then determine the limitations of agency power. Rules promulgated by agencies can be divided into two categories: legislative and interpretive.

1. Legislative Rules

Legislative rules are issued by an agency under a delegated legislative power. When interpretations of legislative rules are reviewed, the agency's interpretation is given more weight than for interpretive rules.

2. Interpretive Rules

Interpretive rules do not stem from a delegated legislative power. Rather, they are interpretations of congressional statutes. Interpretive rule constructions by an agency may persuade the judiciary but do not carry the same weight as legislative rules. The duty of the judiciary is to ensure that the agency has as much authority as, but not more than, Congress intended.

III. QUESTIONS OF FACT

A. Substantial Evidence: APA § 706(2)(E)

The dominant standard for reviewing questions of fact is whether there is "substantial evidence," looking at the whole record, to support the agency's findings. See *Universal Camera v. NLRB*. This standard only applies to formal rulemaking and adjudication. Some states use a "clearly erroneous" standard instead of the "substantial evidence" test. This makes it less difficult for the judge to overturn an agency decision, requiring only a firm conviction that a mistake has been made, regardless of whether there is substantial evidence to support the agency decision. See *Defries v. Association of Owners, 999 Wilder*.

B. Independent Judgment or *De Novo* Review

Only a few specific categories of cases have invoked a substitution of judicial judgment for agency judgment. These categories developed in the 1920's and 1930's and have not expanded. Though none of these rulings has been explicitly overturned, the validity of these doctrines has been questioned.

1. Constitutional Facts
   Early cases in this area suggested that constitutional rights ought to be protected by a judicial trial *de novo*. Thus, in ratesetting cases, utilities claimed that their Fifth Amendment right to not have property taken without due process was violated by agency ratesetting decisions. See *Ohio Valley Water Co. v. Ben Avon Borough*. The Supreme Court did not extend this doctrine, and later cases made it inapplicable even to ratesetting. (In *FPC v. Hope Natural Gas Co.*, the Court ruled that only the result, not the method, of a ratemaking decision can be reviewed.)

2. Jurisdictional Facts
   The jurisdictional fact doctrine has been applied in two types of cases: claims of citizenship and claims of employment relationship under the Longshoremen's Act. See *Crowell v. Benson* and *Public Service Commn v. General Telephone Co.* Jurisdictional facts are facts that must exist to invoke the statutory claim in question. Although the claims of employment status have never been extended beyond the Longshoremen's Act, the claims of citizenship are still given *de novo* trials today. People facing deportation who claim to be citizens are entitled to a judicial trial on the citizenship issue.

3. Vested Fundamental Rights
   Some states, such as California, have statutes providing for either *de novo* or independent judgment review when an agency decision "substantially affects a vested, fundamental right." The theory behind this review is that the judiciary is best equipped to protect individual rights against the majority will. Rights to which a person is entitled (vested rights) and rights that are

fundamental deserve greater judicial protection than other rights. See *Frink v. Prod*.

IV. DISCRETION: APPLICATION OF LAW TO FACTS

A. Arbitrary and Capricious

Judicial review of agency discretion is governed by the "arbitrary and capricious" test of APA §706(2)(A). Under this test, the agency decision may not be reversed unless there is no possible ground for upholding it. See *Citizens to Preserve Overton Park v. Volpe*.

B. "Hard Look"

Agencies are considered experts in their fields. When they make or change policy, they are given a significant amount of deference. However, the public has an interest in fair and consistent policy-making from the agency. So, when agencies act inconsistently, or without logical reason for change, the courts must step in to protect the public interest and prevent abuse of agency discretion. In *State Farm*, the Court reversed a Department of Transportation decision to rescind a safety standard, claiming that the Department had failed to give adequate reasons for the change. The Court took a "hard look" at the record and found no reasonable basis for the decision.

"Hard look" review requires the agency to prove that it has done its homework on the issue at hand. Even if the record shows a complete inquiry into the subject matter, it must be given a "hard look" by the judge. A court must examine the rationality of the conclusions reached by the agency and the justifications offered in support of these conclusions. In addition, a court must ensure that the agency has considered all possible courses of action, or, if the agency failed to do so, that the agency satisfactorily explained the omission.

CASE CLIPS

Universal Camera Corp. v. NLRB (S.Ct. 1951) BA, BS, GB, S
Facts: The NLRB ruled that Universal fired an employee in retaliation for the employee's testimony at an NLRB hearing. Universal claimed the employee was fired for insubordination. Evidence supporting both conclusions was in the record. Interpretations of the Taft-Hartley Act suggested that the "substantial evidence" test only required the court to consider evidence that supported the agency's decision, rather than all evidence, whether supporting or detracting.
Issue: Must the court find substantial evidence in the whole record when reviewing an agency decision?
Rule: (Frankfurter, J.) The substantial evidence test must take into account the whole record, including evidence that detracts from the agency's position.

Defries v. Association of Owners, 999 Wilder (1976) BA
Facts: The Labor and Industrial Relations Board did not find plaintiff's claim of work-related injury credible, resulting in a denial of workers' compensation benefits. Plaintiff sought review of the factual finding that his testimony lacked credibility.
Issue: What standard of judicial review should govern disputes over an agency's finding of fact?
Rule: A court may reverse the factual conclusions of an agency if they are "clearly erroneous" or if the appellate court reaches a "definite and firm conviction that a mistake has been made," regardless of supporting evidence that, by itself, would be substantial.
Dissent: The Board should not be required to resolve all reasonable doubts in the claimant's favor. The decision of the Board was not "clearly erroneous."
Note: While some states still use a "clearly erroneous" standard, the Model State APA, in 1981, changed to the "substantial evidence" standard used in the federal APA.

Frink v. Prod (1982) BA

Facts: An agency denied welfare benefits to the plaintiff. The superior court denied relief using the substantial evidence standard. Petitioner claimed the trial court should have exercised its independent judgment in reviewing the agency's action.

Issue: When an application for welfare benefits is denied, what standard of review applies?

Rule: When vested, fundamental rights, such as welfare benefits, are at stake, a court must review the record and issue an independent judgment. To decide if a vested, fundamental right is at stake, a court must weigh the importance and effect of the right, as well as the degree to which it is possessed.

Dissent: It is not left to the courts to decide the scope of review. The statute mandates substantial evidence review, not independent judgment.

Madison v. Alaska Dept. of Fish and Game (1985) BA

Facts: The Board of Fisheries denied a fishing permit to Madison based on its construction of "subsistence fishing" in the applicable statute.

Issue: What standard of review should apply to agency interpretations of statutes?

Rule: When reviewing an agency's statutory interpretation, a court may substitute its independent judgment for the agency's, even if the agency's interpretation has a reasonable basis in law.

Chevron v. Natural Resources Defense Council
(S.Ct. 1984) BA, GB, CD, MM

Facts: The Environmental Protection Agency (EPA) promulgated regulations to implement the Clean Air Act Amendments of 1977. The Court of Appeals invalidated the EPA regulations on the grounds that the agency's interpretation of the Act was contrary to congressional purpose.

Issue: What standard of review should apply to agency interpretations of statutes?

Rule: (Stevens, J.) Courts should apply a two-part reasonableness test to agency interpretation of statutes. Where available, clear congressional intent is dispositive. But if Congress has been ambiguous or has not addressed the matter, then the question is whether the agency's construction of the statute is "permissible." A court may not substitute its own construction where it finds an agency decision to be bad policy.

McPherson v. Employment Division (1979) BA

Facts: McPherson claimed she left her job for "good cause," entitling her to unemployment benefits, but the Employment Division interpreted "good cause" in a way that excluded her claim. She sought judicial review of the Division's application of the statutory term to the facts of her case.

Issue: When an agency's application of law to facts is challenged, must a reviewing court grant deference to the agency interpretation?

Rule: When reviewing the application of law to facts, a court must determine whether the statute entrusts interpretation of the law to agency discretion. If the agency is responsible for defining a broad term, then judicial review will be deferential. If not, then the court may substitute its judgment.

Motor Vehicle Manufacturers Association v.
State Farm Mutual Automobile Insurance Co.
(S.Ct. 1983) BA, BS, GB, CD, MM

Facts: Under authority of the National Traffic and Motor Vehicle Safety Act, the Transportation Secretary promulgated Standard 208 requiring passive restraint systems in automobiles. Before the standard became effective, the agency rescinded the standard, claiming that it would not produce the expected benefits.

Issue: Must an agency that rescinds a rule satisfy the same standards applied to an agency's refusal to promulgate a rule initially?

Rule: (White, J.) When an agency rescinds a standard, it must offer a reasoned analysis more detailed than required for the "arbitrary and capricious" standard. The agency must articulate "a rational connection between the facts found and the choice made."

Dissent in part: (Rehnquist, J.) A political party change in the White House is an acceptable reason for the agency to change its mind. The agency satisfied the arbitrary and capricious standard and its actions should not be subject to further review.

Note: This case represents the "hard look" approach to review of agency discretion.

Borden, Inc. v. Commissioner of Public Health (1983) BA
Facts: The Commissioner issued a regulation banning UFFI, a substance believed to be toxic, under a statute permitting bans where labelling is insufficient. The manufacturer claimed that the record did not support the finding of toxicity. The trial court overturned the ban.
Issue: What standard of judicial review applies to agency regulations?
Rule: A properly promulgated regulation has the force of law and may not be revoked unless plaintiff proves that it is arbitrary or capricious, i.e., that there is no conceivable ground for upholding the rule.

Smyth v. Ames (S.Ct. 1898) BS
Facts: The Nebraska state legislature set maximum railroad rates at a value so low that the companies claimed they could not cover operating costs. The lower court ruled that the statute effected an unconstitutional deprivation of property.
Issue: What standard should be used to determine the reasonableness of rates?
Rule: (Harlan, J.) The reasonableness of rates should be determined by the fair value of the property used for the convenience of the public.

Missouri ex rel. Southwestern Bell Tel. Co.
v. Public Serv. Commn. (S.Ct. 1923) BS
Facts: Southwestern Bell appealed from a Missouri Supreme Court ruling affirming a rate set by the state commission that did not take into account the greatly enhanced costs of materials and labor over time.
Issue: What constitutes a just return for the use of property that may not be deprived without due process of law?
Rule: (McReynolds, J.) A just return for the use of property involves the recognition of a fair value of the property if it is more than its original cost.
Concurrence: (Brandeis, J.) The rule of *Smyth v. Ames* sets the impossible task of finding the present value of a utility and should be abandoned.

FPC v. Hope Natural Gas Co. (S.Ct. 1944)   BS

Facts: The Natural Gas Act gave the Federal Power Commission authority to determine reasonable rates but did not insist on the use of specific formulas.

Issue: To what extent will a reviewing court examine the methods used in ratesetting?

Rule: (Douglas, J.)   Under the statutory standard of "just and reasonable," the result reached, rather than the method used, determines the fairness of the ratesetting.   If the total effect of the rate order cannot be said to be unjust and unreasonable then the judicial inquiry ends.

East Tennessee Natural Gas Co. v. FERC (1982)   BS

Facts: East Tennessee disputed the low rate of return set by the Federal Energy Regulation Commission (FERC).

Issue: What is the scope of judicial review in ratesetting cases?

Rule: In a simple rate case, a reviewing court may only determine whether the end result of the rate proceedings is reasonable.

U.S. v. Fifty-Three Eclectus Parrots (1982)   BS

Facts: Appellant did not know that Indonesian law and, therefore, American customs law prohibited the importation of eclectus parrots. The Government construed "wild" in the applicable statute to include these parrots. Appellant did not present any evidence that the species is not normally found in a wild state.

Issue: Absent a genuine issue of material fact, is an agency's definition of a statutory term subject to judicial review?

Rule: As a matter of law, an agency's definition of a statutory term is not subject to judicial review when there is no genuine issue of material fact.

NLRB v. Hearst Publications, Inc.
(S.Ct. 1944) BS, GB, CD, S, MM

Facts: Respondents, publishers of four newspapers, refused to bargain collectively with newsboy employees through a union representative, claiming that the paper sellers were not "employees" under the National Labor Relations Act.

Issue: Under what circumstances should an agency interpretation of a statute that has a reasonable basis in law be upheld?

Rule: (Rutledge, J.) Where an agency is responsible for initially determining the meaning of a broad statutory term, a court should uphold any interpretation that has a reasonable basis in law and is supported by the facts.

Dissent: (Roberts, J.) Deciding who is an "employee" within the meaning of the Act is a judicial function. Congress meant to refer to a common, national understanding of the term employee, which does not cover the newsboys in this case.

Packard Motor Car Co. v. NLRB (S.Ct. 1947) BS

Facts: Packard tried to deny foremen employee benefits by not classifying them as "employees." The National Labor Relations Board ruled that foremen are "employees" entitled to benefits under the applicable statute.

Issue: What standard of review should apply to agency interpretations of statutes?

Rule: (Jackson, J.) A reviewing court may resolve questions of statutory interpretation on its own judgment.

Dissent: (Douglas, J.) The agency's interpretation, upheld by the majority, represents a drastic policy change. It is unlikely Congress intended this result.

Note: The review standard articulated in this case is inconsistent with the deference given to agency interpretations in *Hearst*, though both cases upheld the agency decision.

Pittston Stevedoring Corp. v. Dellaventura (1976) BS

Facts: The Benefits Review Board granted compensation to four employees under the Longshoremen's and Harbor Workers' Compensation Act. The Board claimed its interpretation of coverage was entitled to special deference.

Issue: Under what circumstances will a reviewing court not give deference to an agency interpretation of a statutory term?

Rule: If an agency is primarily involved in "umpiring" rather than policy making, and its judgment is not rendered on a full record, then a reviewing court should not defer to the agency's construction.

Addison v. Holly Hill Fruit Products, Inc. (S.Ct. 1944) BS

Facts: The Fair Labor Standards Act required employers to pay minimum wage, with exceptions including the canning of agricultural products "within the area" of agricultural production. The agency interpreted this exception to refer to size of employer as well as location.

Issue: When construing the terms of a statute, may an agency attach additional requirements not prescribed by the statute?

Rule: (Frankfurter, J.) An agency's discretion to interpret a statute is limited by its congressionally delegated authority. Here, Congress did not delegate the authority to consider factors other than geographical area in granting exemptions.

Dissent: (Rutledge, J.) The agency's power is discretionary. The question of size is part of a complex decision-making process and should not be extricated. The majority decision requires the agency to use geography and other factors as a proxy for size, hiding the real distinctions used.

Skidmore v. Swift & Co. (S.Ct. 1944) BS, GB

Facts: Employees were not paid wages for "waiting time" on call at work and demanded compensation under the Fair Labor Standards Act. The appointed Administrator's guidelines indicated that "waiting time" was not work time, but no agency had jurisdiction over the issue.

Issue: When no agency exists to interpret a statute, must the courts give deference to guidelines published by an appointed Administrator?

Rule: (Jackson, J.) Congress intended for the courts to decide questions of statutory interpretation using independent judgment. An appointed administrator's guidelines on a subject are useful but not controlling, absent an agency with statutory jurisdiction.

Social Security Board v. Nierotko (S.Ct. 1946) BS

Facts: The Social Security Board ruled that "back pay" is excluded from "wages" under the Labor Act. On appeal, the Board urged that its decision be viewed as conclusive.

Issue: Is an agency's interpretation of a statutory term conclusive?

Rule: (Frankfurter, J.) Where an agency interpretation of a statutory term goes beyond its delegated powers, it is not entitled to judicial deference.

Kent v. Dulles (S.Ct. 1958) BS
Facts: The Secretary of State denied passports to citizens based on their affiliations with the Communist Party. Although the Secretary of State's power to issue passports was stated in broad terms, it had only been exercised in two narrow categories, which did not apply to plaintiffs here.
Issue: Must delegated powers curtailing basic liberties be construed narrowly?
Rule: (Douglas, J.) Delegated powers that curtail basic liberties, such as the right to travel, should be construed narrowly, since it cannot be readily inferred that Congress intended to grant agencies unbridled discretion to curtail freedoms.

Hampton v. Mow Sun Wong (S.Ct. 1976) BS
Facts: Five aliens challenged the Civil Service Commission (CSC) policy excluding them from federal civil service jobs, allegedly for national security reasons. The aliens contended that the CSC's decision was arbitrary and violated due process.
Issue: When an agency rule is discriminatory, may a court review the agency's justifications for the rule?
Rule: (Stevens, J.) A court may review justifications for a discriminatory rule where the agency alleges an overriding national interest. To satisfy due process, the agency must either have direct responsibility for protecting that interest or prove the rule was intended to serve the interest asserted.

Citizens to Preserve Overton Park v.
Volpe (S.Ct. 1971) BS, GB, CD, S
Facts: The Department of Transportation Act required that the Secretary of Transportation not approve federal funds for highway projects that extend through public parks if a "feasible and prudent" alternative existed. Petitioners contended that proposed highway I-40 could have been routed around Overton Park and the plan for the project did not include "all possible" methods of reducing harm to the park, as required by statute. Respondents argued that the Secretary of Transportation's plan was sufficient and the decision was not reviewable.

Issue: In reviewing agency discretion, what standard of review applies?

Rule: (Marshall, J.) In reviewing agency discretion, a court must decide if the action was within the agency's scope of authority; if the action was "arbitrary, capricious, an abuse of discretion, or otherwise not in accordance with law"; and if the agency followed procedural requirements.

Industrial Union Dept., AFL/CIO v.
American Petroleum Institute (The Benzene Case)
(S.Ct. 1980) BS, CD, MM

Facts: The Occupational Safety and Health Act of 1970 gave OSHA the authority to set standards for toxic chemical use in the work place. In 1977, OSHA tried to reduce its standard for Benzene from 10ppm to 1ppm, based on assumptions that the reduction would lessen the risk of leukemia from exposure. American Petroleum Institute contended that the agency failed to prove that the new standard would prevent a significant risk of harm.

Issue: Where an agency has discretion to formulate standards, may a reviewing court examine the agency's record for substantial evidence that a new standard is needed?

Rule: (Stevens, J.) Where an agency uses discretion to promulgate rules, a court may give the record a "hard look" to determine whether abuse of discretion has occurred. This review may amount to an equivalent of the "substantial evidence" test used for adjudicatory hearings.

Dissent: (Marshall, J.) The agency's determination should be upheld if there is substantial evidence in the record to support it. The court may not substitute its judgment in place of the agency's. In this case, the agency decision was reasonable and supported by evidence.

American Textile Manufacturers Institute v.
Donovan (The Cotton Dust Case)
(S.Ct. 1981)   BS, CD, S

Facts: The Occupational Safety and Health Administration set the permissible standard for cotton dust, known to cause "brown lung disease", by using the "most protective standard that was technologically and economically feasible." Manufacturers claimed there was not substantial evidence in the record proving the agency's standard was "economically feasible." The Court of Appeals disagreed.

Issue: When a court of appeals finds substantial evidence to support an agency decision, may the Supreme Court, on appeal, exercise its independent judgment?

Rule: (Brennan, J.) Where a statute places responsibility for determining substantial evidence questions in the courts of appeals, the only issue for the Supreme Court is whether the substantial evidence standard was "misapprehended or grossly misapplied."

Dissent: (Stewart, J.) The Court of Appeals grossly misapplied the substantial evidence test, since there was only unsupported speculation that the new regulation was economically feasible. OSHA failed to justify its estimate of the costs involved with substantial evidence.

Baltimore Gas and Electric Co. v.
Natural Resources Defense Council
(S.Ct. 1983) BS

Facts: The Nuclear Regulatory Commission instructed licensing boards not to consider the negative environmental risks of radiation escape when they reviewed applications for new plants. Plaintiffs contended that the National Environmental Policy Act required federal agencies to consider the environmental consequences of their actions. The Court of Appeals held the agency's disregard of the statutory requirement to be arbitrary and capricious.

Issue: Where an agency makes predictions within its area of expertise and acts within the bounds of reasoned decisionmaking, are its decisions entitled to judicial deference?

Rule: (O'Connor, J.) In reviewing agency decisions made within their field of expertise, a court's role is only to determine whether an agency has considered the relevant factors and articulated a rational connection between the facts found and the choice made.

Scenic Hudson Preservation Conf. v. FPC (I) (1965) BS

Facts: The Federal Power Commission issued a license for Consolidated Edison to build a power plant on the Hudson River. Under the Federal Power Act, the Commission could only license projects "best adapted to a comprehensive plan for improving a waterway." Petitioners claimed the Commission did not fulfill its statutory duties in the licensing process.

Issue: Where an agency fails to meet statutory obligations in issuing a decision, may a court deem the decision "arbitrary and capricious"?

Rule: Where an agency has ignored relevant factors and failed to compile a record sufficient to support its decision, as required by statute, a court may overturn the agency's actions as arbitrary and capricious.

Note: Although the Commission had not fulfilled its statutory duties in this case, five years later, in *Scenic Hudson (II)*, the court held that it had.

Penasquitos Village, Inc. v. NLRB (1977) GB

Facts: A Penasquitos supervisor fired two employees for slow work. They contended they were fired for union organizing. The National Labor Relations Board, overturning the administrative law judge's decision, found that Penasquitos had wrongfully discharged the employees. Testimony of the events was disputed.

Issue: Must a reviewing court give deference to agency decisions based on inferences drawn from discredited testimony?

Rule: While agency inferences generally deserve judicial deference, decisions primarily based on inferences from discredited testimony are not supported by substantial evidence on the whole record and cannot be sustained.

Dissent in part: Although the substantial evidence test is properly applied, the decision puts undue weight on the reliability of testimonial inferences.

O'Leary v. Brown-Pacific-Maxon, Inc. (S.Ct. 1951) GB

Facts: An employee died while stationed at a job overseas. Compensation benefits could only be collected if the employee died in the "course of employment," which was disputed. The agency ruled in favor of the employee. The appellate court substituted its own findings and reversed.

Issue: When an agency makes a finding based on the application of a statutory term to the facts, what standard of judicial review applies?

Rule: (Frankfurter, J.) When an issue revolves around agency expertise, such as employment, then it is treated as a question of fact and reviewed under the substantial evidence standard, prohibiting the court from substituting its findings for the agency's where there is sufficient supporting evidence.

Dissent: (Minton, J.) The majority ruling finds liability based on the employer-employee relationship alone, no causal link is necessary. The "factual" finding that the employee died in the course of employment is unsupported by evidence.

Ford Motor Credit Co v. Milhollin (S.Ct. 1980) GB

Facts: The Truth in Lending Act was construed by the Federal Reserve Board not to require disclosure of acceleration clauses in credit agreements. Congress delegated expansive authority to the Board to elaborate on the legal framework.

Issue: Where Congress delegates broad powers to an agency to interpret a statute and promulgate regulations under it, may a reviewing court substitute its judgment on statutory construction?

Rule: (Brennan, J.) When an agency has promulgated substantive regulations under a statute that is not dispositive on an issue, a court should uphold the agency's statutory interpretations on the issue unless they are arbitrary and capricious.

Concurrence: (Blackmun, J.) Other readings of the statute are preferable, but since the agency's reading is reasonable it should not be overturned.

Association of Data Processing Service Organizations v. Board of Governors (1984) GB, S

Facts: The Bank Holding Company Act required all bank holding companies to seek prior regulatory approval before engaging in non-banking activities. Citicorp applied for approval, and the Board of Governors conducted informal rulemaking procedures as well as a formal hearing before approving. Under § 1848, the findings of the Board as to the facts, if supported by substantial evidence, were conclusive. Petitioners sought substantial evidence review of both the adjudication and the informal rulemaking.

Issue: Are the standards for judicial review of adjudication and informal rulemaking essentially the same?

Rule: The substantial evidence standard for formal adjudication requires the same amount of evidence as the "arbitrary and capricious" standard for informal rulemaking. As long as there is some ground on which the case could reasonably be upheld, a court must uphold it.

Independent U.S. Tanker Owners Committee v. Lewis (1982) GB

Facts: The Maritime Administration changed its construction of two statutes governing permission for carriers to engage in domestic trade. Domestic carriers appealed to prevent unwanted competition. The agency action was an informal adjudication because the statute did not require a hearing on the record.

Issue: When reviewing an agency informal adjudication, must a court examine the agency's procedures as well as its conclusions?

Rule: In reviewing informal adjudication, a court must ensure that 1) the agency decision is not "arbitrary, capricious, an abuse of discretion, or otherwise not in accordance with law" and 2) that the agency made all relevant evidence available for comment, produced an adequate explanation for its action, reviewed competing comments, and explained its resolution of conflicting comments.

Portmann v. United States (1982) GB

Facts: Portmann was told by a postal employee that a package was insured when it was not. She sued to recover the insurance money.

Issue: Is equitable estoppel ever available against the federal government?

Rule: Equitable estoppel is available against the United States Postal Service because it is an independent establishment with quasi-private status competing against other private enterprises. The Postal Service is not immune, as is the federal government generally, from commercial or judicial garnishment proceedings.

Heckler v. Day (S.Ct. 1984) S

Facts: In a class action, plaintiffs sought injunctive relief against unreasonably long delays in hearings to determine disability benefits.

Issue: May a court impose mandatory deadlines for agency hearings that are not being held within a reasonable time?

Rule: (Powell, J.) Since Congress has considered and expressly rejected imposing mandatory deadlines for agency hearings, it would contradict congressional intent for federal courts to issue injunctions imposing deadlines.

Dissent: (Marshall, J.) A statewide time limit would not be inconsistent with congressional intent. A court-ordered timetable is more flexible than a congressional statute, and there is no evidence that Congress would disapprove of this remedy.

Public Service Commn. v. General Telephone Co. (1977) S

Facts: The lower court, substituting its independent judgment for the Commission's decision, ordered the Public Service Commission to fix minimum rates for the General Telephone Co. at a rate that would avoid a confiscation under the Takings Clause. The Commission contested the independent judgment standard of judicial review used by the lower court, claiming it had essentially been overruled.

Issue: Must courts give full review and an independent judgment when an issue of constitutional fact is raised?

Rule: Since the "constitutional fact" rule has been all but overruled by the Supreme Court, no independent judgment is necessary when a constitutional right is an issue. The substantial evidence standard is sufficient.

Strumsky v. San Diego Employees Retirement Assn. (1974) S

Facts: Plaintiff sought her husband's death allowance from the Retirement Association and was denied. The trial court upheld the Association's ruling using the "substantial evidence" standard. Plaintiff claimed the findings were not supported by evidence.

Issue: When a claim of unsupported findings is made regarding adjudicatory orders or decisions, what is the scope of judicial review?

Rule: In cases where an order affects a vested, fundamental right, a court must exercise its independent judgment on the evidence, finding abuse of discretion if the "weight of the evidence" does not support the decision. In all other cases, a trial court's inquiry is limited to a determination of whether the findings are supported by "substantial evidence in light of the whole record."

Crowell v. Benson (S.Ct. 1932) S

Facts: The Longshoremen's and Harbor Workers' Act provided worker's compensation to injured longshoremen. To qualify, the employee must have been injured in the course of employment and while in navigable waters.

Issue: Where the facts as determined by the agency are pivotal to its jurisdiction, must a reviewing court exercise its independent judgment?
Rule: (Hughes, J.) When jurisdictional facts are at issue, a court must determine the agency's jurisdiction with a trial *de novo*.
Dissent: (Brandeis, J.) Congress clearly did not intend *de novo* fact finding by a reviewing court.

NLRB v. Marcus Trucking Co. (1961) S

Facts: The National Labor Relations Board found that an employer had violated a contract-bar protection rule while bound by contract to a union.
Issue: Is the application of undisputed non-statutory legal terms to the facts a "question of fact"?
Rule: The application of undisputed legal terms to facts is a "question of fact" subject to substantial evidence review, even if those legal terms are not statutory.

O'Keefe v. Smith, Hinchman, & Grylls Assoc., Inc. (S.Ct. 1965) S

Facts: The Bureau of Employees Compensation determined that an employee had died in the course of employment.
Issue: May a court overturn inferences drawn by an agency when they are rational and supported by substantial evidence?
Rule: (Per Curiam) Inferences drawn by an agency are to be upheld unless they are irrational or unsupported by substantial evidence on the record as a whole.
Dissent: (Harlan, J.) This ruling invalidates the meaning of the statute by eliminating the "job-connected" emphasis that was clearly intended.

National Labor Relations Board v.
Bell Aerospace Co., Division of Textron, Inc.
(S.Ct. 1974) MM

Facts: The United Automobile, Aerospace, and Agricultural Implement Workers of America wished to represent employees of Bell Aerospace's purchasing and procurement department in collective bargaining proceedings. Bell opposed the union's petition to the NLRB, claiming that the workers in the department were "managerial employees" and not eligible for union representation under the

National Labor Relations Act. The Board ruled that the employees were not "managerial" under the Act.

Issue: Where an agency construes a statute contrary to its prior consistent interpretations, must the court uphold a construction that is reasonable?

Rule: (Powell, J.) Where, as here, an agency's prior interpretations of a statute were broad, a court may prevent the agency from reading a more restrictive meaning into the statute now.

Dissent: (White, J.) The Board's decision should be upheld if it has a reasonable basis in law. The Court may not restrict the Board based on its prior decisions, which may have been erroneous.

Pacific States Box & Basket Co. v. White (S.Ct. 1935) MM

Facts: An Oregon agency prescribed the size and shape of containers in which raspberries and strawberries could be sold in that state, making plaintiff's containers unusable. Pacific States charged that the rule was an arbitrary and capricious use of the police power in violation of its due process rights under the 14th Amendment.

Issue: Where due process rights are at stake, must a reviewing court grant a presumption of validity to agency rules as well as statutes?

Rule: (Brandeis, J.) Where an agency rule is properly within a delegated legislative power, the same presumption of validity that supports statutes applies. Plaintiff has the burden of proving the rule is not "an appropriate means for attaining a permissible end" and is therefore an arbitrary and capricious use of police power violating due process.

Note: This case was decided prior to the enactment of the Administrative Procedure Act, which codified the arbitrary and capricious test in § 706.

Automotive Parts & Accessories Association v. Boyd (1968) MM

Facts: Motor Vehicle Safety Standard No. 202 required new cars to be equipped while in the factory with head rests. Plaintiff challenged the standard on procedural and substantive grounds.

Issue: Where an agency has engaged in informal rulemaking, is the informal record subject to judicial scrutiny?

Rule: When an agency issues a rule, it must include a written explanation of the basis and purpose of the rule, so a reviewing court can take a hard look at the proceedings and determine whether the agency engaged in "reasoned decisionmaking."

National Tire Dealers & Retreaders Assoc. v. Brinegar (1974) MM
Facts: Federal Motor Vehicle Safety Standard No. 117 required tires to have certain information permanently molded onto the side. The benefits of this requirement had not been proven and the cost of implementation would be high.
Issue: Where an agency has not justified its promulgation of a rule, may a reviewing court find the rule arbitrary and capricious?
Rule: Where an agency fails to show proof that a rule meets the purpose of the related statute, a reviewing court may give the record a hard look and find the rule arbitrary and capricious.

Chapter 9

AVAILABILITY OF JUDICIAL REVIEW

I. JURISDICTION

Since federal courts have limited jurisdiction, statutory authority is needed to gain access to judicial review of agency decisions. The two basic sources for jurisdiction are called statutory and non-statutory review, but these terms are misleading since all jurisdiction must come from a statute. Non-statutory review simply refers to jurisdiction stemming from general statutes rather than specific enabling statutes for agencies. Note: the federal APA does not confer jurisdiction.

A. Statutory Review

An agency's organic, or enabling, statute will often provide jurisdiction for judicial review. Review may be sought by petition against the agency or by the agency to enforce its orders.

B. Non-Statutory Review

1. Federal Question Jurisdiction Statute, 28 U.S.C.A. § 1331
   If no specific statute governs the review of a particular agency's actions, then ordinary jurisdictional rules apply. Jurisdiction in federal district court may be sought under 28 U.S.C.A. § 1331, covering actions "arising under the Constitution, laws or treaties of the United States."

2. Mandamus and Venue Act, 28 U.S.C.A. § 1361
   This statute confers jurisdiction on the federal district courts to hear actions to compel government officers or agencies to perform a duty owed to the plaintiff. Mandamus stems from the old English prerogative writ. This statute applies only to agency actions that are ministerial rather than discretionary.

Distinguishing these two types of functions is a difficult task. Most plaintiffs prefer to use § 1331.

II. DAMAGE ACTIONS

While the APA waives sovereign immunity for the government in cases seeking injunction or mandamus, monetary damage claims are treated differently. Plaintiffs may not seek monetary damages from the government unless the government consents to be sued under a specific statute. The liability of the government is somewhat different from the liability of government officials.

A. Government Liability

1. Federal Torts Claims Act (FTCA)
   The FTCA permits tort claims against the federal government, with several exceptions. The broadest exception prohibits tort claims against the government when an agency is exercising a discretionary function that is a "permissible exercise of policy judgment." This exemption from FTCA liability is designed to permit agencies to perform their jobs without fear of monetary punishment. See *United States v. Varig Airlines.*

2. Tucker Act
   The Tucker Act, 28 U.S.C.A. § 1491, confers jurisdiction on the Court of Claims for claims founded on the Constitution, a congressional statute, an agency regulation, a contract with the United States, or involving damages not in tort. It also waives sovereign immunity for these types of cases. While this appears to be a broad statute, the courts have construed it quite narrowly. The Tucker Act has been interpreted as a jurisdictional statute that does not create a substantive right of action. A right of action must be found in other statutes and regulations. See *United States v. Mitchell.*

B. Liability of Government Officials

1. Common Law Torts
   Generally, government officers have absolute immunity from common law tort liability within the "outer perimeter of [their] line of duty." See *Barr v. Matteo.*

2. Constitutional Torts

   a. Official Immunity
      When a government official violates the Constitution, he has only a qualified immunity from liability, unless he is performing judicial functions, where absolute immunity is provided. Qualified immunity provides protection from liability when officials believe they are acting lawfully and that belief is in good faith. See *Butz v. Economou.* In *Harlow v. Fitzgerald,* the Court made the test for qualified immunity objective rather than subjective, dropping the good faith belief standard. Now officials are only liable if they violate a "clearly established statutory or constitutional right of which a reasonable person should have known."

   b. 42 U.S.C.A. § 1983 Actions
      The Civil Rights Act of 1871, 42 U.S.C.A. § 1983, makes liable state officials who, under the color of state law, deprive any person of rights guaranteed by the Constitution or any federal law.

   c. *Bivens* Actions
      In *Bivens v. Six Unknown Federal Narcotics Agents,* the Court ruled that federal officials could be sued for damages for violating a constitutional right. The Court inferred a cause of action from the Fourth Amendment of the Constitution. Subsequent cases expanded *Bivens* actions, suggesting a private right of action for any constitutional violation for which Congress has not specifically provided other relief.

III. REVIEWABILITY

A. Presumption of Reviewability

Under the APA § 10, a general presumption of reviewability applies to all agency actions. This presumption may be rebutted under two exceptions provided in APA § 701(a). Agency inaction does not carry the same presumption of reviewability. An agency's failure to prosecute a violation or investigate a hazard is presumed unreviewable. See *Heckler v. Chaney.*

B. Exceptions

1. Precluded by Statute

   a. Implied
   The presumption of reviewability is not easily overcome. If there is no explicit mention of preclusion in the statute, silence does not imply preclusion. The courts will look for clear and convincing evidence that Congress intended to preclude review.

   b. Express
   Even where a statute expressly precludes judicial review, the courts may interpret the statutory language to provide at least a partial review. Total preclusion is rare.

2. Committed to Agency Discretion
   Agency discretion may be reviewable under APA § 706(2)(a) (arbitrary and capricious standard) or unreviewable under § 701(a)(2) (committed to agency discretion). A decision may fall under both provisions, with some parts reviewable and others committed to agency discretion. In *Citizens to Preserve Overton Park v. Volpe*, the Court ruled that a decision is committed to agency discretion when the statute contains such broad terms that there is "no law to apply" to pass judgment on the agency's decision.

IV. STANDING

Standing to bring suit for judicial review stems from three sources: Article III of the Constitution, common law rules, and legislative enactments. The Article III case or controversy requirement demands that the plaintiff have a personal stake in the litigation. This injury in fact requirement has been interpreted by the courts to mean that plaintiffs who are not personally injured may not assert the rights of injured third parties. Congressional statutes may confer standing on individuals where they otherwise would not have met the appropriate criteria.

A. Legal Right Test

Historically, plaintiffs could only gain standing to challenge agency action if a legal right had been violated. This meant that only government actions that would be private wrongs if performed by an individual could be used to gain standing. In *FCC v. Sanders Brothers Radio Station*, the Court ruled that "persons aggrieved" under the statute providing review for FCC decisions could include persons who did not have their legal rights violated. The APA incorporated the "aggrieved person" right to review in § 702, suggesting that any plaintiff who could prove he was aggrieved in fact could gain standing. The Court decided not to adopt the APA's formulation, but the idea served as a basis for the modern rule.

B. *Data Processing* Test

The legal right test was replaced by a two-part inquiry in *Association of Data Processing Service Organizations v. Camp*. The Court held that the plaintiff must show "injury in fact" and that his interest is within the "zone of interests" contemplated by the statutory or constitutional guarantee in question.

1. Injury in Fact

   a. Non-economic injury
      The injury in fact requirement is the most important factor in gaining standing. The injury need not be economic; it can be injury to aesthetic or recreational enjoyment or environmental damage to plaintiff's surroundings. See *Duke Power Co. v. Carolina Environmental Study Group, Inc.* and *United States v. Students Challenging Regulatory Agency Procedures (SCRAP)*.

   b. Personal Injury
      Plaintiff must allege direct injury to himself, not to third parties or abstract interests. An environmental group may not bring a general claim to preserve the environment from some imminent harm unless it alleges personal injury to its members. It cannot bring suit on behalf of an injured environment. See *Sierra Club v. Morton*.

   c. Causation
      The injury alleged must be "fairly traceable" to the agency conduct involved. If the connection between the wrongful conduct and the injury is tenuous or strained, then standing is denied. See *Allen v. Wright*.

   d. Redressability
      The relief sought against the agency must be capable of redressing the injury alleged. If it is purely speculative whether the relief will achieve the desired effect, then the parties will not gain standing. See *Simon v. Eastern Kentucky Welfare Rights Organization*.

2. Zone of Interests
   The zone of interests test requires that the plaintiff's interest be one that Congress was trying to protect through the relevant statute. In *Clarke v. Securities Industry Ass'n.*, the Court weakened the zone of interest test by eliminating the need to show that Congress intended to benefit the plaintiff under the relevant statute. Lower courts have traditionally had trouble

applying the zone of interest test, and while *Clarke* did not overrule it, it is no longer an issue in most cases.

V. TIMING

The concepts of ripeness and exhaustion overlap and are often confused. Generally, exhaustion refers to the extent that a plaintiff has taken advantage of administrative review procedures, while ripeness looks to the substance of an issue to see whether it is ready for review.

A. Ripeness

1. *Abbott* test
   Abbott Laboratories v. Gardner is the leading ripeness case, establishing a two-part analysis that considers the "fitness" of issues for judicial decision and the "hardship" to the parties if review were withdrawn. In determining "fitness", an important factor to be considered is whether the agency's action or decision is final. The finality of agency action is difficult to ascertain, but the courts have ruled that there is a presumption of finality in agency action that is overcome only by specific statutory language to the contrary. See *National Automatic Laundry & Cleaning Council v. Shultz*.

2. Pre-enforcement
   Prior to *Abbott*, agency rules were not reviewable before enforcement action was taken against an offender. The offender could not challenge a regulation or notice promulgated by an agency until it was used in an adjudicatory proceeding. Today, pre-enforcement review is standard.

3. Judicial Stays
   While an agency action is under review, an appellate court may stay the action under APA § 705. A judicial stay may prevent irreparable injury to the petitioner. But the harm can run both ways. If agency enforcement is stayed pending judicial review, serious harm to the public interest may occur in the months or

years it takes to litigate. Courts have discretion to use judicial stays and they can be extremely important in determining the outcome of a case.

B. Exhaustion

1. No Agency Action

The classic exhaustion case is one where plaintiff has not sought an administrative remedy from the appropriate agency at all, choosing to bring suit in court instead. Courts have an interest in forcing plaintiffs to go through administrative channels before permitting them to seek judicial review. Agencies are experts in their fields and courts benefit from their factfinding conclusions. Courts rarely hear a case where agency remedies were not invoked at all or prior to completion of an agency hearing in process. See *Myers v. Bethlehem Shipbuilding Corp.*

2. Interlocutory Review

Exceptions to the exhaustion rule are made on a discretionary basis when there seems to be pressing need to review a case prior to completion of agency actions. Generally these exceptions have occurred in cases where the agency clearly has exceeded its jurisdiction or where only a legal issue is disputed and factfinding expertise is not necessary.

3. Waiver

Courts may waive the exhaustion requirement if a party has failed to exhaust an administrative remedy that is now not available. In this case, exhaustion would be tantamount to preclusion. When judicial review is the only option available to prevent a miscarriage of justice, courts are more likely to waive exhaustion. This is especially true when the litigant is a defendant to criminal charges with no administrative avenues open for appeal. See *McKart v. United States.* If denial of review would be extremely harsh on the litigant, review will be permitted. Otherwise courts prefer not to override agency decisions that were not made in error.

Exception: Plaintiffs bringing civil rights actions under § 1983 are not required to exhaust state agency remedies.

C. Primary Jurisdiction

1. Generally
Primary jurisdiction is not a question concerning timing of judicial review. Rather, it raises the question of who should go first when an agency and the courts have concurrent original jurisdiction.

2. Determinative Factors
Usually an agency has primary jurisdiction, and will hear the case first, when agency jurisdiction stems from a delegated authority, when details beyond the conventional experience of judges are involved, or when uniformity of agency decisions is needed. In *United States v. Western Pacific Railroad*, the Court referred the issue of ratesetting to the Interstate Commerce Commission, which had experience in interpreting the tariff rates in dispute. But in *Nader v. Allegheny Airlines*, the Court decided that the issue did not require factual expertise and was an issue of law within the competence of the courts.

3. Antitrust Cases

a. Defined
Antitrust laws seek to eliminate monopolies and increase competition. Regulatory agencies preserve monopolies but control their activities to simulate the public interest benefits competition might bring about. Antitrust and regulation are two opposing ways of protecting the public from the negative effects of monopolies.

b. Jurisdiction
If industry behavior is protected by regulation, then it is not bound by antitrust laws. When primary jurisdiction is an issue, courts will allow the agency to determine whether the disputed behavior is protected, by statute or agency regulation, from general antitrust laws. If it is protected, the courts only have judicial review powers. If it is not protected, then antitrust laws may be applied in court. Each case

is unique, and interpreting which behavior is protected by regulation is a difficult task.

CASE CLIPS

Commonwealth of Kentucky,
Dept. of Banking and Securities v. Brown (1980) BA

Facts: The Commonwealth was charged with negligence in regulating several loan associations. The government claimed sovereign immunity. The Board of Claims Act waived part of the constitutional immunity granted to the state government. Plaintiff contended, and the lower courts held, that the common law immunity granted to the government was also waived by the Act, leaving the state liable in tort as an individual or corporation.

Issue: When a state government performs a regulatory function negligently, is it protected by constitutional and common law sovereign immunity?

Rule: The Board of Claims Act waives constitutional immunity for state governments, but retains the common law sovereign immunity traditionally granted to local governments in the performance of their general public obligations.

Butz v. Economou (S.Ct. 1978) BA, BS, GB, CD, S, MM

Facts: Plaintiff sued federal agency officials for initiating agency proceedings against him without proper due process. The officials claimed absolute immunity from liability.

Issue: Are federal officials entitled to a higher degree of immunity against constitutional claims than state officials?

Rule: (White, J.) In a suit for damages arising from unconstitutional action, federal executive officials exercising discretion are not absolutely immune from liability. Federal and state officials have only a qualified immunity from damages liability. Only federal officials involved in adjudication are absolutely immune from liability.

Dissent: (Rehnquist, J.) Refusal to give federal officials absolute immunity leaves the courts open to fraudulent constitutional claims that use valuable resources and threaten the autonomy of officials.

Pennsylvania v. Delaware Valley Citizens' Council for Clean Air (S.Ct. 1986) BA

Facts: Under the Clean Air Act, reasonable attorney's fees may be awarded to the winner of a citizen-initiated suit when appropriate.

Issue: Is payment for non-traditional attorney work excluded from the recovery of attorney's fees permitted by statute?

Rule: (White, J.) A fee for work done by counsel outside the context of traditional judicial litigation is eligible for inclusion in an award of reasonable attorney's fees as granted by statute.

Bowen v. Michigan Academy of Family Physicians (S.Ct. 1986) BA

Facts: A rule promulgated under Part B of the Medicare program provided lower payments for a certain group of doctors. They sought judicial review of the regulation, but the government contended that review had been precluded when Congress specified review for Part A and was silent regarding Part B.

Issue: When Congress has not specifically provided for judicial review, may its silence be evidence of intent to preclude review?

Rule: (Stevens, J.) A showing of "clear and convincing evidence" that Congress intended to preclude judicial review is necessary to overcome the strong presumption that agency action is reviewable. Congressional silence in language or legislative history is not clear and convincing evidence.

Heckler v. Chaney (S.Ct. 1985) BA, GB, CD, S, MM

Facts: A prisoner sentenced to death by lethal injection claimed that using the lethal drug to execute him was an unapproved use under food and drug laws. He petitioned the Food and Drug Administration to enforce the rules governing new drug use. The FDA claimed the right to refuse enforcement since no public health threat existed and there was no blatant fraud.

Issue: Is an agency's refusal to take enforcement action a decision subject to judicial review?

Rule: (Rehnquist, J.) An agency's decision not to enforce a rule is a decision committed to agency discretion under the APA § 701(a)(2) and is presumptively unreviewable.

Concurrence: (Marshall, J.) Refusals to enforce, like other agency actions, are reviewable in the absence of "clear and convincing" congressional intent to the contrary. However, these refusals should be given deference when there is no evidence of abuse of discretion.

Association of Data Processing Service Organizations v. Camp (S.Ct. 1970) BA, BS, GB, CD, S, MM

Facts: The Comptroller of the Currency ruled that national banks could offer data processing services to other banks and customers under § 4 of the Bank Services Corporation Act. Petitioners challenged the ruling, which created more competitors for their businesses. The District Court held no standing to sue.

Issue: Does a competitor suffering economic injury in fact have standing to sue?

Rule: (Douglas, J.) To gain standing, a competitor must, as here, suffer injury in fact and fall within the "zone of interests" protected by the statute.

Concurrence: (Brennan, J.) Standing should be granted on the basis of injury in fact alone. The zone of interests test is unnecessary.

Iowa Bankers Assn. v. Iowa Credit Union Dept. (1983) BA

Facts: The Bankers Assn. challenged rules promulgated by the Credit Union Dept. allowing credit unions to perform several functions that would compete with traditional banking functions. The Iowa APA provided judicial review for persons aggrieved by a final agency action.

Issue: Is injury in fact sufficient to gain standing where a state APA intends to provide standing to all injured parties?

Rule: The federal zone of interests test is inapplicable where a state statute demonstrates intent to provide standing for those with a specific, personal and legal interest that has been injured.

Allen v. Wright (S.Ct. 1984) BA

Facts: The parents of black public school children charged the Internal Revenue Service (IRS) with failure to enforce rules denying tax-exempt status to discriminatory private schools. They alleged that tax exemptions for these private schools were taking white students from the public schools and preventing desegregation. The Court of Appeals granted standing.

Issue: What constitutes a sufficient degree of causation between challenged conduct and an alleged injury to grant standing?

Rule: (O'Connor, J.) An alleged injury must be "fairly traceable" to the conduct challenged in order to gain standing. The effectiveness of the remedy sought cannot depend on third parties beyond the court's control, and alleviation of the problem by the remedy must not be purely speculative.

Dissent: (Stevens, J.) The injury alleged is fairly traceable to the government's wrongful conduct. The tax exemptions are cash grants to private schools engaged in discrimination. Taking away the cash grants will lessen their competitiveness with public schools and enrollment will drop. An economically feasible racially segregated alternative to public schools will be denied to parents, resulting in a direct remedy to the aggrieved plaintiffs in the case.

Federal Trade Commission v.Standard
Oil Company of California (S.Ct. 1980) BA, BS, GB, MM

Facts: The Federal Trade Commission served a complaint on Standard Oil averring that the Commission had "reason to believe" the company had violated the Federal Trade Commission Act. Standard Oil sought a declaration in federal district court that the issuance of the complaint was unsubstantiated and illegal.

Issue: Is an agency complaint averring reason to believe a "final agency action" subject to interlocutory review?

Rule: (Powell, J.) An agency statement that it has "reason to believe" a violation occurred is not "final agency action" reviewable prior to conclusion of agency proceedings.

Concurrence: (Stevens, J.) Congress did not intend to authorize any judicial review of decisions to initiate administrative proceedings.

Abbott Laboratories v. Gardner (S.Ct. 1967) BA, BS, GB, MM

Facts: The Commissioner of Food and Drugs, under the Federal Food, Drug, and Cosmetic Act, promulgated a regulation requiring new labelling procedures. Abbott sued to enjoin enforcement of the regulation. The government claimed that pre-enforcement review was impliedly precluded.

Issue: May an agency regulation be ripe for judicial review before it is enforced?

Rule: (Harlan, J.) An agency regulation is ripe for review prior to enforcement if the issues are "fit" for judicial decision-making and there would be "hardship to the parties" absent court review.

Note: This leading case significantly relaxed the requirements for ripeness. Pre-enforcement review of regulations has become the norm, not the exception.

Myers v. Bethlehem Shipbuilding Corp.
(S.Ct. 1938) BA, BS, GB, S

Facts: Bethlehem sought review in federal district court to enjoin the National Labor Relations Board (NLRB) from holding a hearing in response to a complaint about one of its plants. Bethlehem claimed the NLRB had no jurisdiction and the hearing would result in irreparable damage. The District Court granted the injunction.

Issue: Is judicial review available to a party seeking relief from administrative action before that action is completed?

Rule: (Brandeis, J.) Once agency enforcement has begun, a party is not entitled to judicial relief for a supposed or threatened injury until the statutorily prescribed administrative remedy has been exhausted. This rule cannot be circumvented by charging that the complaint is groundless or that the mere holding of a hearing would result in irreparable damage.

New Jersey Civil Service Assn (NJCSA) v. State (1982) BA

Facts: Former Hearing Officers at the Division of Motor Vehicles claimed they had been denied appointment as Administrative Law Judges under the new act creating the Office of Administrative Law. The State Agency Transfer Act entitled agency officers to jobs in a new division if their duties were transferred there. The Attorney General concluded that this Act did not apply to the Hearing Officers. Plaintiffs sought judicial review rather than pursuing their claim with the Civil Service Commission.

Issue: Where the question is purely one of law, does failure to exhaust all administrative remedies bar judicial review?

Rule: In a case involving only legal questions, the doctrine of exhaustion of administrative remedies does not apply.

Note: This rule is specific to New Jersey and differs from the laws of most states and the federal government.

Nader v. Allegheny Airlines (S.Ct. 1976) BA, BS, CD, MM
Facts: Airlines routinely over-booked passengers without notifying them and planned to "bump" extra passengers off a flight if necessary. Ralph Nader was "bumped" from an Allegheny flight and sued for fraudulent misrepresentation of booking practices. The Court of Appeals ordered the District Court to stay judgment pending rulemaking action by the Civil Aeronautics Board.
Issue: Must an agency rule on the issue of fraudulent misrepresentation before a common-law action can be brought?
Rule: (Powell, J.) Where the standards to be applied are within the conventional competence of the courts, prior agency ruling on the issue is not necessary.
Concurrence: (White, J.) It seems unlikely that the agency would rule differently in this case since it has not chosen to issue rules to the contrary.

Foree v. Crown Central Petroleum Corp. (1968) BA
Facts: The Texas Railroad Commission investigated a claim by the owner of an oil field that defendant, a common purchaser of oil, had discriminated against him by refusing to run a pipeline to his field. Another pipeline became available before the Commission reached a conclusion, and the point became moot. Plaintiff brought suit under the governing statute providing a cause of action for damages against a common purchaser who discriminates. The trial court dismissed on the basis of primary jurisdiction.
Issue: Where an agency and a court have concurrent jurisdiction and an issue becomes moot, does the agency have primary jurisdiction?
Rule: An agency has the power to conduct hearings only when it acts pursuant to its statutory power. When an issue becomes moot, the agency no longer has statutory power and cannot have exclusive primary jurisdiction.

Dalehite v. United States (S.Ct. 1953) BS
Facts: Injured by an exploding package of fertilizer, plaintiffs charged the government with negligence in manufacturing and packaging the fertilizer. The federal government claimed immunity under the exceptions to the Federal Tort Claims Act (FTCA).

Issue: Does the "discretionary function" exemption in § 2680(a) of the FTCA extend to actions of subordinates?

Rule: (Reed, J.) Discretionary acts in the performance of government functions, including policy-making and implementation by subordinate federal officials, are exempt from liability by the FTCA.

Dissent: (Jackson, J.) When the government acts as a private enterprise, such as a landowner, manufacturer, or shipper, it should not be exempt from the liabilities that are imposed on private individuals.

Barr v. Matteo (S.Ct. 1959) BS, CD, S, MM

Facts: Matteo was suspended from an executive agency by his boss, Barr. Barr issued a press release denouncing Matteo. Matteo alleged malice and sued for defamation.

Issue: Are all executive officers absolutely immune from civil suits, or does official immunity apply only to Cabinet-level officials?

Rule: (Harlan, J.) All federal employees are absolutely immune from common law tort liability for acts performed "within the outer perimeter" of their line of duty.

Concurrence: (Black, J.) If federal employees are subjected to restraints, the restraints must be expressly imposed by Congress and not by common law.

Dissent: (Warren, C.J.) One should have the opportunity to criticize the government and the actions of its officials without being subjected to unfair retorts.

Dissent: (Brennan, J.) Only a qualified privilege is necessary to protect government officials. If the official's actions are defamatory, untrue, and malicious, then immunity should not apply.

Dissent: (Stewart, J.) Petitioner's actions were not within "the outer perimeter of [his] line of duty."

Harlow v. Fitzgerald (S.Ct. 1982) BS, CD

Facts: After his discharge from the Defense Department, Fitzgerald sued President Nixon and his assistants on charges of conspiracy to violate his constitutional and statutory rights. Nixon's assistants could only claim a "qualified immunity."

Issue: When qualified or "good faith" immunity is offered as an affirmative defense by a government official, must "good faith" be measured by subjective or objective standards?

Rule: (Powell, J.) Government officials performing discretionary functions are shielded from liability for civil damages as long as their conduct does not violate clearly established statutory or constitutional rights of which a reasonable person would have known.

American School of Magnetic Healing
v. McAnnulty (S.Ct. 1902) BS

Facts: The Postmaster General believed that the plaintiff's mail-order business was fraudulent and ordered all mail returned to sender. Plaintiff's business was not forbidden by statute, so the Postmaster General's action was mistaken.

Issue: If a government officer acts beyond the scope of statutory authority, is the action subject to judicial review?

Rule: (Peckham, J.) Judicial relief is available where a party is injured by a government officer acting beyond his express or implied powers.

Switchmen's Union v. National Mediation Board (S.Ct. 1943) BS

Facts: Two unions disagreed over who should participate in elections for union representatives. The National Mediation Board, following the Railway Labor Act, ruled against the Switchmen's Union, which brought suit in federal district court to have the Board's decision canceled. The lower courts affirmed the Board ruling.

Issue: Can judicial review be precluded when the governing statute does not expressly authorize or prohibit it?

Rule: (Douglas, J.) Where a statute shows evidence of intent to make an agency's rulings final, then judicial review may be deemed precluded.

Note: The expansive view of judicial review expressed in *McAnnulty*, above, has prevailed, and silence regarding review is not generally interpreted to preclude it.

Harmon v. Brucker (S.Ct. 1958) BS

Facts: The Secretary of the Army gave petitioners a less than honorable discharge from military service, basing his decision on factors other than their military records. Petitioners sued, charging that the Secretary had exceeded his powers. The District Court held that it lacked jurisdiction to review the decision.

Issue: If a statute declares agency decisions to be final, may a court review the decision to determine whether the administrator exceeded his powers?

Rule: (Per Curiam) Administrative decisions are judicially reviewable to determine whether the administrator acted within statutorily prescribed limits, even if the governing statute declares agency decisions final.

Dissent: (Clark, J.) Where a statute specifically describes an agency decision as final, then Congress intended no judicial review.

Johnson v. Robison (S.Ct. 1974) BS, GB, MM

Facts: Conscientious objectors who completed alternative service were denied educational benefits by the Veterans' Administration (VA). The relevant statutes made the VA the final arbitrator and precluded judicial review. Plaintiff sued for benefits on constitutional grounds.

Issue: Does a statute that precludes judicial review preclude review of constitutional issues?

Rule: (Brennan, J.) A statute which precludes judicial review of agency decisions does not preclude challenging a question of law arising under the Constitution rather than the statute.

Panama Canal Co. v. Grace Line, Inc. (S.Ct. 1958) BS

Facts: Shipping companies sued the Panama Canal Co. for overcharging on tolls by misapplying the ratesetting formula set by statute.

Issue: Is judicial review available for issues left to agency discretion by statute?

Rule: (Douglas, J.) Where an issue is unclear and experts might reasonably disagree over the proper outcome, agency action involving informed discretion is not reviewable.

United States ex rel. Schonbrun v. Commanding Officer (1968) BS

Facts: Schonbrun, a reservist, sought exemption from active duty based on "extreme personal hardship." When his request was denied, he sought a writ of habeas corpus.

Issue: May a reservist seeking to avoid active duty receive judicial review of an exemption denial?

Rule: Exemptions from military service are granted on a discretionary basis and are not subject to judicial review.

Hahn v. Gottlieb (1970) BS
Facts: The Federal Housing Authority (FHA) approved rent increases for landlords renting out publicly financed housing. Plaintiffs sought judicial review of the rent increase. The National Housing Act did not explicitly bar judicial review, but the FHA claimed its decision was "committed to agency discretion" and non-reviewable.
Issue: Under what circumstances will clear and convincing evidence exist that Congress intended an issue to be "committed to agency discretion"?
Rule: Where the text of a statute does not provide clear and convincing evidence that Congress intended to preclude review, courts will use three factors to determine preclusion: 1) whether the issue is appropriate for review by courts, 2) whether judicial supervision is needed to protect plaintiff's rights, and 3) whether review will significantly affect agency efficiency.

Langevin v. Chenango Court, Inc. (1971) BS
Facts: The Federal Housing Authority (FHA) must approve rent increases by landlords renting low-income housing. Plaintiffs claimed the FHA abused its discretion by allowing rent increases on their apartments. The FHA contended that its actions were "committed to agency action" by statute and non-reviewable.
Issue: Are charges of abuse of discretion sufficient to gain review of agency actions "committed to agency discretion" by law?
Rule: A mere claim of abuse is not enough to overcome the "committed to agency discretion" exemption from judicial review.

Alabama Power Co. v. Ickes (S.Ct. 1938) BS
Facts: Alabama Power, a private company, contended that federal grants to municipal power companies under a federal public works program were illegal. Plaintiff claimed standing to sue based on either federal taxpayer status or direct injury from the agency action.
Issue 1: Is injury in fact sufficient grounds to obtain federal standing?
Rule 1: (Sutherland, J.) To obtain federal standing, a plaintiff must suffer a direct injury caused by the violation of a legally protected right.
Issue 2: Is taxpayer status sufficient to obtain federal standing?

Rule 2: A taxpayer's interest in the spending of money from the federal treasury does not confer the personal stake necessary for standing to sue.

The Chicago Junction Case (S.Ct. 1924) BS
Facts: The Transportation Act of 1920 required the Interstate Commerce Commission (ICC) to approve railroad consolidations to ensure that the "public interest" was served. The ICC approved a consolidation giving New York Central a disproportionate share of rail traffic through Chicago. Six competitors filed suit, but the District Court denied standing.
Issue: Where a statutory scheme gives a private business an unfair advantage over its competitors, do the disadvantaged parties have standing to obtain judicial review?
Rule: (Brandeis, J.) When a statutory scheme denies fair treatment to some private parties, those injured by the scheme have a special legal interest in obtaining judicial review.
Dissent: (Sutherland, J.) The Transportation Act concerns the "public interest" and does not create a right of action for private competitors who are economically injured.

FCC v. Sanders Brothers Radio Station (S.Ct. 1940) BS
Facts: Sanders Brothers objected to the Federal Communications Commission's licensing of a new station in its area. The Federal Communications Act provided for review of FCC actions at the request of any "person aggrieved or whose interests are adversely affected by any decision of the Commission" regarding license applications.
Issue: Where a statute grants judicial review to aggrieved persons, is economic injury a sufficient legal interest to gain standing?
Rule: (Roberts, J.)   Although economic injury is generally not sufficient to obtain standing, Congress has the power to confer such standing through statutes.

Sierra Club v. Morton (S.Ct. 1972) BS, MM
Facts: Sierra Club alleged that a proposed highway would destroy the natural beauty of the Sequoia National Park and impair enjoyment of the park by future generations.

Issue: May an organization gain standing by demonstrating an organizational interest in a problem without showing direct personal injury?

Rule: (Stewart, J.) To ensure that parties seeking review have a direct stake in the outcome, members of an organization must suffer direct injury in fact from the contested action to gain standing.

Dissent: (Douglas, J.) The community of those permitted standing should be broadened to include soil, water, plants, animals, and the collective land. The voice of the inanimate object should not be stilled.

Dissent: (Blackmun, J.) The Sierra Club should be granted standing and permitted to amend its complaint to include members. Furthermore, standing should be granted to organizations based on proven dedication and interest in a subject area, such as the environment.

Simon v. Eastern Kentucky Welfare
Rights Organization (S.Ct. 1976) BS, GB, CD, MM

Facts: The Internal Revenue Service issued a new regulation permitting tax-exempt hospitals to refuse non-emergency service to indigents. The Eastern Kentucky Welfare Rights Organization claimed the regulation encouraged hospitals to refuse indigents, violating the tax exempt status provisions. The lower courts upheld standing.

Issue: Does Article III of the Constitution require a showing of redressable injury to gain standing?

Rule: (Powell, J.) To gain standing, citizens must show a personal injury that is fairly traceable to the defendant's actions and likely to be redressed by a favorable decision.

Concurrence: (Stewart, J.) A person whose own tax liability is not affected cannot have standing to litigate the federal tax liability of someone else.

Concurrence: (Brennan, J. and Marshall, J.) The majority is correct in the judgment but on grounds of ripeness, not standing. Respondents made a sufficient showing of injury in fact to gain standing.

Duke Power Co. v. North Carolina
Environmental Group, Inc. (S.Ct. 1978) BS, GB

Facts: Duke Power was licensed by the Atomic Energy Commission to build a nuclear power plant in North Carolina. The Price-Anderson Act limited the liability for a nuclear accident to $560 million. Two groups of individuals living near the proposed site challenged the constitutionality of the Price-Anderson Act, claiming that the liability cap made the building of the plant economically feasible. Duke Power contended the plaintiffs had no standing.

Issue: Must a plaintiff show injury in fact and a causal relationship between injury and conduct in order to obtain standing?

Rule: (Burger, C.J.) To obtain standing a plaintiff must show a "distinct and palpable" injury and a "fairly traceable" causal connection between the injury and the conduct. The prudential concerns underlying the standing doctrine are generally met when the constitutional requirements are satisfied.

Concurrence: (Stewart, J.) Apart from a loose "but for" causation, there is no relationship at all between the injury alleged for standing purposes and the plaintiff's federal claim.

Concurrence: (Rehnquist, J.) No actual controversy has been made out against the Commission. Where the actions of a third party determine prospects for relief against a defendant, no justiciable controversy exists.

Concurrence: (Stevens, J.) This series of speculations is insufficient to establish standing.

Columbia Broadcasting System, Inc.
v. United States (S.Ct. 1942) BS

Facts: The Federal Communications Commission (FCC) promulgated "Chain Broadcasting Regulations" prohibiting network affiliation contracts with stations agreeing to carry one network exclusively. CBS had over one hundred such contracts with local radio stations. CBS sought immediate judicial review under § 402(a) of the Federal Communications Act, permitting review of FCC "orders." The District Court denied jurisdiction.

Issue: Are agency regulations ripe for review as "orders" prior to adjudicatory proceedings?

Rule: (Stone, C.J.) Regulations that penalize for non-compliance, and therefore alter behavior, are ripe for review as "orders" even before enforcement takes place.

Dissent: (Frankfurter, J.) This type of agency regulation has no more enforcement power than a press release and is not ripe for review until administrative adjudication is complete.

National Automatic Laundry and
Cleaning Council v. Shultz (1971) BS, GB

Facts: Amendments to the Fair Labor Standards Act changed the wage requirements for laundry establishments. The trade association applied to the Federal Wage and Hour Administration for an informal advisory opinion on the interpretation of the new law. They disagreed with the Administrator's conclusions of law and sought judicial review.

Issue: Are informal agency actions, such as advisory opinions, considered "final actions" of an agency and ripe for review?

Rule: The ruling of a board, commission, or head of agency is presumptively final for purposes of establishing ripeness for review. Only if it indicates on its face that it is tentative will it be considered inappropriate for judicial review.

McKart v. United States (S.Ct. 1969) BS, MM

Facts: When the Selective Service reclassified McKart as eligible for military service, he failed to attend the reclassification hearing provided. Since he did not report for induction, he was convicted. The government claimed judicial review was barred since he had not exhausted administrative remedies.

Issue: Does failure to exhaust all administrative remedies bar judicial review when proper resolution of the issue might prevent a criminal conviction?

Rule: (Marshall, J.) The exhaustion requirement is waived where agency expertise and discretion are not necessary to resolve an issue and the government's interest in requiring exhaustion does not outweigh the severe burden on the petitioner caused by barring judicial review. Eliminating a defense to a criminal conviction would create a severe burden on the petitioner.

United States v. Western Pacific Railroad Co.
(S.Ct. 1956) BS, GB, S

Facts: Western Pacific brought suit in the Court of Claims to recover transportation fees from the Army for shipments of napalm. The railroad contended that the higher "incendiary bomb" rate could be charged. The government asked for the question of interpretation of rates to be sent to the Interstate Commerce Commission for resolution.

Issue: When may a claim brought in court be referred to an agency for resolution of specific issues?

Rule: (Harlan, J.) An agency may have primary jurisdiction over certain issues when uniformity is necessary and the agency has "expert and specialized knowledge" of the issues.

Far East Conference v. United States (S.Ct. 1952) BS, GB, S

Facts: An association of steamship companies agreed to a two-tier ratesetting system, giving discounts to customers who agreed to use the association's ships exclusively. The government alleged violations of the Sherman Antitrust Act and brought suit in federal district court. The Far East Conference claimed the matter had to be addressed first by the Federal Maritime Board before judicial action.

Issue: Does an agency have primary jurisdiction when the subject matter of a case requires administrative expertise?

Rule: (Frankfurter, J.) Cases that raise facts not within the traditional experience of judges or that require administrative discretion should pass through the appropriate agencies before reaching the courts.

Dissent: (Douglas, J.) The defendants did not seek approval of their rate system from the Federal Maritime Board as required by Congress. The association is not exempt from the Sherman Act, and the courts have jurisdiction to decide Sherman antitrust questions.

Ricci v. Chicago Mercantile Exchange (S.Ct. 1973) BS, S

Facts: Ricci tried to buy a seat on the Exchange with money borrowed from Siegel Trading Co. Siegel allegedly transferred the seat to someone else over Ricci's objection. Ricci charged Siegel and the Exchange with conspiracy to deny him a seat. The Court of Appeals stayed the action, claiming that the Commodities Exchange

Commission had primary jurisdiction to determine whether the action violated antitrust laws.

Issue: When conduct that is seemingly within the reach of antitrust laws is also arguably protected by a regulatory statute, does the governing agency have primary jurisdiction to determine the scope of the statute's protection?

Rule: (White, J.) A regulatory statute may exempt certain conduct from antitrust laws, thus denying a cause of action. Primary jurisdiction may be granted to an administrative agency to decide whether the statute covers that conduct.

Dissent: (Douglas, J.) Through its inaction, the agency has expressed its opinion that this conduct is legal. By remanding the case to the agency, the regulators must admit that they have been negligent for plaintiff to prevail.

Dissent: (Marshall, J.) Courts should retain primary jurisdiction where the plaintiff has no means of invoking agency jurisdiction, where the agency rules do not guarantee the plaintiff a means of participation in the administrative proceedings, or where the likelihood of a meaningful agency input into the judicial process is remote.

Block v. Community Nutrition Institute (S.Ct. 1984) GB, S

Facts: Under the Agricultural Marketing Agreement Act of 1937, the Secretary of Agriculture could issue milk-market orders to fix minimum prices that handlers must pay to producers. Consumers contended that the Act made certain types of milk prohibitively expensive and sought judicial review under APA § 701. Since review was not expressly precluded, defendant claimed implied preclusion.

Issue: Does statutory specification that certain groups may seek judicial review constitute "clear and convincing evidence" of congressional intent to preclude review by others?

Rule: (O'Connor, J.) When a statute specifically provides for judicial review at the behest of particular individuals, review by other individuals may be found to be impliedly precluded. The "clear and convincing evidence" standard does not require unambiguous proof in the traditional evidentiary sense, but rather "fairly discernable" congressional intent to preclude review.

Associated Industries of New York State, Inc. v. Ickes
(1943) GB

Facts: The Bituminous Coal Act permitted "any person aggrieved by an order issued by the [Bituminous Coal Division] Commission" to seek judicial review. Associated Industries sought review of the Commission's order fixing minimum prices for coal. Respondents contended that consumers could not be "aggrieved persons" with standing to sue.

Issue: May Congress confer standing to sue on individuals who have no direct legal interest in challenging administrative rulings?

Rule: Ordinarily, a citizen suing a government official must first show that some "substantive legally protected interest" has been violated by the official. However, Congress may confer standing by statute, permitting any "person aggrieved" to vindicate the public interest by suing an officer acting in violation of his statutory powers.

Barlow v. Collins (S.Ct. 1970) GB, MM

Facts: A regulation promulgated by the Secretary of Agriculture permitted landlords to hike the rents of tenant farmers. The farmers sued, charging economic injury due to the regulation. The District Court denied standing based on lack of a legally protected interest.

Issue: Is injury in fact from an administrative regulation sufficient to gain standing to sue?

Rule: (Douglas, J.) A party has standing to sue an administrative agency if he is injured in fact, satisfying the Article III requirement, and if the interest at stake is within the "zone of interests" protected by the statute.

Concurrence: (Brennan, J.) The two-pronged standing test in the majority opinion incorrectly addresses the question of reviewability as well as standing. The first question regarding injury in fact is sufficient for standing; the question regarding "zone of interests" is confusing and unnecessary.

Control Data Corporation v. Baldridge (1981) GB

Facts: The Secretary of Commerce promulgated standards for the manufacture of automatic data processing equipment (ADP) under the Brooks Act. The Act was designed to lower government costs by promoting competition. Plaintiffs could not meet the new standards without substantial economic loss, but IBM already met the standards. Plaintiffs were IBM's only competition.

Issue: Does the interest of the competitors fall within the zone of interests contemplated by the statute?

Rule: Where a statute is designed to benefit the government, it may not be interpreted to protect the interests of competing manufacturers and create standing.

United States v. Students Challenging Regulatory Agency Procedures (SCRAP) (S.Ct. 1973) GB, S

Facts: The nation's railroads petitioned the Interstate Commerce Commission for a rate increase. SCRAP, a group of students attempting to preserve the environment, contended that the rate hike would discourage recycling and ruin the beautiful parks they enjoyed. They sued to enjoin the increase.

Issue: Does a party have standing if the injury in fact is destruction of aesthetics in the environment?

Rule: (Stewart, J.) A party has standing if he can prove a specific injury to himself, aesthetic, economic, or otherwise, though he need not be the only one suffering from the injury.

Concurrence: (Blackmun, J.) Plaintiffs, as concerned representatives of environmental interests, should not have to show individual and personal injury, only irreparable and substantial injury in fact to the environment.

Dissent: (White, J.) The alleged injuries are too remote to confer standing.

Dissent: (Douglas, J.) The appellees should not have to show individual injury to have standing. The majority is incorrect in its interpretation that the Interstate Commerce Act barred injunctive relief.

Toilet Goods Association v. Gardner (S.Ct. 1967) GB, MM

Facts: The Commissioner of the Food and Drug Administration (FDA) promulgated a regulation giving the FDA free access to inspect all facilities for manufacturing color additives. Toilet Goods sought declaratory and injunctive relief.

Issue: If a case would be reviewed better after the implementation of an agency policy, is it ripe for judicial review prior to enforcement?

Rule: (Harlan, J.)   A regulation is not ripe for review if a court would be able to review the case better after agency policy is implemented and arguments on both sides are more concrete.

Concurrence: (Fortas, J.)   Judicial review of administrative regulations is most effective when based on concrete fact situations.

Larson v. Domestic & Foreign Commerce Corp.
(S.Ct. 1949) GB

Facts: The government entered into a contract to sell surplus coal to plaintiff and later canceled to sell to another party.   Plaintiff sued to enjoin the War Assets Administrator from selling the coal to anyone else.   The District Court dismissed the suit, claiming the United States was an indispensable party unreachable because of sovereign immunity.

Issue: May suit be brought against a government officer for tortious conduct without seeking relief against the sovereign?

Rule: (Vinson, C.J.)   A suit addressed to a government officer does in fact seek relief against the sovereign, since the sovereign can only act through its officers.   Absent consent, a court has no jurisdiction over the government unless the officer's actions are unconstitutional or beyond his statutorily delegated powers.

United States v. S.A. Empresa de Viacao Aerea
Rio Grandense (Varig Airlines), et al. (S.Ct. 1984) GB, CD, MM

Facts: An airplane owned by plaintiff caught fire after it was certified as airworthy by the Federal Aviation Administration.   Varig sued the agency for negligence.   The Federal Torts Claims Act exempted discretionary agency actions from liability.

Issue: Is an agency's method of carrying out its regulatory duties a discretionary agency action immune from tort liability?

Rule: (Burger, C.J.)   When an agency carries out its regulatory duties, its actions are clearly discretionary acts of the "nature and quality" Congress intended to exempt from liability under the Federal Torts Claims Act.

Gott v. Walters (1985) CD

Facts: The Veterans' Administration Act specifically precludes judicial review of "decisions of the Administrator. . . under any law administered by the Veterans' Administration [VA]."   Veterans seeking benefits challenged a VA ruling on compensation for injuries due to radiation exposure, charging violation of the APA rulemaking requirements.

Issue: Do statutes that preclude review of administrative "decisions" apply to agency rules as well as adjudications?

Rule: Statutes precluding judicial review of claims adjudications also preclude review of agency rules applicable in those adjudications.

Environmental Defense Fund v. Hardin (1970) CD, MM

Facts: The Environmental Defense Fund (EDF) sought suspension of registration for all poisons containing DDT, based on evidence of harmful effects of the pesticide on human and animal life. The Secretary of Agriculture took no action on this requested interim relief but began proceedings for permanent relief. The EDF filed an appeal to compel the Secretary to provide the interim relief requested. The Secretary asserted that his failure to act was not reviewable.

Issue: Does administrative inaction qualify as a final administrative order suitable for judicial review?

Rule: When inaction has the same effect on the rights of the parties as denial of relief, an agency cannot preclude judicial review by choosing not to act rather than issuing an order denying relief.

Environmental Defense Fund v. Ruckelshaus (1971) CD, MM

Facts: After making findings on the pesticide DDT, the Secretary of Agriculture refused to suspend its registration or to begin the formal procedures used to terminate registration. The Environmental Defense Fund (EDF) sought judicial review of the order refusing interim relief.

Issue: Where an agency uses discretion in withholding interim relief, are any aspects of the decision reviewable?

Rule: Where an agency's findings meet the statutory requirement for initiating formal agency action, a court may review the findings and direct the agency to begin the administrative process requested. Courts will defer to the agency's fact findings, but will ensure that the standards used to make decisions conform to the legislative purpose and are uniformly applied.

Nor-Am Agricultural Products, Inc. v. Hardin (1970) CD

Facts: The Secretary of Agriculture suspended the registration of certain "economic poisons" after an accident involving ingestion. Nor-Am was granted expedited administrative hearings on the case, but chose to seek a preliminary injunction in court prior to the hearings. Defendants tried to dismiss for failure to exhaust administrative remedies. The preliminary injunction was granted and the Secretary appealed.

Issue: Is an agency's grant of interim relief reviewable prior to exhaustion of administrative remedies?

Rule: A grant of interim relief is not reviewable since it is not final action until the formal administrative procedures are completed.

United States v. Mendoza (S.Ct. 1984) CD

Facts: Respondent filed a petition for naturalization under the Nationality Act of 1942, which made non-citizens who fought for the U.S. in World War II exempt from some requirements for naturalization. Filipino servicemen aiding the United States in the Philippines were denied this privilege because of objections from the Philippine government. Mendoza claimed he was denied due process of law. The government lost a prior case on the same issue against sixty-eight Filipino war veterans. The District Court granted Mendoza's petition on grounds that the government could not re-litigate an issue it had lost previously.

Issue: May the government re-litigate an issue it lost in a prior suit with different litigants?

Rule: (Rehnquist, J.) Non-mutual offensive collateral estoppel does not apply against the government to preclude the re-litigation of issues.

Note: Policy considerations and sheer volume of government cases justify a different standard for the government than for individuals regarding collateral estoppel.

Moog Industries, Inc. v. Federal Trade Commission (S.Ct. 1958) CD

Facts: The Federal Trade Commission ordered Moog to cease and desist in various price discrimination practices that violated the Clayton Act. Moog sought postponement of the order, claiming it would put the company out of business since its competitors would not be similarly restrained. The lower courts affirmed the order.

Issue: May a reviewing court modify a valid administrative order absent abuse of discretion?

Rule: (Per Curiam) An agency decision to take action against one party but not others is reviewable only for abuse of discretion. Agencies have special competence to develop enforcement policies best calculated to achieve the ends contemplated by Congress and to allocate their available funds and personnel in the manner they deem most efficient.

Federal Trade Commission v.
Universal-Rundle Corp. (S.Ct. 1967) CD

Facts: The Federal Trade Commission ordered Universal-Rundle to cease and desist various price discrimination practices that violated the Clayton Act. Universal-Rundle petitioned to stay the order until its competitors could be similarly restrained. The lower courts stayed the order, claiming it would be contrary to the Act's purpose to put a small company out of business for practices common to the industry giants.

Issue: May a reviewing court modify a valid administrative order absent abuse of discretion?

Rule: (Warren, C.J.) The rule in *Moog Industries* stands: a reviewing court may not modify a valid administrative order absent a patent abuse of discretion.

Dunlop v. Bachowski (S.Ct. 1975) CD, MM

Facts: See *Bachowski v. Brennan* below.

Issue: Is an agency's decision not to prosecute a violation subject to judicial review?

Rule: (Brennan, J.) A decision not to enforce is not committed to agency discretion, but is reviewable under the arbitrary and capricious standard.

Concurrence: (Burger, C.J.) The permissible scope of review for agency refusal to act should be extremely narrow.

Dissent in part: (Rehnquist, J.) Previous cases in this Court have decided that agency decisions not to act are committed to agency discretion under the APA and are not reviewable.

J.I. Case Co. v. Borak (S.Ct. 1964) CD, MM

Facts: Borak, a stockholder in Case Co., brought suit charging Case with deprivation of preemptive rights by reason of a merger. Borak alleged that the merger was effected by circulating a false and misleading proxy statement, a violation of the Securities Exchange Act § 14(a). The Act conferred jurisdiction on federal courts for all actions brought to enforce any liability or duty created under the Act. Case Co. contended that no private right of action existed since Congress did not specifically provide for one.

Issue: Where a statute has the broad remedial purpose of protecting individual investors, but makes no specific reference to a private right of action, may a right of action be implied?

Rule: (Clark, J.) When Congress intends to protect individuals from certain misconduct, the availability of judicial relief to ensure that protection can be implied.

Ash v. Cort (1974) CD

Facts: Under 18 U.S.C. § 610, corporations were prohibited from contributing money to presidential and vice-presidential elections. Ash, a corporate stockholder, tried to enforce this criminal statute against the corporate directors. Cort contended that no private cause of action existed to enforce the statute.

Issue: Where a federal, criminal statute does not provide a private cause of action and the relationship between plaintiff and defendant is generally governed by state law, may a federal private cause of action be implied?

Rule: A private cause of action may be implied where the plaintiff is a member of the class that the statute was designed to benefit and where the remedy sought is appropriate for the statute's purposes.

Cort v. Ash (S.Ct. 1975) MM

Facts: See *Ash v. Cort* above. The Court of Appeals held that respondent had a private cause of action as a stockholder.

Issue: Where a federal criminal statute does not provide a private cause of action and the relationship between plaintiff and defendant is generally governed by state law, may a federal private cause of action be implied?

Rule: (Brennan, J.) A federal private cause of action is usually implied when there is a clearly articulated federal right in favor of the plaintiff, a pervasive legislative scheme governing the relationship between plaintiff class and the defendant, an underlying purpose in the statute consistent with an implied right, or an area of the law not traditionally left to states where federal action would not be inappropriate.

Note: Since *Cort*, few Court cases have implied federal private causes of action under statutes that do not expressly provide a remedy.

Silkwood v. Kerr-McGee Corp. (S.Ct. 1984) CD

Facts: Silkwood was contaminated with plutonium while working at Kerr-McGee's Cimarron nuclear plant. Many of her personal belongings had to be destroyed due to the high level of contamination at her apartment. Kerr-McGee denied allegations that it violated safety regulations set by the Nuclear Regulatory Commission, claiming Silkwood intentionally contaminated herself to embarrass the company. The day she returned to work following contamination tests at the Los Alamos Laboratory, she was killed in a car accident. Her estate sued for personal and punitive damages under state law. Kerr-McGee contended that punitive damages were preempted by federal regulation.

Issue: Where federal statutes regulate an industry, is state tort law preempted?

Rule: (White, J.) State law is preempted if Congress intends to occupy a given field or if Congress occupies part of a field, making it impossible to comply with both federal and state law without compromising congressional purposes.

Dissent: (Blackmun, J.) Punitive, but not compensatory, damages are preempted because federal law seeks to regulate safety but not to compensate victims.

Dissent: (Powell, J.) The jury system is operating here as an unauthorized regulatory medium by awarding punitive damages where no malicious or grossly negligent conduct has been proven.

Paul v. Davis (S.Ct. 1976) CD

Facts: Davis was identified in a police flyer as an "active shoplifter" though he had never been convicted of shoplifting. After his boss confronted him regarding the flyer, Davis brought an action against the police department under 42 U.S.C. § 1983 seeking relief for a violation of his constitutional rights. The District Court dismissed the action on grounds that defamation by the police did not deprive Davis of a constitutional right.

Issue: Under § 1983, are wrongs actionable if inflicted by government employees and previously subject only to state-law tort claims?

Rule: (Rehnquist, J.)   Government officers are not liable for constitutional wrongs, such as defamation, except under state tort law. A body of general federal tort law may not be derived from congressional civil rights statutes.

<h3 style="text-align:center">Bivens v. Six Unknown Named Agents
of the Federal Bureau of Narcotics
(S.Ct. 1971) CD, MM</h3>

Facts: Federal narcotics agents entered the plaintiff's home without reasonable cause or a warrant and arrested him in front of his family, causing damage to the home and emotional suffering.   Plaintiff brought federal charges against the officers based on a violation of the Fourth Amendment right to be free from unreasonable search and seizure.   The lower court dismissed on the grounds that no federal cause of action existed.

Issue: Does the violation of a constitutional right by federal agents provide a cause of action for damages against the agents?

Rule: (Brennan, J.) Where federally protected rights are invaded by government officers, individuals have a cause of action against the officers, and the courts may impose any available remedy, including money damages.

Concurrence: (Harlan, J.) That an interest is constitutionally rather than statutorily protected does not deprive the federal courts of the power to grant damages without express congressional approval. The government's claim that congressional approval is needed is at cross-purposes with the Bill of Rights, which is designed to protect the rights of the individual from the popular will.

Dissent: (Burger, C.J.) Congress should develop an administrative remedy against the government to compensate persons whose Fourth Amendment rights have been violated. A judicially created damage remedy violates separation of powers.

Dissent: (Black, J.) Congress has created a federal cause of action against state officials acting under state law, but declined to create a similar cause of action against federal officials who violate constitutional rights. For this court to do so violates the Constitution. The business of the judiciary is to interpret laws, not make them.

Carlson v. Green (S.Ct. 1980) CD

Facts: Respondent brought suit against federal prison officials on behalf of her son, who died when the officials intentionally withheld proper medical care while he was in prison. Respondent seeks relief against the United States under the Federal Tort Claims Act (FTCA), and against the officers, under the Constitution.

Issue: Is a constitutional claim against a federal officer barred by the FTCA?

Rule: (Brennan, J.) Unless the defendants can show that Congress intended an alternative remedy to replace constitutional claims or that "special factors counsel hesitation," victims of any constitutional violation by a federal agent may recover damages against the agent in federal court. Since Congress is explicit when it intends the FTCA to be an exclusive remedy, that Act does not bar a *Bivens* claim.

Concurrence: (Powell, J.) The majority imposes unnecessarily rigid conditions for the defendant by requiring a showing that Congress intended an alternative remedy to be a substitute for recovery under the Constitution.

Dissent: (Burger, C.J.) The Federal Tort Claims Act provides adequate remedy for victims. The majority's expansion of the *Bivens* doctrine is unwarranted.

Dissent: (Rehnquist, J.) The majority expands Bivens by adding to the list of constitutional amendments from which civil damage remedies may be inferred. This expansion infringes on the legislative domain by creating damage remedies.

Stark v. Wickard (S.Ct. 1944) S

Facts: Milk producers filed a class action suit, charging that the Secretary of Agriculture acted beyond his statutory power by issuing an order setting minimum prices on milk sold by producers to handlers. The governing statute created a right for the producers to avail themselves of minimum price protection but did not specifically provide for judicial review of administrative orders.

Issue: When Congress is silent regarding the availability of judicial review, may review be impliedly precluded?

Rule: (Reed, J.) Where definite personal rights have been created by federal statute, congressional silence is not to be construed as denial of review.

Shaughnessy v. Pedreiro (S.Ct. 1955) S

Facts: The Attorney General ordered Pedreiro, an alien, deported under the Immigration and Nationality Act of 1952. The Act provided that deportation orders of the Attorney General were "final." The Court of Appeals held that "final" meant only that no further agency action would be taken and decided that APA § 10 conferred judicial review.

Issue: When interpretation of a statutory term determines preclusion of review, should it be interpreted narrowly?

Rule: (Black, J.) Where a statute contains provisions that appear to restrict judicial review, these provisions should be interpreted narrowly, consistent with the APA intent to make judicial review more available generally.

Ortwein v. Schwab (S.Ct. 1973) S

Facts: Appellant Ortwein sustained a reduction in welfare benefits and appealed to the Public Welfare Division. After a hearing, the agency decided against Ortwein. State law authorized judicial review of the decision, but Ortwein could not afford the state's twenty-five dollar appellate court filing fee.

Issue: Must a court fee be waived for indigents to provide access to statutorily granted judicial review?

Rule: (Per Curiam) Appellate court fees do not violate due process for the indigent, since states are not required to provide appellate systems even for criminal cases.

Dissent: (Douglas, J.) Judicial review of agency action is not appellate in nature. Rather, it is initial access to the courts that, if denied, violates due process.

Dissent: (Marshall, J.) It is extremely doubtful that due process permits states to shield administrative agencies from all judicial review.

Lindahl v. OPM (S.Ct. 1985) S

Facts: The Office of Personnel Management denied Lindahl disability benefits. After administrative review by the Merit Systems Protection Board failed, he sought judicial review. The lower court held the review to be barred, relying on statutory language that determinations "concerning these matters are final and conclusive and are not subject to review."

Issue: Is statutory language that seems to absolutely preclude judicial review clear and convincing evidence that all review is to be denied?

Rule: (Brennan, J.) Agency decisions absolutely precluded from judicial review by statute may nonetheless be reviewed, except for factual determinations, if the statutory scheme and objectives permit a more limited reading of the preclusion language.

Clarke v. Securities Industry Assn. (S.Ct. 1987) S, MM

Facts: The Securities Industry Assn. brought suit in federal district court challenging the Comptroller's decision, under the McFadden Act, to permit Security Pacific National Bank to engage in discount brokerage services. The Comptroller contended that the Association did not have standing because it was not within the "zone of interests" protected by the McFadden Act.

Issue: Must Congress have intended to benefit a class of plaintiffs for them to be within the "zone of interests" required for standing?

Rule: (White, J.) To confer standing on a class of plaintiffs, the "zone of interests" test requires congressional intent to rely upon that class of plaintiffs to challenge agency disregard of the law. However, the test is not especially demanding, and no indication of congressional intent to benefit the plaintiff is needed.

Ward v. Keenan (1949) S

Facts: The plaintiff took a leave of absence from his job as a police officer to run for a position in the city government. In several campaign speeches, he revealed knowledge of corruption and misconduct in the police force. Upon return to work, he was charged with failing to report this knowledge to his superior officers. Plaintiff sought judicial review to enjoin the Director of Public Safety from conducting hearings.

Issue: When may a plaintiff seek judicial review prior to exhausting administrative remedies?

Rule: In New Jersey, there are two exceptions to the federal exhaustion of administrative remedies requirement: 1) when the jurisdiction of the agency is challenged, and 2) when the agency asserts jurisdiction based upon defective charges.

Ciba-Geigy Corp. v. EPA (1986) S

Facts: The Environmental Protection Agency (EPA) issued a new "Registration Standard" changing the labelling requirement on pesticides made by Ciba-Geigy. Ciba-Geigy contended that the EPA could not mandate new labels without following the notice and hearing requirements in the governing statute. The District Court dismissed the appeal for lack of ripeness.

Issue: What constitutes final agency action ripe for review?

Rule: An agency's interpretation of its governing statute, with the expectation that regulated parties will conform to and rely on this interpretation, is final agency action ripe for judicial review.

Degge v. Hitchcock (S.Ct. 1913) S

Facts: Petitioner contended that the Postmaster General, acting in a judicial capacity, exceeded his jurisdiction by ordering Degge's mail returned as "fraudulent." Since the Postmaster's actions deprived petitioner of a valuable right, petitioner asserted that the common-law certiorari writ made judicial review available.

Issue: May the federal courts grant certiorari as a nonstatutory remedy?

Rule: A writ of certiorari may only be issued to review the decisions of inferior courts. Any attempt to use the writ of certiorari for the purpose of reviewing an administrative order would be an invasion of the executive branch and cannot be permitted. Certiorari as a nonstatutory remedy has been eliminated.

Califano v. Sanders (S.Ct. 1977) S

Facts: Respondent filed a claim for disability benefits under the Social Security Act, but the administrative law judge found him ineligible. Seven years later, he filed the same claim, and the administrative law judge refused to reopen the case, finding no error. He then filed suit to force the case to be reopened, but the District Court dismissed the suit for lack of jurisdiction. The Court of Appeals held that § 10 of the APA conferred jurisdiction.

Issue 1: Does the federal Administrative Procedure Act afford an implied grant of subject matter jurisdiction permitting federal judicial review of agency action?

Rule 1: (Brennan, J.) The federal Administrative Procedure Act does not, expressly or impliedly, confer an independent grant of subject matter jurisdiction for the federal courts to review agency actions.

Issue 2: Where a petition to reopen a prior final agency decision is sought, does the Social Security Act confer subject matter jurisdiction?

Rule 2: The Social Security Act does not confer subject matter jurisdiction.

Note: Compare with *Shaughnessy v. Pedreiro* where a review action was permitted under the APA for cases that previously required a habeas corpus proceeding.

United States v. Mendoza-Lopez (S.Ct. 1987) S

Facts: Respondents, Mexican nationals, were arrested by the Immigration and Naturalization Service (INS) and given a group deportation hearing. They were deported and notified that re-entry to the United States would constitute a felony. Respondents re-entered the U.S. and were arrested again. They were indicted for the felony of re-entry, and moved to dismiss their indictments on the ground that they were denied fair deportation hearings, since they unknowingly waived their right to apply for suspension.

Issue: Where criminal charges are brought on the basis of prior agency proceedings, may the defendant collaterally attack the legality of the proceedings?

Rule: (Marshall, J.) A collateral challenge to the use of a deportation proceeding as an element of a criminal offense must be permitted where the agency proceeding effectively eliminates an alien's right to judicial review.

Laird v. Nelms (S.Ct. 1972) S

Facts: Respondent sought recovery under the Federal Tort Claims Act (FTCA) for property damages allegedly caused by a sonic boom from United States military planes. The Court of Appeals held that the case could proceed under a theory of strict liability for ultrahazardous activities engaged in by the government. The government contended that the FTCA did not allow suits unless plaintiff could prove negligence or wrongful acts.

Issue: Does the Federal Tort Claims Act permit strict liability suits against the government?

Rule: (Rehnquist, J.) Government liability must be based on negligence or wrongful acts; the FTCA does not authorize claims of strict liability for ultrahazardous activity.

Dissent: (Stewart, J.) There is nothing in the language or history of the FTCA to suggest that strict liability alone was precluded.

Citizens to Preserve Overton Park, Inc. v. Volpe
(S.Ct. 1971) MM

Facts: The Department of Transportation Act required that the Secretary of Transportation not approve federal funds for highway projects that extend through public parks if a "feasible and prudent" alternative existed. Petitioners contended that proposed highway I-40 could have been routed around Overton Park and that the plan for the project did not include "all possible" methods of reducing harm to the park, as required by statute. Respondents argued that the Secretary of Transportation's plan was sufficient and the decision was not reviewable.

Issue: Where Congress has not specifically authorized judicial review, may review be presumed?

Rule: (Marshall, J.) Agency actions are presumptively reviewable, and review may only be precluded expressly by statute or when an action is "committed to agency discretion" and there is no law to apply.

Valley Forge Christian College v.
Americans United for Separation of Church and State
(S.Ct. 1982) MM

Facts: The Secretary of Health, Education, and Welfare transferred property to Valley Forge under a federal property statute, setting the price at zero. Plaintiffs charged that the giving of property to a religious organization denied them "fair and constitutional" use of their tax dollars under the First Amendment. The lower court denied taxpayer standing but granted standing based on a citizen's interest in protecting his right to a government that adheres to the Establishment Clause.

Issue: Does alleging a legal right to proper government conduct satisfy the Article III requirements for standing?
Rule: (Rehnquist, J.) To satisfy the Article III requirement of injury in fact, plaintiffs must show personal injury as a result of the alleged conduct. Claiming that the Constitution has been violated by government conduct does not create a personal injury sufficient to confer standing.
Dissent: (Brennan, J.) The relationship of the taxpayer to the breach of the Establishment Clause should confer standing.

Havens Realty Corp. v. Coleman (S.Ct. 1982) MM

Facts: Havens Realty owned apartment complexes and allegedly engaged in "racial steering" by falsely telling black renters that no apartments were available. Plaintiffs included black and white "testers" used to prove that Havens engaged in discriminatory policies, as well as HOME, a nonprofit corporation trying to improve equal opportunity in housing. The plaintiffs claimed standing as "testers" receiving false information under the Fair Housing Act and as residents of a neighborhood denied the benefits of integrated housing.
Issue 1: Are residents of a neighborhood injured in fact by discriminatory housing practices in the area?
Rule 1: (Brennan, J.) While it is implausible that one owner's practices could affect an entire metropolitan area, if injury in fact cannot, as a matter of law, be disproven, then standing is granted.
Issue 2: Is the invasion of a statutory right sufficient to satisfy the injury in fact requirement for standing?
Rule 2: Where a statute establishes an enforceable right, an Article III injury in fact is created solely by invading that right.
Issue 3: May an organization bring suit in its own right seeking damages from a defendant who has hurt its interests?
Rule 3: While an organization may not claim injury to its abstract social interests to gain standing, it can gain standing when it proves concrete and demonstrable injury to its practice or services.
Concurrence: (Powell, J.) The metropolitan area is not too large to feel the effects of discriminatory practices. The respondents could have claimed to be residents of Virginia and would have had standing to contest the discriminatory practices.

Dunn v. Retail Clerks International Association (1962) MM

Facts: The Regional Director of the Labor Board set aside election results from a union vote because of charges of intimidation. The store that had won the vote brought suit to force the Regional Director to do his duty to investigate the false charges and reinstate the election results. The National Labor Relations Act provided for review of the Director's decisions by the General Counsel of the Board.

Issue: Where the relevant statute provides for intra-agency review of agency decisions, is judicial review available to examine an agency decision not to act on alleged violations?

Rule: Congress has provided for intra-agency review; thus judicial review of the agency's enforcement discretion is precluded.

Bachowski v. Brennan (1974) MM

Facts: Bachowski ran for a union office, lost the election, and filed a complaint with the Department of Labor alleging election irregularities. The Secretary of Labor investigated the charges and chose not to set aside the election. Bachowski brought suit against the Secretary, charging that the decision was arbitrary and capricious.

Issue: Is an agency's decision not to prosecute a violation subject to judicial review?

Rule: Where a governing statute does not show clear and convincing evidence that Congress intended to preclude review or to commit the decision to enforce absolutely to agency discretion, an administrative decision not to enforce a regulation is not shielded from review as is prosecutorial discretion.

Chaney v. Heckler (1983) MM

Facts: See *Heckler v. Chaney* above.

Issue: Is an agency's refusal to take enforcement action a decision subject to judicial review?

Rule: The "committed to agency discretion" exception to reviewability must be construed narrowly and applied only when a court finds there is "no law to apply" in reviewing an agency decision.

Natural Resources Defense Council v. SEC (1979) MM

Facts: After seven years of hearings, the Securities and Exchange Commission (SEC) refused to issue a rule requiring corporations to disclose certain equal opportunity and environmental policies. The SEC contended that its decision not to adopt a rule was non-reviewable. The District Court held that the SEC proceedings were inadequate and remanded for fuller proceedings.

Issue: Is an agency's refusal to promulgate a rule "committed to agency discretion" and non-reviewable?

Rule: Discretionary decisions not to adopt rules are reviewable where the agency has in fact held a rulemaking proceeding and compiled a record narrowly focused on the particular rule suggested but not adopted.

Note: The court upheld the SEC's decision after review. Generally, the courts have permitted review of decisions not to promulgate rules but have been deferential to the agency's decisions.

Ticor Title Insurance Co. v. Federal Trade Commission
(1987) MM

Facts: The Federal Trade Commission Act authorized the Federal Trade Commission (FTC) to initiate and prosecute claims against persons suspected of unfair methods of competition. The FTC issued a complaint against Ticor and five other insurance companies, charging that they illegally restrained competition by price-fixing. Appellants argued that Article II of the Constitution prohibited the FTC, as an independent federal agency, from exercising the law enforcement activities specified by the Act.

Issue: Where a party challenges an agency's authority on constitutional grounds, must the party exhaust agency remedies prior to judicial review?

Rule: The exhaustion doctrine applies even when a collateral judicial action challenges the constitutionality of the basic statute under which the agency functions.

United States v. Mitchell (S.Ct 1983) MM

Facts: The government gave timber land to various Indians under a trust allotment agreement dating back to the late 19th century. The government exercised comprehensive control over the land. Four Indians sued to recover damages based on allegations of waste and mismanagement of the timber lands. The respondents alleged that the government owed them a fiduciary duty as trustee under various statutes. The Court of Claims held the government liable for money damages.

Issue: Where a fiduciary trust relationship exists between the government and a beneficiary, is the government liable for damages for breach of trust?

Rule: (Marshall, J.) Since a trustee is accountable in damages for breach of trust, the government acting as a trustee is liable for damages to its beneficiaries. The Tucker Act constitutes a waiver of sovereign immunity for this case.

Dissent: (Powell, J.) A cause of action for damages against the United States cannot be implied but must be unequivocally expressed.

Berkovitz v. United States (S.Ct. 1988) MM

Facts: Berkovitz contracted polio after ingesting a defective oral polio vaccine. The disease left him completely paralyzed. Berkovitz and his parents sued the government, since the National Institute of Health licensed the company that produced the defective vaccines and the Food and Drug Administration acted wrongfully in releasing that particular batch of vaccine. The government contended that the agency actions fell within the "discretionary function" exception of the Federal Tort Claims Act.

Issue: Does the "discretionary function" exemption in the Federal Tort Claims Act preclude government liability for all agency actions?

Rule: (Marshall, J.) The "discretionary function" exemption from the Federal Tort Claims Act applies only to agency conduct that involves the permissible exercise of policy judgment. It does not preclude liability for all acts arising out of the regulatory programs of federal agencies.

Gregoire v. Biddle (1949) MM

Facts: A Frenchman was arrested and kept in custody for four years on the pretense that he was German and therefore an enemy alien. The defendants kept the plaintiff in custody maliciously despite a ruling by the Enemy Alien Board that he was a Frenchman. The lower court held that the defendants had an absolute immunity from liability even though they acted out of personal ill-will.

Issue: Can government officials be sued for misuse of their official powers?

Rule: Government officials are absolutely immune from liability for any actions where they use their power in official capacity, regardless of whether that use can be shown at trial to be malicious or against the public interest. Officers should be punished for such conduct, but not through trials that deter the innocent from doing their job.

National Railroad Passenger Corp. v.
National Assoc. of Railroad Passengers
(S.Ct. 1974) MM

Facts: The National Railroad Passenger Corp. (Amtrak) announced discontinuance of certain passenger trains. Plaintiffs contended that the Rail Passenger Service Act (Amtrak Act) prohibited the discontinuance of service. The District Court denied standing to plaintiffs based on § 307 of the Act. The Court of Appeals reversed, holding that § 307 does not bar a suit by a private party who is allegedly aggrieved.
Issue: Where a statute confers jurisdiction for a public cause of action, is a private cause of action impliedly precluded?
Rule: (Stewart, J.) Where the legislative history and text of a statute conferring a public cause of action indicate that Congress intended to preclude private causes of action, no such action may be implied.
Concurrence: (Brennan, J.) The question whether a private suit for mandamus under § 1361 could be maintained against the Attorney General if his refusal to act went beyond "any rational exercise of discretion" should be left open.
Dissent: (Douglas, J.) In this case, the question of cause of action is identical to the question of standing. The majority's construction of the statute is strained. Passengers satisfy the tests for standing and are the logical choice for enforcement of the statute.

Cannon v. University of Chicago (S.Ct. 1979) MM

Facts: Cannon claimed that she was excluded from the University of Chicago's medical program because of her gender. Since the medical program received federal financial assistance, she charged the University with violation of Title IX of the Education Amendments, which prohibits gender discrimination by schools receiving federal aid. The District Court concluded that Title IX did not provide for a private cause of action by aggrieved persons and dismissed the case.

Issue: May a federal statute designed to discourage discrimination through the withholding of federal funds be interpreted as creating a private cause of action for those discriminated against?

Rule: (Stevens, J.) In the rare case where all four of the *Cort* factors support an implied cause of action, no express statutory authorization is necessary for a federal, private cause of action.

Concurrence: (Rehnquist, J.) In the future, this Court should be very reluctant to imply a cause of action without legislative authority.

Dissent: (White, J.) The majority concludes that a remedy should be inferred in Title IX because, prior to its enactment, several lower courts heard private suits to enforce the prohibition on racial discrimination in Title VI. This conclusion confuses the existing § 1983 right of action, remedying denial of federal rights under color of state law, with the creation of a new right of action against private discrimination.

Dissent: (Powell, J.) Under Article III, Congress alone has the responsibility to determine the jurisdiction of lower federal courts. When Congress does not provide a private civil remedy, federal courts should not enlarge their own jurisdiction by creating a new remedy. Thus, the *Cort* analysis is unconstitutional and the implication doctrine should be abandoned.

Maine v. Thiboutot (S.Ct. 1979) MM

Facts: Respondents alleged that the State of Maine violated 42 U.S.C. § 1983 by depriving them of welfare benefits to which they were entitled under the federal Social Security Act. The dispute over benefits arose from Maine's interpretation of the governing law. Petitioners claimed that § 1983 did not encompass purely statutory violations of federal law.

Issue: Does § 1983 encompass all laws of the United States?

Rule: (Brennan, J.)   The statutory language and subsequent interpretations clearly indicate that § 1983 protects deprivation of any rights secured by the Constitution or any federal law.

Dissent: (Powell, J.) The Court transforms purely statutory claims into "civil rights" action under § 1983. When placed in historical context, the clear meaning of the statutory language is hardly clear. This decision dramatically expands the liability of state and local officials.

Pennhurst State School and Hospital
v. Halderman (S.Ct. 1981) MM

Facts: Plaintiffs contended that Pennhurst State School, a state-run institution for the mentally retarded, violated the Developmentally Disabled Assistance and Bill of Rights Act by failing to provide minimally adequate habilitation for its patients. The District Court found substantial abuse and held that the mentally retarded have a federal constitutional right to habilitation and a least restrictive environment. The Court of Appeals held that the Act created statutory substantive rights for the mentally retarded that were judicially enforceable.

Issue: Where a statute does not specifically create a cause of action, but refers to "rights" of its beneficiaries, may a cause of action be implied?

Rule: (Rehnquist, J.) An implicit cause of action may exist where a statute refers to beneficiaries, but the case for inferring intent to provide a cause of action is at its weakest where the "rights" asserted impose affirmative obligations on the states to fund certain services, since it may be assumed that Congress will not implicitly attempt to impose massive financial obligations on the states.

Dissent in part: (White, J.) The majority has misconceived the purpose Congress intended the statute to serve. The legislative history indicates that Congress intended to establish requirements for participating states to meet in providing care to the developmentally disabled.

Atascadero State Hospital v. Scanlon (S.Ct. 1985) MM

Facts: Respondent accused Atascadero State Hospital of denying him employment based on physical handicap. Petitioners sought dismissal on grounds that the Eleventh Amendment barred suit against the State of California in federal court. The Court of Appeals held that the action was not barred since California consented to be sued as a recipient of federal funds under the Rehabilitation Act.

Issue: Does the Eleventh Amendment bar suits against states in federal court?

Rule: (Powell, J.) Federal suits against states are barred unless a state, in a specific waiver of immunity, consents to be sued, or Congress abrogates a state's constitutionally secured immunity from suit in federal court by making its intention unmistakably clear in statutory language. A general authorization for suit that does not specify the states is not sufficient.

Dissent: (Brennan, J.) The Court's Eleventh Amendment doctrine is misguided and pernicious. The states should not be exempt from compliance with laws that bind every other legal actor in our nation.

Dissent: (Blackmun, J.) The Court today compounds a longstanding constitutional mistake. Shielding the states through this interpretation of the Eleventh Amendment cannot be reconciled with the federal system envisioned by the Constitution. Congress intended for the states to be sued under the Fourteenth Amendment, and California, in this case, gave its consent to be sued by accepting federal funds.

Dissent: (Stevens, J.) The Eleventh Amendment doctrine should be re-examined.

Wright v. Roanoke Redevelopment & Housing Authority (S.Ct. 1987) MM

Facts: Petitioners, tenants in apartments owned by the Housing Authority, brought suit under § 1983 claiming that respondent over-billed them for utilities, violating the rent ceiling imposed by the Brooke Amendment to the Housing Act of 1937 and regulations of the Department of Housing and Urban Development (HUD). The District Court held that a private cause of action was not available. The Court of Appeals held that the tenants' rights were only enforceable by HUD, not private tenants.

Issue: Where there is state deprivation of a "right" secured by federal statute, does § 1983 provide a remedial cause of action?

Rule: (White, J.) Where the relevant federal statute creates individual substantive rights and shows no congressional intent to preclude § 1983 claims by private persons against a state agency, then a § 1983 action is permitted.

Dissent: (O'Connor, J.) Neither the Brooke Amendment language its legislative history, nor its interpretation by HUD, supports the conclusion that Congress intended to create an entitlement to reasonable utility fees. Additionally, the HUD regulations in question are not judicially enforceable.

Middlesex County Sewerage Authority v.
National Sea Clammers Association (S.Ct. 1981) MM

Facts: Respondents fished off the coast of New York and New Jersey. They brought suit against various government officials alleging that sewage and sludge were being dumped into the Atlantic Ocean, injuring the fishing business. Respondents tried to base their claims on the Federal Water Pollution Control Act (FWPCA), which provides for citizen suits. Since they failed to meet the prescribed deadlines and notice requirement, the lower court refused to allow them to proceed under the citizen suit or the general jurisdictional statute.

Issue: Where a statute specifically confers enforcement authority on government officials and private citizens, may the courts imply further judicial remedies for citizens?

Rule: (Powell, J.) In the absence of strong congressional intent to the contrary, courts must assume that where Congress specified some citizen remedies it did not intend to permit others.

Dissent: (Stevens, J.) Both the FWPCA and the Clean Water Act specifically preserve all existing judicial remedies, including private remedies under § 1983.

WHAT YOU AREN'T SUPPOSED TO KNOW ABOUT THE LEGAL PROFESSION

You're going through the mill of learning to mispronounce Latin words, present cases before the King's Bench, and think like a Greek philosopher who could not save himself from the death penalty.

Your social relationships are a mess. If you were married when you began law school, you are probably divorced; if you were single, you are probably desperately trying to marry prior to launching a career not known for promoting love.

Fear of passing the bar exam keeps you awake at night more frequently than any Stephen King novel. Your mind flutters with degrees, security interests, consideration, and other tortuous interference, yet somewhere over that rainbow is a land of law, which is not like any other profession. It smells of freshly mowed ethics and power, and you're prepared to devote yourself to the common weal (whatever that is).

Fortunately, the practice of law is not like that. Ethics are displaced by billable hours. Your friends become your associates, and therefore competitors. Your seniors set you up to be scapegoats. Female lawyers discover that making it in law can sometimes mean making it. Principles fly out the window (if the window can even be opened) while you spend weekends inflating a frivolous matter into a hundred thousand dollar firm revenue.

WHAT YOU AREN'T SUPPOSED TO KNOW... by Laurens Schwartz, a graduate of Yale and NYU Law, tells you HOW:
- To make it through law school and remain sane.
- To regain command of the English language.
- Professors, partners, and senior associates "train" you.
- Headhunters can screw up your career.

184 pp., 6 x 9, hardbound, $14.95

Note: this book is a realistic and often blunt look at legal education and practice and therefore does not always paint the profession in the rosiest of terms. Sulzburger & Graham Publishing feels that this book expresses an important viewpoint, and therefore we are marketing it exclusively to lawyers and law students.

How am I doing?

The question that plagues every law student. They often find out the answer when it is too late. Law school is very different from your previous education. You don't have exams before finals to make sure you are on the right track. Many bright students work very hard, but are disappointed with grades that could have been much higher had they realized a little sooner that they should have been doing things a little differently.

The answer: BLOND'S MULTISTATE QUESTIONS

- More than 1000 multiple choice questions
- Answers and detailed explanations
- Divided by course and subject
- One volume covers Torts, Property, Contracts, Criminal Procedure, Criminal Law, Constitutional Law, and Evidence

Used for years by Bar Exam candidates, we found that more and more students were using Blond's Multistate for their final exams. Short fact patterns before each question will help you practice issue spotting. The detailed explanations will teach and reinforce the law and let you know how you are doing.

Research has shown that material learned by active studying, such as taking practice exams, is retained longer than material passively learned. Find out how you are doing, and do better.

100% Cotton, the finest quality.
Available at your law school bookstore or directly from the publisher. $9.95 per shirt plus $2.25 shipping per order. (Postpaid with book order.)   Please specify size: M, L, XL.
After
receipt of order, please allow 2-7 working days for delivery.
MasterCard, Visa, American Express, and DiscoverCard phone orders
accepted.

BLOND'S™ LAW GUIDES

Precisely What You Need to Know

Civil Procedure
Cound
Field
Rosenberg
Louisell

Contracts
Farnsworth
Dawson
Kessler
Fuller
Murphy

Criminal Procedure
Kamisar
Saltzburg
Weinreb/Crim.Process
Weinreb/Crim.Justice
Miller

Evidence
McCormick
Green
Weinstein
Kaplan
Cleary

Property
Dukeminier
Browder
Casner
Cribbet

Torts
Prosser
Epstein
Keeton
Franklin

Constitutional Law
Barrett
Brest
Ducat
Gunther
Lockhart
Rotunda
Stone

Criminal Law
Kadish
LaFave
Kaplan
Weinreb
Dix
Johnson
Inbau

Corporate Tax
Lind
Kahn
Wolfman
Surrey

Corporations
Cary
Choper
Hamilton
Henn
Jennings
Solomon
Vagts

Family Law
Areen
Foote
Krause
Wadlington

Administrative Law
Bonfield
Breyer
Gellhorn
Cass
Schwartz
Mashaw

International Law
Sweeney
Henkin

Income Tax
Klein
Andrews
Surrey
Kragen
Freeland
Graetz

ORDER FORM

Sulzburger & Graham Publishing
P.O. Box 20058
Park West Station
New York NY 10025

(800)366-7086
Orders shipped
within 24 hours

BLOND'S LAW GUIDES @ $13.95 per copy.
Name of book

——— $ _____
———   _____
———   _____
———   _____
———   _____
———   _____
———   _____

——— BLOND'S MULTISTATE @ $26.95 per copy   _____

——— BLOND'S T-SHIRT @ $9.95   _____

——— WHAT YOU AREN'T... @ $14.95 per copy   _____

Shipping and handling @ 2.25   _____
Total $ _____

☐ Check or money order (payable to Sulzburger & Graham)
☐ MasterCard   ☐ Visa   ☐ American Express   ☐ DiscoverCard
Charge Card No. _____
Exp. Date _____   Signature _____

Name _____
Address _____
City/State/Zip _____
Phone # _____
Law School _____
Graduation Date _____

All orders are shipped UPS same or next business day. Delivery time will vary, based on distance from New York City. Washington/Boston corridor can expect delivery 2 working days after shipment. West Coast should allow 6 working days. UPS overnight, Federal Express, and 2d day air available at extra cost.

NOTES

NOTES

NOTES

NOTES

NOTES